FIRE OF LOVE

Encountering the Holy Spirit

Donald J. Goergen, OP

Paulist Press
New York/Mahwah, N.J.

Book and cover design by Lynn Else

Library of Congress Cataloging-in-Publication Data

Goergen, Donald.
   Fire of love : encountering the Holy Spirit / Donald J. Goergen.
     p.   cm.
   Includes bibliographical references.
   ISBN 0-8091-4408-5 (alk. paper)
   1. Holy Spirit. I. Title.
BT121.3.G64 2006
231'.3—dc22

2006015390

Published by Paulist Press
997 Macarthur Boulevard
Mahwah, New Jersey 07430

www.paulistpress.com

Printed and bound in the
United States of America

CONTENTS

As the years have passed, I have realized that some things can be told and others not. Telling diminishes what is told. Only what has been integrated by the human aspect of ourselves can be shared with others. I have also come to believe that things stay alive proportionally to how much silence there is around them. Meaning does not need words to exist.

The speech of silence is achieved when words, and their potential ability to hurt meaning, are done away with. Words entrap meaning, torture it, slice it into pieces the way a butcher cuts the meat of a slaughtered animal and serves it to us. The speech of silence has profound respect for the integrity of meaning as an entity separate from language. In silence, meaning is no longer heard, but felt; and feeling is the best hearing, the best instrument for recording meaning. Meaning is made welcome as it is and treated with respect.

—Malidoma Patrice Somé, *Of Water and the Spirit*

PREFACE

Jesus Christ has been the subject of my teaching on three different continents, in four books, and in a number of articles for over thirty years. A result of that extensive period of research and reflection was the conclusion that we need comparable attentiveness to the Holy Spirit. Who do we say the Spirit is? The Spirit excites, ignites, energizes, challenges, consoles, and disturbs. Were it not for the Spirit, things would fall apart.

There is a text in the Acts of the Apostles in which St. Paul, while passing through Ephesus on one of his journeys, comes upon some followers of Jesus (Acts 19:1–3). Paul asks them: "Did you receive the Holy Spirit when you became believers?" They replied, "No, we have not even heard that there is a Holy Spirit." It is noteworthy that Paul asks the question. Even more significant is their response, since Jesus' baptism was particularly a baptism with the Spirit.

Today, of course, we have heard of the Holy Spirit, but does this make a difference in our lives? In the life of the church? In dialogue between Christians and other religious and spiritual traditions? What difference does the Holy Spirit make? A quotation attributed to William James, which I have never been able to locate, comes to mind, "A difference that makes no difference is no difference." Does the Holy Spirit make a difference? This book is something of an introduction to the Spirit. Who do we say the Spirit is? How does the Spirit make a difference?

In the Orthodox churches of the East, the theology of the Holy Spirit has been more emphasized than in the Latin West. In the West, however, the Holy Spirit has become prominent in the past century through varied Pentecostal and charismatic movements. Their strength has been a focused attentiveness to the gift of the Spirit. To a great degree "life in the Spirit" is often associated with these churches and movements. It would be a mistake, however, if we limited our awareness of the Spirit to the Pentecostal and charismatic movements alone. My focus here is on the Spirit as at work in a series of concentric circles or, to borrow an image from Pierre Teilhard de Chardin, at the core of a dynamic spiral moving upward and forward.[1]

There are a variety of spheres in which we find the Spirit at work: within the human person, in ecclesial communities, in the wider range of religious and spiritual traditions, in the world itself, even in the so-called secular world, as well as in the whole cosmos and all of creation. In each case the Holy Spirit is at the core—of a cosmology, a theology of history, a theology of religions, ecclesiology, and human psychology. Failure to see the breadth and depth and height of the Spirit's work is to not know the Spirit. The Spirit transforms one's personal life but is equally the Spirit of social transformation. We recognize a prophetic Spirit who acts in our human history as well as a cosmic Spirit at work in all creation. The Spirit undergirds and energizes the evolution and transformation of consciousness.

Our purpose in life involves discerning this Spirit, becoming aligned with it, and letting it be the deepest source from within which our own lives take shape and form. We let ourselves be instruments of this Most Holy Spirit. Once we become increasingly aware of the Holy Spirit, that intense ubiquitous divine presence, our lives begin to change, and so does the way we see the world. Our sense of wonder grows. Our hope becomes more secure. We find ourselves capable of loving in ways unimagined. As the prophet Isaiah instructs us, we widen the space of our tents (Isa 54:2). We deepen and widen our vision.

This work is an invitation to encounter the Spirit. Before continuing, I want to say something about theological language. *Apophatic theology* refers to theological and spiritual traditions that proceed by way of unknowing (from the Greek *apophatikos*). Given the transcendence of God, apophaticism affirms that we can know only what God is not. By way of contrast, *cataphatic theology* proceeds by way of affirmations and analogy, aware that our language about God communicates truth that God has revealed. Nevertheless, God surpasses whatever a word means. This is important when it comes to the question of the gender of pronouns in references to the Spirit.

In reflecting on Denys the Areopagite's *Divine Names*, Denys Turner points out that the very nature of God requires reflection on how we talk about God, indeed whether we can talk about God at all. God-talk, or theological language, in order to approach adequacy, requires maximizing our ways of speaking, even if that be at times shocking, rather than limiting ourselves to unshocking, customary speech. Naming God is important and necessary, but equally important and necessary is the awareness that ultimately our language about God fails. This is particularly true when it comes to attributing sex or gender to God.

> It is less misleading…if we describe God both as male and as female, then we force upon our materialistic imaginations a concrete sense of the collapse of gender-language as such. For no person can be *both* male *and* female. Hence, if God has to be described in both ways, then he cannot possibly be either male or female; and if God is neither, then also she cannot possibly be a "person" in any sense we know of, for every person we know of is one or the other. It is in the collapse of ordinary language, brought to our attention by the necessity of ascribing incompatible attributes, that the transcendence of God above all language is best approached.[2]

The Spirit is neither *he* nor *she* nor *it*, and yet speak of the Spirit we must, however inadequate our speaking may be. Rather than err in our references to the Spirit by limiting ourselves to one pronoun alone, it is better to use all the pronouns at our disposal so as to subvert the tendency to think of our theological language as adequate. St. Augustine acknowledged that God has no sex,[3] and we cannot communicate the genderlessness of the divine by making our language about God or the Spirit gender-specific. The ancient Syriac Christian tradition depicted the Spirit as feminine and sometimes even as mother.[4] Jessica Powers (1905–88) picks up this maternal side when she speaks of the Holy Spirit as "Love Who seeks to mother."[5] In truth, neither God nor the Spirit is feminine or masculine. Theologically it is more appropriate to retain "the full range of gender possibilities"[6] rather than confine ourselves, or confine the unconfinable Spirit, to a specific gender.

I would like to take this opportunity to express deep gratitude to Paulist Press, especially Lawrence Boadt, Nancy de Flon, and Paul McMahon, as well as to those who have assisted in editing and reading the manuscript along the way or who have offered continuing encouragement and support, particularly Margaret Bunkers, Diana Culbertson, Albert Nolan, Ed Ruane, as well as my provincial and his socius, Michael Mascari and John Meany. I also thank members of my Dominican Ashram community during these past years who assisted me with their prayer, encouragement, and editing: Jim Barnett, Maureen Cannon, Deb Clark, Richard de Ranitz, Stan Drongowski, Rosemary Henley (now deceased), Marie Therese Kalb, Giles Klapperich, and Kathy Smith. The confidence and support of all of you have meant a lot to me. I also wish to thank librarians at the Salzmann Library, St. Francis Seminary, Milwaukee, for their assistance. I dedicate this book to God's friends everywhere.

Notes

1. See Pierre Teilhard de Chardin, "The Heart of the Problem" (1949), in *The Future of Man* (New York: Harper & Row, 1964), 260–69. Don Beck, based on work by Clare Graves, has developed the theory of spiral dynamics. See Don Beck and Christopher Cowan, *Spiral Dynamics* (Oxford: Blackwell, 1996).

2. Denys Turner, *The Darkness of God: Negativity in Christian Mysticism* (Cambridge: Cambridge University Press, 1995), 26; see pp. 24–26 for a more extended reflection.

3. Augustine, *The Trinity*, trans. Edmund Hill (Brooklyn, NY: New City Press, 2000), 329.

4. Kilian McDonnell, "A Trinitarian Theology of the Holy Spirit?" *Theological Studies* 46 (1985): 200–203.

5. *Selected Poetry of Jessica Powers*, ed. Regina Siegfried and Robert Morneau (Kansas City, MO: Sheed & Ward, 1989), 33.

6. McDonnell, "A Trinitarian Theology...?" 203.

Chapter One
AWAKENING THE HUMAN SPIRIT

God creates human beings for participation in divine life. We have been structured in the very core of our being for unity with God. Nothing less than this can bring happiness. Not all religious traditions name the source and goal of our being *God*, but they all recognize that there is something profound for which we are destined. Amal Kiran (K. D. Sethna), a disciple of Sri Aurobindo (1872–1950), spoke about "the ache for the infinite."[1] The classic Christian statement of this belief in the West is that of St. Augustine: "you have made us for yourself, [O Lord], and our heart is restless until it rests in you" (*Confessions* 1.1).[2] The psalmist in the Hebrew Scriptures sang: "For God alone my soul waits in silence; from him comes my salvation" (Ps 62:1). What is it in a human person that yearns for God? We begin our reflection on God's Spirit with this yearning of the human spirit.

Pauline Anthropology

St. Paul writes, "But you are not in the flesh; you are in the Spirit, since the Spirit of God dwells in you" (Rom 8:9). He continues: "For all who are led by the Spirit of God are children of God. For you did not receive a spirit of slavery to fall back into fear, but you have received a spirit of adoption. When we cry, 'Abba! Father!' it is that very Spirit bearing witness with our spirit that we are children of God" (Rom 8:14–16).

St. Paul contrasts flesh *(sarx)* with S/spirit *(P/pneuma)*. He speaks of the Spirit as dwelling within us (1 Cor 6:19). This indwelling Spirit pours God's love into us (Rom 5:5). Being "in the

1

Spirit" means that we are God's children. The Fourth Gospel speaks about "being born again from above" (John 3:1–10). The Spirit is also the source of our prayer. When we pray "Abba," it is the Spirit who is praying within us. Not only, however, is there the Spirit of God, but there is also a human spirit. When we pray, it is the Spirit of God bearing witness *with our spirit*. What is this human spirit (*pneuma*) of which Paul speaks?

Paul speaks of "our spirit" earlier in Romans as well: "For God, whom I serve with my spirit by announcing the gospel of his Son, is my witness…" (1:9). The close of the First Letter to the Thessalonians reads: "May the God of peace himself sanctify you entirely; and may your spirit and soul and body be kept sound and blameless at the coming of our Lord Jesus Christ" (1 Thess 5:23). This is not a division of the human person into parts but dimensions of our humanity, varied words adding nuances to our understanding of what being human means.

In some texts from Paul there is such a close relationship between the Holy Spirit and the human spirit that it is difficult to know to which Paul refers. Yet there are clear references to the *human* spirit (Rom 1:9; 8:16; 1 Cor 2:11; 5:3–5; 7:34; 14:14; 16:18; 2 Cor 7:1; Gal 6:18; Eph 4:23; Phil 4:23; Col 2:5; 1 Thess 5:23; 2 Tim 4:22; Phlm 25, and others). For example:

- "For what human being knows what is truly human except the human spirit that is within?" (1 Cor 2:11)

- "For if I pray in a tongue, my spirit prays but my mind is unproductive." (1 Cor 14:14)

- "May the grace of our Lord Jesus Christ be with your spirit, brothers and sisters." (Gal 6:18)

For Paul, spirit (*pneuma*) is not the same as soul (*psychē*) or mind (*nous*). Paul speaks not only about body (*sōma*), soul (*psychē*), and spirit (*pneuma*) but also about mind (*nous*), heart (*kardia*), and flesh (*sarx*). These are varied facets of the human person or lenses through which Paul sees us.[3] *Body*, an important Pauline word, means not simply the physical body but rather the whole person as a corporeal, embodied, interactive being. My bodiliness is not a part of me but rather my whole being considered under the aspect of its corporeality. In his discussion of resurrection in First Corinthians, Paul distinguishes a *sōma psychikos* and *sōma pneumatikos* (15:44), the human person as embodying natural life as we know it and the human person as embodying spirit or the Spirit.

Flesh (sarx) occurs frequently in Paul and, like many Pauline words, covers a range of meanings, in this case from neutral to sinful. Less frequent in Paul than *sarx* are *mind* and *heart*. *Nous* (mind) refers to the human being as a thinking person, connoting what some think of as the most noble aspect of one's humanity. *Kardia* (heart) denotes a deeper, inner dimension, in one sense the seat of emotion but more than that. "Rather, a person is a Jew who is one inwardly, and real circumcision is a matter of the heart—it is spiritual and not literal" (Rom 2:29). "God's love has been poured into our hearts through the Holy Spirit" (Rom 5:5). "And God, who searches the heart, knows what is the mind of the Spirit, because the Spirit intercedes for the saints according to the will of God" (Rom 8:27). Sometimes "heart" and "spirit" are difficult to differentiate.

Psychē (soul) corresponds to the Hebrew *nephesh*. It denotes a human being as alive, connoting soul as source of natural life. A *sōma psychikos*, a besouled body, cannot inherit the reign of God, only the *sōma pneumatikos*, or inspirited body, can (1 Cor 15:44–50). How often Paul refers to "human spirit" is difficult to say since there are so many references to the Holy Spirit, then to the human spirit, and then those references where it is difficult to tell to which Paul is referring (e.g., 1 Cor 4:21; 14:15; 2 Cor 4:13; Gal 6:1; Eph 1:17; Phil 1:27). It is through *pneuma*, the person as a pneumatic being (rather than as an embodied, corporeal, somatic being *[sōma]*, or intelligent, mental, thinking being *[nous]*, or living, natural, psychic being *[psychē]*, or fleshly, worldly being *[sarx]*), that one is most directly in contact with God: "God, whom I serve with my spirit" (Rom 1:9).

Pneuma is that dimension of our humanness which is higher than *nous*, deeper than *kardia*, and more than *psychē*. Pneumatology (the study of s/Spirit) complements psychology (the study of psychic life). *Pneuma*, or spirit, is the innermost, deepest core of ourselves, wherein we are connected to the divine Spirit. The *New Jerusalem Bible* comments that "spirit" can be taken "as the divine presence in a human being, giving new life in union with Christ" or "as the innermost depths of the human being, open and awake to the Spirit."[4]

Paul also distinguishes between the inward and the outward self: "For I delight in the law of God in my inmost self, but I see in my members another law at war with the law of my mind, making me captive to the law of sin that dwells in my members" (Rom 7:22–23). "So we do not lose heart. Even though our outer nature is wasting away, our inner nature is being renewed day by day" (2 Cor 4:16). Paul's language for articulating his understanding of the human person and human condition cannot always be pinned down to one precise meaning. *Sōma, sarx, nous, kardia, psychē, pneuma* can have varied associations and nuances. Nevertheless, Paul has a psychology, a pneumatology, or an anthropology that recognizes both interiority and exteriority in the multifaceted complexity of the human person. The human person has both an inner dimension and an innermost dimension. The latter is our pneumatic or spiritual core.

The Life of the Soul

Asian spiritual traditions have developed extensively the psychology of the human spirit. This is less true of modern empirical Western psychologies. A simple framework for reflecting on our interior lives can include five facets of humanness—body, mind, heart, soul, and spirit.

We are all bodily beings, embodied persons, and our embodiment with its sorrows and joys should never be denied, nor its importance diminished. We are also intelligent creatures, no matter how unintelligent we may sometimes be, and the life of the mind is a sacred gift. Mentality gives witness to the fact that we, while embodied, are more than bodies alone. We are embodied beings but also mental and affective beings. "Mind" indicates that there is more to us than bodiliness, and "heart" indicates that there is still more than body and mind.

There is more to the life of the soul than its intelligence, intellect, reason, even including intuitiveness, imagination, and memory. There is also more to the soul than its affective life, vitality, emotions, feelings, connectedness to others, all symbolized by the word *heart* understood in a more modern sense. Intellectual development and affective development must be held together in a delicate balance lest the life of one eclipse that of the other. The head center and the heart center respect each other. Each requires the other. Each is incomplete by itself alone. In an analogous way, this is true also of persons and society. The social, relational continuations, or extensions of our bodiliness show that we can move ever outward in a rhythm of continuing, pulsating excentration, going out of ourselves, refusing to be self-preoccupied and falsely self-centered. But we can likewise—indeed we must—plumb the inner depths of that deeper self beyond mind, beyond heart, at the very depths of soul.

"Indeed," the author of the Letter to the Hebrews writes, "the word of God is living and active, sharper than any two-edged sword, piercing until it divides soul from spirit, joints from marrow" (4:12). Here again we see the distinction between "soul" and "spirit" that we found in St. Paul. There is inseparability but nevertheless distinguishability between "soul" and "spirit," *psychē* and *pneuma*, where psychology and pneumatology merge and differentiate themselves.

Psychē: life, soul, mind, heart, head, consciousness, subconsciousness, collective unconsciousness; and *pneuma:* the depth of the soul, spirit, the abyss within, the opening to the life divine—these two are not exactly the same. Biblical anthropologies, especially Pauline, interpreted the human person in terms of three principles—body, soul, and spirit—and not simply two, body and soul, a bipartite understanding that goes back to Aristotle. Nevertheless, an exploration of the *human* spirit has been neglected. The soul's life and energy can be channeled toward the formation of the ego or focused on a deeper energy coming forth from life-giving spirit. I am not using ego here in the sense of modern post-Freudian ego psychologies but rather in the sense of false self, the self-preoccupied self, the separate or individualistic self. The true self, by contrast, knows that it is not who it is apart from the other, that a person is always a person-in-community, relational, open to both self-affirmation and self-denial, self-actualization and self-negation.

There is more to life than biological life alone. A rosebush does not appreciate the expansive life of a deer. A dog does not fathom the worlds open to human beings. Just as there is more to life than biological life, so there is more to life than psychological life. A lion does not know the joys and sorrows of humankind, and a human person might not always know how much more to life there can be—what it is to be fully alive, pneumatic life.

The Human Person's Innermost Sanctum

It is not a question of the language we use to articulate our understanding and experience of soul, but rather of our awareness of a depth within the human person. This awareness has permeated mystical traditions and spiritual wisdom through the centuries. "By prayer," wrote a certain Hesychius in the fifth or sixth century, "I mean the prayer which is constantly active in the innermost secret places of the soul."[5] Earlier St. Augustine (354–430) had written his *Confessions*, manifesting his awareness of this depth within the soul:[6]

- "But you [my God] were more inward than my most inward part and higher than the highest element within me."

- "With you as my guide I entered into my innermost citadel."

- "But where in my consciousness, Lord, do you dwell? Where in it do you make your home? What resting-place have you made for yourself? What kind of sanctuary have you built for yourself?...Late have I loved you, beauty so old and so new: late have I loved you. And see, you were within and I was in the external world and sought you there....You were with me, and I was not with you."

We find references to the soul of the soul, the core of the soul, the ground of soul, the innermost dimension of the self, the true self, the cave of the heart, along with many other expressions in the language of saints past and present. This innermost aspect of the soul, this "human spirit," goes by many names. Varied thinkers and saints, in their own ways, have witnessed to this inner depth or human spirit within the human person. Teresa of Avila spoke about the "center of the soul,"[7] "the most intimate part of the soul,"[8] "the extreme interior, in some place very deep within,"[9] and "a difference clearly recognized between the soul and the spirit."[10]

Only two popes have written encyclicals on the Holy Spirit, Pope Leo XIII (1810–1903) and Pope John Paul II (1920-2005).[11] John Paul II wrote: "Thus human life becomes permeated, through participation, by the divine life, and itself acquires a divine, supernatural dimension....Thus there is a close relationship *between the Spirit* who gives life and *sanctifying grace* and the manifold *supernatural vitality* which derives from it...: between the uncreated Spirit and the created human spirit" (*Dominum et Vivificantem* 52.3).[12] For John Paul II, with respect to God's salvific work following the death of Jesus, "the Holy Spirit remains the transcendent principal agent of the accomplishment of this work in the human spirit and in the history of the world" (ibid., 42.1). John Paul II was aware of the close association between the Holy Spirit and the human spirit as well as the action of the Holy Spirit beyond the world of personal interiority in the history of the world.

Let us take, by way of elaboration, a particular spiritual tradition, that of the Rhineland in the fourteenth century. Meister Eckhart (1260–1328), indebted as he was to the religious women's movement and beguine mysticism of the twelfth and early thirteenth centuries,[13] is especially significant.[14]

Eckhart speaks about the ground *(grunt)* of the soul wherein God is present, sometimes referred to as "the inmost person," "the silent middle," the soul's "essence."[15] Closely related to the ground of the soul, at times practically interchangeable with it, are Eckhart's references to "the summit of the soul," "the spark," "the apex of the mind," "the topmost summit of the soul," "the citadel," "the highest peak."[16] These latter expressions can sometimes be distinguished from the ground; at other times not. The "highest" or "topmost" refers to the intellect and the higher powers of the intellect whereby we grasp or are grasped by God, in one sense the point of access to the ground. But this seems simply to be an aspect of the ground of the soul itself, by which the ground is entered. The innermost ground and the highest peak are almost synonymous.

> God is nowhere so truly as in the soul, and in the angels if you will, in the inmost soul, in the summit of the soul. And when I say the inmost, I mean the highest, and when I say the highest, I mean the inmost part of the soul. In the inmost and highest part of the soul—there I mean them both together in one.... All that God works in all the saints, that He works in the inmost part of the soul.[17]

There is for Eckhart, as there will be for Johannes Tauler, his disciple, a threefold birth of the Word: the birth of the Word in eternity within the Trinity; the birth of the Word in time, in history, on earth, from Mary; and the birth of the Word in each of us, in the soul, in the innermost part of the soul. It is the latter that is a major theme in Eckhart's spirituality.[18] The birth of the Word in the ground of the soul prompts a breakthrough *(durchbruch)* of the soul into the Godhead and of God into the soul. "Just as God breaks through into me, so I break through in turn into Him. God leads this spirit into the desert and into the unity of Himself, where He is simply One and welling up in Himself."[19] The breakthrough, the birth, and the ground are all the Spirit's encounter with the human spirit. By whatever name we name this ineffable inner sanctum of our being, and Eckhart certainly struggled to name it while recognizing the inadequacy of all its names, there is something in human nature, within the human person, whereby that person is connected to God as Spirit, call it human spirit or call it something else.

Johannes Tauler (ca. 1300–1361), another of the German Dominican mystics of the fourteenth century, was as influential as Eckhart, if not more so. A disciple of Eckhart, whom he had most probably met personally in both Strasbourg and Cologne, Tauler was a spiritual guide for the Friends of God movement.[20] He attempted in his preaching both to open up the life of the soul and to explore its depths. He referred to "this wonderful divine spark deeper inside us and closer to us than we are ourselves," "the very depths of the soul where God is infinitely closer to the soul and more integral to it than is the soul itself," "the most intimate region of the soul, its most secret and inmost depths, where God is present essentially, actually, and substantially," and "God Himself firing the spirit with a spark from the divine abyss."[21]

Tauler, in his own distinctive, pastoral, and practical mystical way, carried on Eckhart's teaching concerning the ground of the soul, the union with God in the ground, and the birth of the Word in the ground.[22]

> It is a genuine ascent to God, a lifting of the spirit upward, so that God may in reality enter the purest, most inward, noblest part of the soul—its deepest ground— where alone there is undifferentiated unity. In regard to this Saint Augustine says that the soul has a hidden abyss, untouched by time and space, which is far superior to anything that gives life and movement to the body. Into this noble and wondrous ground, this secret realm, there descends that bliss of which we have spoken.[23]

This deepest ground of the soul is one's human spirit at its highest and most noble, wherein, we might say again, human spirit becomes one with Holy Spirit.

Not only did Tauler's preaching have a widespread influence in his lifetime but his writing continued to exert great influence through the centuries—more than Eckhart's, whose legacy had become tainted because of the condemnation of some propositions extracted from his works and taken out of context.[24] Paul Francis Danei (1694-1775), better known as Paul of the Cross, the founder of the Congregation of the Passion (or Passionists), was deeply influenced by Tauler.[25] He speaks of the sanctuary of the soul, the temple of the soul, the interior chamber, the most intimate chamber of the soul, the inner tabernacle, the interior solitude, and the interior desert.[26]

The Christian mystical tradition has frequently testified to an awareness of an innermost dimension to the human soul, the spirit within, which manifests a similitude to the Holy Spirit, the former being the temple of the latter. This "human spirit," this "ground of the soul," is a great link with Indian religious traditions whose psychologies point in a similar direction. Abhishiktananda, the French monk Henri Le Saux who lived in India from 1948 until his death in 1973, spoke about this "still point" within the human person. The Holy Spirit, he writes, "dwells in us in the innermost recesses of our hearts" and "is present at the core of each being, at the centre of the human heart."[27] In these texts Abhishiktananda is speaking not only out of his own mystical experience but also out of his careful reading of the Hindu Scriptures. That God resides in "the cave of the heart" is a central teaching of the Upanishads, written in Sanskrit between 800 and 400 BC and considered the last books of the Indian Vedas or Hindu Scriptures.

Translations of the Upanishads vary in their search for the right word. Swami Prabhavananda and Frederick Manchester prefer "the lotus of the heart."[28] Swami Nikhilananda prefers "cave of the heart" or at times simply "heart,"[29] as is also the case in the translation by F. Max Müller.[30] "The radiant Brahman dwells in the cave of the heart and is known to move there."[31] Sri Aurobindo's translation speaks about "the secret heart," "our secret being," or just "the heart."[32]

I am not suggesting that *pneuma*, or "spirit," in St. Paul, "ground of the soul" in Eckhart and Tauler, Teresa of Avila's "innermost part of the soul," and the Upanishads' "cave of the heart" are to be equated with one another. They all indicate, how-ever, an awareness of spiritual depth within the human person. And there is a close relationship, as Pope John Paul II affirmed (*Dominum et Vivificantem* 52), between that created "human spirit" and the uncreated Holy Spirit. The human spirit, with its ache for the infinite, yearns for an ever-deepening union with the Holy Spirit, who comes to dwell within us in the innermost core of our being.

Spirit: Human and Holy

It is difficult in some texts of St. Paul to determine whether the reference is to the human spirit or the Holy Spirit. The human spirit is also holy in that the human spirit is where the human and divine most immediately come together and make contact. It is the innermost sanctum that the Holy Spirit indwells. Yet human spirit and Holy Spirit are not the same, although experientially at times it is difficult to distinguish them. Is it now my spirit or your Spirit, O God? And apart from conceptually, how important is it to distin-guish them? It is now not me, my God, but your Spirit who lives within me. According to the Christian faith, we are truly temples of the Holy Spirit. "Do you not know that you are God's temple and that God's Spirit dwells in you?" (1 Cor 3:16). "Do you not know that your body is a temple of the Holy Spirit within you, which you have from God, and that you are not your own?" (1 Cor 6:19).

Our human spirit is the capacity created within us to be recep-tive to the Holy Gift. We remain incomplete by ourselves alone. When God's Spirit has embraced and become one with our spirit, when our human spirit has been awakened by the touch of the divine Spirit, when the Holy Spirit and our spirits have become one, it is now not we who live but God who is living within us.

This closeness between our human nature and the divine is reflected in another verse from Paul: "But anyone united to the Lord becomes one spirit with him" (1 Cor 6:17). When we are united to Christ, or to God through Christ, we become one spirit with God, not two. Just as two become one flesh in an intimate, loving sexual union, so two become one spirit in a spiritual union. Does the human spirit preexist the divine indwelling and receive it, or is it created by the coming of the Holy Spirit as she creates a home for herself within us, or is it simply a manifestation of the divine Spirit dwelling within us? Whatever our understanding, s/Spirit remains the innermost core of the human person.[33]

Within us, at the deepest level, human spirit is touched by the Divine Spirit, human being meets Divine Being, the utterly transcendent one becomes profoundly immanent and intimate, intercourse between God and us takes place. God and we have built a home together—our true and lasting home—where we become the glory of God and the glory of God makes us fully alive.[34]

Let us return to some texts in Paul in which it is difficult to note whether it is the Holy Spirit or the human spirit to which he is referring because they seem almost indistinguishable:

- "Therefore, one who speaks in a tongue should pray for the power to interpret. For if I pray in a tongue, my s/Spirit prays but my mind is unproductive. What should I do then? I will pray with the s/Spirit, but I will pray with the mind also; I will sing praise with the s/Spirit, but I will sing praise with the mind also." (1 Cor 14:13–15)

- "For though I am absent in body, yet I am with you in s/Spirit, and I rejoice to see your morale and the firmness of your faith in Christ." (Col 2:5)

The Holy Spirit is the point of contact between God and ourselves.[35] The Holy Spirit gives us a transfusion of divine life by which we live spiritual lives. Whereas the Holy Spirit is God as

Gift,[36] the human spirit is creature as receptor, the vehicle created by God within the human person that is able to receive the Divine Persons. Through the Holy Spirit, God breathes out. Through our spirits, we breathe God in.

> *Come, Holy Spirit, with your life divine.*
> *Come, awaken, ignite our aching, holy, human spirits.*
> *Enter your dwelling place in the innermost recesses of*
> *   our souls*
> *which you created*
> *so as to have a fitting place in which to dwell.*
> *Let our human spirits, O God, O Love Divine,*
> *and your Holy Spirit, your Holy Gift,*
> *become one within a loving embrace.*
> *For we are not two, not one, but one in You.*
> *Touch our bodies, our minds, our hearts, our souls, our human*
> *   spirits with your energy*
> *and fill us with your love.*

Notes

1. K. D. Sethna, *The Vision and Work of Sri Aurobindo*, 2nd rev. and enl. ed. (Pondicherry: Sri Aurobindo Ashram, 1992), 4. Sri Aurobindo Ghose is twentieth-century India's greatest mystic-philosopher-sage.

2. Augustine, *Confessions*, trans. Henry Chadwick (Oxford University Press, 1991), 3.

3. See James D. G. Dunn, *The Theology of Paul the Apostle* (Grand Rapids: Eerdmans, 1998), 51–78.

4. Note h on 1 Thess 5:23. *The New Jerusalem Bible* (Garden City, NY: Doubleday, 1985), 1955.

5. In *Writings from the Philokalia on Prayer of the Heart*, trans. E. Kadloubovsky and G. E. H. Palmer (London: Faber & Faber, 1973), 283.

6. The following texts are taken from Augustine, *Confessions*, 43 (III, 6[11]), 123 (VII, 10[6]), 200–201 (X, 25–27[36–38]).

7. Teresa of Avila, *The Interior Castle*, trans. Kieran Kavanaugh and Otilio Rodriguez, Classics of Western Spirituality (New York: Paulist Press, 1979), 74–75 (IV.2.5).

8. *The Life of Teresa of Jesus: The Autobiography of St. Teresa of Avila*, trans. E. Allison Peers (Garden City, NY: Doubleday, 1960), 150 (chap. 14).

9. Teresa of Avila, *The Interior Castle*, 175 (VII.1.7).

10. Ibid., 177 (VII.1.11). Such references can also be found in John of the Cross. See *The Collected Works of St. John of the Cross*, trans. Kieran Kavanaugh and Otilio Rodriguez (Washington, DC: Institute of Carmelite Studies, 1973). For example, in "The Dark Night," he speaks of "the spirit, the superior part of the soul," 304.

11. Pope Leo XIII, encyclical *Divinum Illud Munus* (1897). See *The Papal Encyclicals*, ed. Claudia Carlen, 5 vols. (Wilmington, NC: McGrath, 1981), 2:409–18. Pope John Paul II, encyclical *Dominum et Vivificantem* (1986). Available on the Vatican Web site at http://www.vatican.va/holy_father/john_paul_ii/encyclicals/documents/hf_jp-ii_enc_18051986_dominum-et-vivificantem_en.html.

12. Translation revised for the purpose of inclusive language.

13. See *Meister Eckhart and the Beguine Mystics*, ed. Bernard McGinn (New York: Continuum, 1997); and Amy Hollywood, *The Soul as Virgin Wife, Mechthild of Magdeburg, Marguerite Porete, and Meister Eckhart* (Notre Dame, IN: University of Notre Dame Press, 1995).

14. For Eckhart's works themselves, see *Meister Eckhart: The Essential Sermons, Commentaries, Treatises and Defense*, trans. Edmund Colledge and Bernard McGinn, Classics of Western Spirituality (New York: Paulist Press, 1981); *Meister Eckhart: Teacher and Preacher*, trans. Bernard McGinn, Frank Tobin, and Elvira Borgstadt, Classics of Western Spirituality (New York: Paulist Press, 1986); and *Meister Eckhart: German Sermons and Treatises*, trans. M. O'C. Walshe, 3 vols. (London: Watkins, 1979, 1981, 1987). Excellent introductions to Eckhart include Cyprian Smith, *The Way of Paradox: Spiritual Life as Taught by Meister Eckhart* (New York: Paulist Press, 1987); and Richard Woods, *Eckhart's Way* (Wilmington, DE: Michael Glazier, 1986). Other significant studies include Oliver Davies, *Meister Eckhart: Mystical Theologian* (London: SPCK, 1991); Robert K. C. Forman, *Meister Eckhart: Mystic as Theologian*

(Rockport, MA: Element, 1991); Bernard McGinn, *The Mystical Thought of Meister Eckhart: The Man from Whom God Hid Nothing* (New York: Crossroad, 2001); Reiner Schürmann, *Meister Eckhart: Mystic and Philosopher* (Bloomington: Indiana University Press, 1978), reprinted as *Wandering Joy: Meister Eckhart's Mystical Philosophy* (Great Barrington, MA: Lindisfarne Books, 2001); and Frank Tobin, *Meister Eckhart: Thought and Language* (Philadelphia: University of Pennsylvania Press, 1986).

15. For some references, see *Meister Eckhart*, trans. M. O'C. Walshe, I:3, 5, 9–10, 15–18, 25, 39, 84, 86, 128, 171–72, among many others.

16. Ibid., 64, 76–77, 80, 97, 99, 107, 136, 147–48, 179, 183, among others.

17. Ibid., 147–48.

18. Ibid., 1–47, 67, 76, 93–94, 99, 106–7, 111, 117, 138, 145, 148, 164–65, 179–80, and many other references.

19. Ibid., 136.

20. For the sermons of Tauler in English translation, see Johann Tauler, *Spiritual Conferences*, trans. and ed. Eric Colledge and Sister M. Jane (Rockford, IL: Tan Books, 1978); and Johannes Tauler, *Sermons*, trans. Maria Shrady with an introduction by Josef Schmidt, Classics of Western Spirituality (New York: Paulist Press, 1985). Sermon 15, for the Eve of Palm Sunday, refers to Eckhart, "one great teacher who taught you and told you about these things" and " a famous teacher who spoke of these matters" (*Spiritual Conferences*, 238).

21. Johann Tauler, *Spiritual Conferences*, trans. Colledge, 40, 76, 142, 166–67.

22. E.g., see Sermons 1, 5, 24 in Johannes Tauler, *Sermons*, trans. Shrady, 38, 48–49, 89–90.

23. Ibid., 89.

24. Concerning the condemnation, see Oliver Davies, "Why Were Eckhart's Propositions Condemned?" *New Blackfriars* 71 (1990): 433–45; Woods, *Eckhart's Way*, 151–77; idem, "The Condemnation of Meister Eckhart," *Spirituality* 6 (Nov.-Dec., 2000): 342–47.

25. See Martin Bialas, *The Mysticism of the Passion in St. Paul of the Cross* (San Francisco: Ignatius Press, 1990). With respect to the influence of Tauler, see pp. 123–46.

26. Ibid., 138 and 177 n. 93.

27. Abhishiktananda, *Prayer,* new ed. (New Delhi: ISPCK, 1999), 13, 14.

28. *The Upanishads: Breath of the Eternal,* trans. Swami Prabhavananda and Frederick Manchester (Hollywood, CA: Vedanta Press, 1983), a very readable translation. For references to "the lotus of the heart," see pp. 25, 48, 63–65, 149, 192, among many others.

29. *The Upanishads,* trans. and ed. Swami Nikhilananda (New York: Harper Torchbooks, 1964), e.g., 114, 152.

30. *The Upanishads,* trans. F. Max Müller, in two parts (New York: Dover Publications, 1962).

31. *The Upanishads,* trans. and ed. Swami Nikhilananda, 114. Mundaka Upanishad, II, 2, 1.

32. Sri Aurobindo, *The Upanishads: Texts, Translations, and Commentaries* (Pondicherry, India: Sri Aurobindo Ashram, 1994), e.g., pp. 201, 202, 222, 305.

33. On the innermost spirit in Eastern Orthodox spirituality, see Tomás Spidlík, *The Spirituality of the Christian East,* trans. Anthony P. Gythiel (Kalamazoo, MI: Cistercian Publications, 1986), 60–61, 94. On "the heart" in relationship to "spirit" in Russian spirituality, see pp. 103–6. It is difficult to distinguish "heart" from "spirit" in the scriptures as well as in the writings of many of the fathers. Biblically as well as later they are often interchangeable and each can refer to the innermost core of the person, depending on the context.

34. Irenaeus, *Adversus Haereses* 4.20.7.

35. Kilian McDonnell speaks about the Holy Spirit as a contact point ("A Trinitarian Theology of the Holy Spirit?" *Theological Studies* 46 [1985]: 191–227, esp. 193, 200, 208–12). He writes, "the Spirit is the point of contact between God and humankind" and "that point where the one 'touches' the other" (p. 208). Also see Kilian McDonnell, *The Other Hand of God: The Holy Spirit as the Universal Touch and Goal* (Collegeville, MN: Liturgical

Press, 2003), 114–18, 216–21. Previously Tomás Spidlík had written in a somewhat similar vein, "As the pupil of the eye is, so to speak, the point of intersection between two worlds, the outer and the inner, so—the Fathers thought—there must be in man a mysterious point through which God enters the human heart with all his riches" (*Spirituality*, 104).

36. "Gift" is one of the traditional names for the Holy Spirit going back as far as Augustine. It will be taken up in more detail in chap. 12.

Chapter Two
JESUS, THE ANOINTED ONE

Jesus is paradigmatic of who we as human beings are created to be. As our human spirits are awakened by contact with God's Spirit, so was Jesus' humanity anointed by the Spirit. In the workings of the Trinity in creation, the Spirit and the Word accompany each other.[1] Irenaeus spoke of them as the two hands of God.[2] Jesus of Nazareth is the embodiment of the Word, but Jesus is also a work of the Holy Spirit. He is the Christ, the Anointed One of God.

In this chapter we will turn primarily to the Synoptic Gospels. Jesus is God's Spirit at work in the world, and this is to a great degree how the Synoptic Gospels understand him. Our focus will be particularly on the Gospel of Luke, in which Jesus and the Spirit take on the contours one of the other. To know the Spirit is to know Christ Jesus, and to know Jesus Christ is to know the Spirit. The Holy Spirit is at work in every phase of the Jesus story.

The Beginnings of the Story

If we ask when Jesus was first associated with the Spirit, the answer according to Mark is at the baptism of Jesus (Mark 1:9–11). The Gospels of Matthew and Luke, while recognizing the significance of this anointing by the Spirit on the occasion of Jesus' baptism, indicate that Jesus is connected to the Spirit from the moment of his conception in the womb of Mary (Luke 1:26–35; Matt 1:18–21). Although the infancy narratives reflect later redactions of Matthew and Luke, the two Gospels as we have them begin the Jesus story with Jesus' conception. "When his mother Mary had been engaged to Joseph, but before they lived together, she was found to be with child from the Holy Spirit" (Matt 1:18).

The role of the Spirit is even more pronounced in the Lucan infancy narrative, where it is clear that Jesus is inseparable from the Spirit. The Holy Spirit is mentioned seven times in Luke before we read of Jesus' baptism. The Holy Spirit appears with John the baptizer. The Spirit enters the scene while John is still in Elizabeth's womb (Luke 1:13–15). Jesus is conceived through the power of the Spirit (Luke 1:34–35). Following the scene of the annunciation to Mary comes the visitation: Mary, now pregnant, visits Elizabeth. "And Elizabeth was filled with the Holy Spirit and exclaimed with a loud cry, 'Blessed are you among women, and blessed is the fruit of your womb'" (Luke 1:41–42).

Elizabeth gives birth to John. "Then his father Zechariah was filled with the Holy Spirit and spoke this prophecy: 'Blessed be the Lord God of Israel…'" (Luke 1:67–68). Next Mary gives birth to Jesus. On the occasion of the young child's being brought to Jerusalem to be presented to the Lord, Simeon prophesies and the Holy Spirit is mentioned three times (Luke 2:25–28).

For both Matthew and Luke, but particularly for Luke, the Jesus story begins with the Spirit. Jesus was conceived through the power of the Spirit. John, his predecessor, is endowed with the Spirit. Simeon, another man of the Spirit, as well as Anna, also a prophet, are the context of Jesus' first trip to the temple in Jerusalem. Thus it should be no surprise that the Spirit is present at Jesus' baptism.

The Gospel of Mark also points out early on that Jesus is associated with the Spirit. John the baptizer distinguishes his baptism from that of Jesus: "I have baptized you with water; but he will baptize you with the Holy Spirit" (Mark 1:8). We see this same distinction in the Gospel of John (John 1:24–34), that Jesus' baptism was seen as a baptism in the Spirit. Then Mark goes immediately to the baptism of Jesus; "And just as he was coming up out of the water, he saw the heavens torn apart and the Spirit descending like a dove on him" (Mark 1:10). The baptism was understood as the occasion during which Jesus was anointed by the Spirit. The Gospel of Luke makes an even stronger statement. "Now when all the people were baptized, and when Jesus also had been baptized and was praying, the heaven was opened, and the Holy Spirit descended upon him in bodily form like a dove" (Luke 3:21–22). In the Lucan account the Holy Spirit descends on Jesus after the immersion during a moment of prayer. Yet it is clear that the baptism leads to Jesus' being endowed with a full measure of the Spirit: "Jesus, full of the Holy Spirit, returned from the Jordan…" (Luke 4:1).

In Mark, the real beginning of the Jesus story is that of the baptism. This is the moment when Jesus is portrayed as becoming the Messiah or is revealed as being the Messiah.[3] Jesus becomes the Messiah through the outpouring of the Holy Spirit upon him. For Matthew and Luke, Jesus had already been Messiah from the moment of his conception. Nevertheless, even in Luke the baptism takes on a significance as another occasion into which the Spirit enters. Jesus may have been conceived through the power of the Spirit, and the Spirit had been hovering over Jesus during the course of his early life; but Jesus is overtaken in a new way by the Spirit at his baptism. If the conception points to the divine origins of Jesus, his baptism in the Spirit points to Jesus' humanity, that it must be permeated with Spirit. For in spite of all that Luke had previously said in his infancy narrative, it remained for Jesus to increase in wisdom and in years (Luke 1:52).

We may never be able to penetrate fully what the experience of the immersion into the Jordan meant for Jesus. We can be sure that it left an indelible mark on his life. When Jesus left Nazareth at that time, did he expect to receive John's baptism, or was he drawn into it by the power of John's preaching? Had Jesus left home expecting to return more or less as he had left, or did he have intimations that this would be a turning point in his life? Had he heard John preach on some previous pilgrimage to Jerusalem or only heard about the baptizer? What drew Jesus to take leave of

Mary at that time, what was he seeking, for what had he already prepared himself? These, of course, are questions we will never answer. We can only imagine. But the texts about the baptism make clear that it was understood as a Spirit-filled event.

The baptism is not only about Jesus but also about the Spirit. The Spirit had already been present to Jesus in Nazareth at prayer, in the synagogue, and during his meditations on the Jewish Scriptures. Yet the baptism was not just another event alongside others in Jesus' life but an experience of the Spirit that changed his life. Jesus is now fully aligned with the Spirit. He has been chosen by the Spirit and anointed by the Spirit to be the Spirit's mouthpiece, as was true of the prophets of old. Jesus was now "prophet of the Most High" (Luke 1:76).

The Wilderness Experience

As overpowering as were the baptism and its experience of the Spirit, so another powerful experience was ahead for Jesus, that of the wilderness, in which *wilderness* is not to be understood primarily as geography.[4] The Gospel of Luke reports: "Jesus, full of the Holy Spirit, returned from the Jordan and was led by the Spirit in the wilderness, where for forty days he was tempted by the devil" (Luke 4:1–2). Jesus was already full of the Spirit and is now led by the Spirit in the wilderness. Led where? Into his own interior anguish of soul? Into a deeper search for the God of Israel? Into wrestling like Jacob with what God has in store for him? Into surrender?

The Gospel of Mark speaks even more strongly: "And the Spirit immediately drove him out into the wilderness" (Mark 1:12). Here the Spirit does not lead but drives Jesus into the wilderness. It is not Jesus but the Spirit who is in charge. The baptism of Jesus concluded with the understanding: "You are my Son, the Beloved; with you I am well pleased" (Mark 1:11; Luke 3:22). The text takes us back to the servant poems in Isaiah and the first servant poem in particular:

> Here is my servant, whom I uphold,
> my chosen, in whom my soul delights;
> I have put my spirit upon him;
> he will bring forth justice to the nations. (Isa 42:1)

The servant is endowed with the Spirit of the Lord. In the wilderness Jesus surrendered to the Spirit. He is now the Spirit's servant. He is letting the Spirit take over. As Luke expresses it, the Spirit leads Jesus through this experience of wilderness, of struggle with demonic powers, of self-questioning and unknowing, of surrender to the Lord.

In the temptation narratives in Matthew and Luke, the texts from scripture that sustain Jesus during this ordeal in the wilderness all come from the Book of Deuteronomy, and from what is now chapters 6 to 8 of Deuteronomy, following the text of the great prayer of Israel, the *Shema:* "Hear, O Israel: The LORD is our God, the LORD alone. You shall love the LORD your God with all your heart, and with all your soul, and with all your might" (Deut 6:4–5). Jesus in the wilderness comes through his test faithful. Jesus is one who loves the Lord with all his heart, a true Israelite. The wilderness is a Spirit story as much as a Jesus story. The Spirit drives Jesus there (Mark 1:12), leads him while there (Luke 4:1), and triumphs there over the powers of evil. It was Jesus' wrestling, to be sure, but never apart from the Spirit who had been given him.

The Mission of the Spirit

Following the ordeal in the wilderness, Jesus returned in the Spirit to Galilee. Mark has Jesus returning to Galilee after John was arrested (Mark 1:14). Likewise Matthew: "Now when Jesus heard that John had been arrested, he withdrew to Galilee" (Matt 4:12). Luke, however, suggests a more immediate return and again highlights the role of the Spirit: "Then Jesus, filled with the power of the Spirit, returned to Galilee, and a report about him spread through all the surrounding country" (Luke 4:14). His life mission had begun. But what was it? How did Jesus himself understand it? We cannot be certain in our responses to these questions. Yet the scriptures provide clues, and in this context Luke allows us an inside view. The Lucan Jesus tells us in a straightforward fashion on the occasion of his first preaching back in Nazareth.

> When he came to Nazareth, where he had been brought up, he went to the synagogue on the sabbath day, as was his custom. He stood up to read, and the scroll of the prophet Isaiah was given to him. He unrolled the scroll and found the place where it was written:
>
> > "The Spirit of the Lord is upon me,
> > > because he has anointed me to bring good news to the poor.
> >
> > He has sent me to proclaim release to the captives
> > > and recovery of sight to the blind
> > > to let the oppressed go free,
> >
> > to proclaim the year of the Lord's favor."
>
> And he rolled up the scroll, gave it back to the attendant, and sat down. The eyes of all in the synagogue were fixed on him. Then he began to say to them, "Today this scripture has been fulfilled in your hearing." (Luke 4:16–21; see Isa 61:1–2)

Take note of what Jesus does, reads, and says. The scroll of the prophet Isaiah was given to him, but Jesus unrolls it with intentionality until he finds this particular text in Isaiah. This text is the Lucan Jesus' chosen self-description. The first thing Jesus proclaims is: "The Spirit of the Lord is upon me." This reflects Jesus' self-awareness following upon the experiences of the Spirit in his baptism and in the wilderness. Jesus knows he belongs to the Spirit. It is the Spirit who has anointed him as prophet, as Messiah, as servant. *Messiah* means "anointed one," and Jesus has been anointed as the prophets of old had been. Anointed for what? Jesus takes the cue from Isaiah: to bring good news to the poor, to proclaim freedom. Then Jesus sits down. He stood up to read; he sits down to preach. His message is brief. All that the Isaian text had envisioned, with its note of hopefulness for those without status in the world, has come to fulfillment. This was Jesus' mission, the mission of the Spirit, the mission of the Spirit through the centuries—to free people and proclaim justice. Jesus was in accord with the long line of the Spirit's prophets who had gone before him.

After these frequent references to the Spirit in the first chapters of the Gospel, Luke does not see the need to mention the Spirit at every Spirit-filled event in the ministry of Jesus. Where Jesus is, there the Spirit is also. Whatever portrait we attempt to draw of the ministry of Jesus, it is clear that the earthly Jesus of the New Testament gave himself predominantly to preaching, healing, and the casting out of demons. Jesus was involved in a social and spiritual struggle with the demonic world. Not much further into the text following Jesus' inaugural preaching in Nazareth, the people, upon witnessing an exorcism, "were all amazed and kept saying to one another, 'What kind of utterance is this? For with authority and power he commands the unclean spirits, and out they come!'" (Luke 4:36–37).

Jesus possesses authority over unclean and demonic spirits. It is by the power of the Holy Spirit that Jesus does this. Following another exorcism, some within the crowd accused Jesus of casting out demons by the power of an evil spirit: "Some of them said, 'He casts out demons by Beelzebul, the ruler of the demons'" (Luke 11:15). Yet Jesus defends himself with the argument that a house divided against itself is not able to survive and with the story of the binding of the strong man. He then goes on to declare that "if it is by the finger of God that I cast out the demons, then the kingdom of God has come to you" (Luke 11:20). Jesus himself affirms that he casts out demons by the power of God, the Spirit of God, the finger of God.

Not only are the exorcisms works of the Spirit, but so are Jesus' healings. Jesus is someone "full of the Holy Spirit" (Luke 4:1), "filled with the power of the Spirit" (Luke 4:14). Jesus was as much a healer as anything, and the power to heal manifested a psycho-pneumatic power at work within him. "Someone touched me; for I noticed that power had gone out from me" (Luke 8:46). Not only the healings, but also Jesus' preaching and teachings, were manifestations of the Spirit. "They were astounded at his teaching, because he spoke with authority" (Luke 4:32). The Lucan Jesus saw his ministry as involving Spirit-filled preaching: "I must proclaim the good news of the kingdom of God to the other cities also; for I was sent for this purpose" (Luke 4:43). This latter text, as much as the earlier one from the scroll of the prophet Isaiah, is one of the clearest statements of Jesus concerning his mission: to proclaim the good news of God.

Jesus' exorcisms, healings, and preaching were of one piece, not three separate ministries. They all came from one source: "the Spirit of the Lord" (Luke 4:18). They were all proclamations or manifestations of the reign of God. The healings were a preaching. Jesus the Healer was Jesus the Preacher. The healings were symbolic actions manifesting God's power, presence, and the reign of the Spirit. Symbolic or parabolic actions often accompanied Jesus' teaching or were the way in which he taught. His table fellowship with sinners was an enacted parable; the reign of God is here. He called the little children to come to him (Mark 9:36–37; 10:13–16). He washed the feet of the disciples (John 13:2–20).

The teaching through symbolic action, the table fellowship, the healings and exorcisms, all made God present to those who were, according to the teaching of some of the Pharisees or Sadducees, outside the pale of salvation, outside the reign of God. Teaching, preaching, healings, dining with sinners were all consistent: both a praxis of God and a proclamation of God. Underneath all the actions and sayings and stories of Jesus was the Spirit of the Lord. The reign of God was God present as Spirit. The reign of God was the Holy Spirit present and active. The Holy Spirit was the gift Jesus had come to give.

In the body of the Gospel of Luke itself, following the inaugural preaching on Isaiah in Nazareth, the Gospel refers explicitly to the Spirit four more times.

> At that same hour Jesus rejoiced in the Holy Spirit and said, "I thank you, Father, Lord of heaven and earth, because you have hidden these things from the wise and the intelligent and have revealed them to infants...." (Luke 10:21)

> "If you then, who are evil, know how to give good gifts to your children, how much more will the heavenly Father give the Holy Spirit to those who ask him!" (Luke 11:13)

> "And everyone who speaks a word against the Son of Man will be forgiven; but whoever blasphemes against the Holy Spirit will not be forgiven." (Luke 12:10)

> "When they bring you before the synagogues, the rulers, and the authorities, do not worry about how you are to defend yourself or what you are to say; for the Holy Spirit will teach you at that very hour what you ought to say." (Luke 12:11–12)

The texts manifest Jesus' awareness of the role of God's Holy Spirit in his mission and ministry.[5] Jesus not only began his mission with a Spirit-consciousness (Luke 4:18), but this awareness of the power and indwelling of the Spirit persisted.

Jesus rejoiced in the Holy Spirit's revelation of God through his ministry. Even we who are sinful give our children what is good; how much more true this is of God, whose gift to us is the Holy Spirit. Just as Jesus teaches that his "Abba" is our Abba too ("When you pray, say: Father" [Luke 11:2]), so his Spirit is also our Spirit. The Holy Spirit will teach us what to say, as he evidently taught Jesus, as he had previously assisted Moses, and as he comes to our aid, according to Paul (Rom 8:26). As a parallel text from Matthew says: "For it is not you who speak but the Spirit of your Father speaking through you" (Matt 10:20//Luke 12:11–12). According to

Luke, Jesus was conceived through the power of the Spirit, baptized with the Spirit, led by the Spirit through the wilderness ordeal, returned to Galilee in the power of the Spirit, declared that the Spirit had been poured out upon him in his first preaching in Nazareth, and continued to preach, teach, heal, and drive out demons through the power of the Spirit. Evil spirits recognized within him the Holy Spirit.

In the Gospel of John the Holy Spirit is breath, wind, advocate, and the Spirit of truth (3:8; 14:16, 17; 15:26; 16:12; 20:22). Breath and wind are both translations of the Hebrew *ruach* (spirit). In the Acts of the Apostles, another Lucan writing, wind is associated with the Spirit on the occasion of Pentecost. It is on that occasion that the Holy Spirit also appears as fire (Acts 2:1–4). The Lucan Pentecost is perhaps the Spirit event par excellence in the New Testament, and we shall come to it in the next chapter. Here we take note of the wind, a violent wind that accompanies the coming of the Holy Spirit, as well as fire. Fire is an image not unlike wind in that it can be soothing and benign—a gentle breeze, soft cool wind, warm fire, candlelight—or destructive and even violent—a tornado, typhoon, something that is on fire, something that burns. Yet Luke pictures fire accompanying the Holy Spirit's Pentecostal inbreaking.

This is not the first time fire appears in Luke in relationship with the Holy Spirit. If we go back to John's water baptism and that of Jesus, John is reported as saying:

> "I baptize you with water; but one who is more powerful than I is coming; I am not worthy to untie the thong of his sandals. He will baptize you with the Holy Spirit and fire. His winnowing fork is in his hand, to clear his threshing floor and to gather the wheat into his granary; but the chaff he will burn with unquenchable fire." (Luke 3:16–17)

The imagery here is apocalyptic. Apocalyptic language and images are more appropriate to John the baptizer's message and mission than they are for that of Jesus, whose life and mission were less characterized by apocalyptic.[6] "Fire" is apocalyptic talk and conjures up a fiery judgment to come. But fire in Luke is also associated with the Spirit, as on the occasion of Pentecost, and here in John's response to those questioning him about the Messiah: He will baptize you with the Holy Spirit and fire. The Holy Spirit brings fire and sets our lives ablaze. There is something passionate and comforting and challenging about fire and also about the Holy Spirit.[7] At Pentecost the Holy Spirit set the disciples on fire.

Within the Gospel of Luke the image of fire is used by Jesus to describe his own mission as well. "I came to bring fire to the earth, and how I wish it were already kindled! I have a baptism with which to be baptized, and what stress I am under until it is completed" (Luke 12:49–50). Here fire is associated with baptism, as in John the baptizer's reference to Jesus. Fire occurs at the beginning of the mission of Jesus, during the course of that mission, and when that mission seems to be completed with Pentecost. According to Luke, Jesus would baptize not with water but with fire. And Jesus identifies his own mission with the bringing of fire, wishing that it were ablaze already. On Pentecost the fire has come at last. Thus one can suggest that the Lucan Jesus is saying, "I have come to bring down the Spirit to earth, and how I wish that she were already here. She is the one with whom we are to be baptized and that will be a baptism indeed. Would that she might be here and my work might be complete."[8] Jesus understood his life as an outpouring of Spirit. The Spirit was breaking through.

Death and Resurrection

We now come to the concluding chapter in the story of the earthly Jesus of Nazareth, a story that began, according to Matthew and Luke, with Jesus' conception through the power of the Holy Spirit and will conclude with his being raised from the dead by the power of that same Spirit. The Spirit remains with Jesus as he comes to his final ordeal, the final wilderness experience from Gethsemane to the cross. The Spirit does not abandon the one whom she has so faithfully aided, guided, and accompanied during Jesus' earthly pilgrimage. Yet, when we come to this point in the story, we are left with Jesus seemingly alone. The Holy Spirit is not mentioned explicitly. There is no denying, however, that she is there, even on the cross.

As Jesus consciously brings the earthly sojourn to a close, his last words from the cross, according to Luke, are: "Father, into your hands I commend my spirit" (Luke 23:46). The same sense is there in the Gospel of John. It is over, at last. "[Jesus] said, 'It is finished.' Then he bowed his head and gave up his spirit" (John 19:30). Whatever the sense of finality, of completion, of accomplishment, of disappointment, of resignation, one final act remained: to surrender his S/spirit and leave his life in the hands of God.

Are we to say "Spirit" or "spirit" in these texts? All translations say spirit. But the Greek text is open to interpretation. It clearly does not say "holy spirit," simply S/spirit, that is, *pneuma*. But one could well speculate at this point whether there was a difference between Jesus' spirit and Jesus' Spirit. Had one not become the other? Were they so united that one could not surrender one without surrendering the other? Is it Jesus' human spirit that is being handed over to the Father? Or the divine Spirit? And is it possible to distinguish, other than conceptually? For indeed handing over, returning, the Spirit to the Father was existentially the same as handing over his own human spirit. In the course of the seemingly long earthly journey, the two had become one. To surrender one's spirit, the abode of the Spirit of God, the Spirit's entry into and contact point with the human life of Jesus, means to surrender one's Spirit.

So the Spirit remained with Jesus through his final ordeal and was returned to the Father with Jesus' parting breath (*ruach*, *pneuma*). The Spirit had clearly put his seal or stamp on Jesus, and Jesus his imprint on the Spirit. Perhaps never have two been so intimately one. It is finished. It is time to let the Spirit go and to go with it. And yet, the Spirit does not abandon Jesus to death. Although Jesus has let go of the S/spirit, the Spirit restores Jesus to

29

life in a totally new and transformed and unimaginable way that eye has not seen (1 Cor 2:9). Jesus is raised from the dead.

The resurrection narratives in the Gospels do not refer to the Spirit explicitly, yet the Spirit is there "to be given" by the risen Christ. The Spirit's Christ has now become the Christ's Spirit. Both are equally true. They belong to each other as they do to the Father. The Spirit of God is now also the Spirit of Christ (Rom 8:9–11). Christ has put his stamp on the Spirit, as the Spirit has on Christ.

Paul had simply said, according to the tradition handed down to him, that Jesus "was raised on the third day" (1 Cor 15:4). For Paul, Christ was alive because God had raised him from the dead. It was God's doing (1 Thess 1:10; 1 Cor 6:14; 15:15; 2 Cor 4:14; Gal 1:1; Rom 4:24; 10:9). The earliest formula for announcing the resurrection was in the passive voice. "He was raised," not "he rose." Thus we naturally inquire: raised by whom or by what? That the Spirit plays a role in the resurrection of Jesus is only intimated by Paul.

> But you are not in the flesh; you are in the Spirit, since the Spirit of God dwells in you. Anyone who does not have the Spirit of Christ does not belong to him. But if Christ is in you, though the body is dead because of sin, the Spirit is life because of righteousness. If the Spirit of him who raised Jesus from the dead dwells in you, he who raised Christ from the dead will give life to your mortal bodies also through his Spirit that dwells in you. (Rom 8:9–11)

The Spirit of God, who raised Jesus from the dead, will also raise us. Here the power of the Spirit is the agent of resurrection.[9] The Spirit will give us life also; we are given the risen life through the power of the Spirit who then dwells within us. In Roman Catholic liturgy, the implicit intimation is made explicit. The sixth preface for Sundays in Ordinary Time in the liturgy of the Eucharist states:

Each day you show us a Father's love;
your Holy Spirit, dwelling within us,
gives us on earth the hope of unending joy.
Your gift of the Spirit,
who raised Jesus from the dead,
is the foretaste and promise
of the paschal feast of heaven....[10]

The Holy Spirit indwells us. The Holy Spirit is God's gift to us. It is the Holy Spirit who raised Jesus from the dead. It is the Holy Spirit who is the foretaste of more to come. The whole Jesus story is an act of the Holy Spirit, whose work began before Jesus was conceived and continued beyond his raising Jesus from the dead. Just as Jesus returned the Spirit to the Father and sent the Spirit to us from the Father, so the Spirit restores Jesus, the Anointed One, to life.

Holy Spirit, risen Christ, in whom we live and move,
may your divine presence anoint our human spirits, ignite our
    souls,
and set our hearts on fire.
Enkindle in us the fire of your love.
Guide us, Holy Spirit,
so that we might conform our lives to that of Christ.
Help us to be prophetic seekers, teachers of wisdom,
and true servants of God and one another.
As you, O Christ, were son of God and son of humanity,
make us also through the power of your Spirit
daughters and sons of God and deeply human through your grace.
Teach us to love.
Pour out upon us once again a full measure of your Spirit.

Notes

1. I discuss the Word and the Spirit at greater length in chap. 12.

2. Irenaeus, *Adversus Haereses*, 4.19.2; 20.1–12; 5.1.3. Also Irenaeus, *Proof of the Apostolic Preaching*, 11. Also see *Catechism of the Catholic Church* (New York: Doubleday, 1995), #704; and John Lawson, *The Biblical Theology of Saint Irenaeus* (London: Epworth Press, 1948).

3. See Raymond E. Brown, *An Introduction to New Testament Christology* (New York: Paulist Press, 1994), 107–8; idem, *The Birth of the Messiah* (Garden City, NY: Doubleday, 1977), 29–32, 134–37, 140–42, 181–82.

4. See Donald J. Goergen, *The Mission and Ministry of Jesus* (Wilmington, DE: Michael Glazier, 1986; reprint, Eugene, OR: Wipf & Stock, 1992) for a more complete exposition of the Jesus material, esp. pp. 116–29 on the wilderness experience in particular. On Jesus and the Spirit, also see the *Catechism of the Catholic Church*, ##717–30.

5. The Lucan text (12:10) on blasphemy against the Holy Spirit is one to which I give greater attention in chap. 9.

6. See Goergen, *Mission and Ministry of Jesus*, 177–204. Edward Schillebeeckx sees John within early prophetic traditions rather than apocalyptic ones; see *Jesus: An Experiment in Christology* (New York: Seabury Press, 1979), 126–36.

7. Fire is one of the predominant images of the Holy Spirit also for Catherine of Siena. See her *Dialogue*, *Prayers*, and *Letters*: Catherine of Siena, *The Dialogue*, trans. Suzanne Noffke, Classics of Western Spirituality (New York: Paulist Press, 1980); *The Prayers of Catherine of Siena*, 2nd ed., trans. Suzanne Noffke (New York: Authors Choice Press, 2001); *The Letters of Catherine of Siena*, trans. Suzanne Noffke (Tempe, AZ: Arizona Center for Medieval and Renaissance Studies, 2000, 2001).

8. Thomas Hopko ("Holy Spirit in Orthodox Theology and Life," *Commonweal* 89 [November 8, 1968]: 186–91) speaks of Mother Maria, a Russian nun in Paris who went to her death in a Nazi gas chamber on Good Friday, 1945. "Mother Maria also said her word to the world, 'If Christianity is not fire,' she said, the Fire which is the Spirit whom Christ has come to cast upon the earth, 'then it does not exist'" (p. 189).

9. Thomas Aquinas interprets Rom 8:11 as indicating the Spirit as agent of the resurrection: "The power of raising to life, of course, belongs to the Holy Spirit" *(On the Truth of the Catholic Faith [Summa contra Gentiles],* Bk. IV, chap. 17, #5 [Garden City, NY: Doubleday, 1957]), 108.

10. From the Sacramentary of the Roman Missal, 1974. Preface for Sundays in Ordinary Time, VI.

Chapter Three
HOLYSPIRIT@ECCLESIA.ORG

We have followed the Holy Spirit from the moment of Jesus' conception through the raising of Jesus from the dead. Now we continue to follow the Spirit as she is poured out upon the post-resurrection Jesus movement. We followed Jesus and the Spirit by staying primarily with the Gospel of Luke. Here we begin with Luke's companion work, the Acts of the Apostles, which mentions the Holy Spirit over fifty times.[1]

The Emergence of the Christian *Ecclesia*

Luke begins: "In the first book [the Gospel], Theophilus, I wrote about all that Jesus did and taught from the beginning until the day when he was taken up to heaven, after giving instructions through the Holy Spirit to the apostles whom he had chosen" (Acts 1:1–2). The apostles were told, "John baptized with water, but you will be baptized with the Holy Spirit not many days from now" (Acts 1:5). Immediately before Jesus' ascension—and Luke is the only New Testament author to speak about Jesus' exaltation in this way—the risen Jesus stated, "You will receive power when the Holy Spirit has come upon you" (Acts 1:8), referring to an imminent outpouring of the Spirit.

Jesus was taken from his disciples' sight. They returned to Jerusalem from the mount of the ascension. Peter addressed a gathering of about 120 of the followers about how the scriptures, which were understood to be a work of the Holy Spirit, had to be fulfilled (Acts 1:16). Then came the Jewish feast of Pentecost.

> When the day of Pentecost had come, they were all together in one place. And suddenly from heaven there came a sound like the rush of a violent wind, and it filled the entire house where they were sitting. Divided tongues, as of fire, appeared among them, and a tongue rested on each of them. All of them were filled with the Holy Spirit and began to speak in other languages, as the Spirit gave them ability. (Acts 2:1–4)

Perhaps the greatest outpouring of Spirit in all of history had taken place. The occasion was a Jewish festival; the setting was Jerusalem. One could hear the Holy Spirit coming. The sound was like that of a violent wind. Here as well as in the Gospel of John, in the story of Jesus with Nicodemus (John 3:8), the Holy Spirit is imaged as wind—and here a violent one. Not only wind, but also fire depicts the presence of the Spirit, as we have already seen. "I have come to bring fire to the earth" (Luke 12:49). Fire, like wind, conveys the uncontrollable God, capable of being experienced as consoling or overwhelming.

On this particular feast of Pentecost, the Holy Spirit who came like wind and fire gave the power to speak in foreign languages. How to explain the event? Peter makes the attempt and sees in it a fulfillment of the scriptures. He interprets the event in the light of a text from the prophet Joel (2:28–32).

> But Peter, standing with the eleven, raised his voice and addressed them....This is what was spoken through the prophet Joel:

> "In the last days it will be, God declares,
> that I will pour out my Spirit upon all flesh,
> and your sons and your daughters shall prophesy,
> and your young men shall see visions,
> and your old men shall dream dreams.
> Even upon my slaves, both men and women,
> in those days I will pour out my Spirit;
> and they shall prophesy...." (Acts 2:14–18)

35

This text is as significant as the description of Pentecost itself (Acts 2:1–13). The one narrates what happened; the other interprets it. What was foretold by the prophet Joel referred to the end times, or a distant future, when there would be an outpouring of God's Spirit. What Peter saw happening on that day was what Joel had envisioned.

The prophetic text from Joel envisions a universal outpouring, not a selective one. All flesh will be the Spirit's recipients. And lest there be any doubt about whether "all" means all, the prophet delineates men and women, young and old, slave and free. Among the works of the Spirit there will be dreams, prophecies, and visions. The Spirit is now available to all. Nothing can confine the Spirit's sphere of influence.

Peter continued his effort to help the people understand. This Jesus God raised up (2:32); this Jesus God has made both Lord and Messiah (2:36); this Jesus had received from the Father the promise of the Holy Spirit (2:33); this Jesus has now poured out this Holy Spirit upon all people (2:33). The next step: "Be baptized" and "receive the gift of the Holy Spirit" (2:38). The invitation to enter this new pneumatic reality was issued. The beginning of the church lay within this outpouring of the Spirit.

The risen Christ's work on earth continues through the power of the Spirit. References to the Spirit in Acts continue. Peter, filled with the Holy Spirit, speaks to the rulers of the people (4:8). Peter and John report to the others. After praying, "the place in which they were gathered together was shaken; and they were all filled with the Holy Spirit and spoke the word of God with boldness" (4:31). In this incident there is no report of baptism, simply "when they had prayed" (4:31).

Shortly, in Acts 6–7, comes the story traditionally considered to be the institution of deacons and their ministry. The Spirit is mentioned six times. The context is still the church in Jerusalem and the need for more assistance with ministry in an expanding church. The widows of the Greek-speaking Jews are being neglected in the daily distribution of food (6:1), and so the decision is

made to choose others to be of assistance with that particular service (6:2–3), since it is important that the ministry of the word not
be neglected (6:2). Those selected are "seven men of good standing, full of the Spirit and of wisdom" (6:3). To qualify for ministry,
one must be filled with the Spirit.

Stephen, one of the seven, is described as "a man full of faith
and the Holy Spirit" (6:5). Stephen is able to hold his own against
those who argue with him because "they could not withstand the wisdom and the Spirit with which he spoke" (6:10). Those who refused
to believe Stephen are described as "forever opposing the Holy
Spirit" (7:51). They became enraged with him, but Stephen was still
"filled with the Holy Spirit" (7:55). As they stoned him, he prayed, as
Jesus had prayed, "Receive my S/spirit" (7:59; Luke 23:46).

The church began to expand into Samaria, and so the church
in Jerusalem sent Peter and John to Samaria. Peter and John prayed
that those hearing the word of God in Samaria might receive the
Holy Spirit (Acts 8:14–15). Followers of Jesus in Samaria had been
baptized in the name of the Lord Jesus but had not as yet received
the Spirit (8:16). "Then Peter and John laid their hands on them,
and they received the Holy Spirit" (8:17). The Spirit was given
through the laying on of hands (8:17–18), although ordinarily the
Spirit is received at baptism (2:38; 19:5–6), or, as we shall see, even
before baptism (10:44), but here the people of Samaria received the
Spirit subsequent to baptism through the laying on of hands. The
Spirit guided Philip to the Ethiopian eunuch and the eunuch's subsequent baptism (8:29, 39).

By now a young man named Saul (7:58), destined to be the
great St. Paul, has entered the scene, with his reputation for assist-
ing in the persecution of the church in Jerusalem and followers
of "the Way" (8:1–3; 9:1–2).[2] En route to Damascus, he had an
extraordinary experience of the risen Christ (Acts 9:3–8; 22:4–11;
26:12–15; 1 Cor 15:8; Gal 1:13–17). After his arrival in Damascus,
still blind from his experience, a disciple of Jesus, Ananias, visited
Saul. "He laid his hands on Saul and said, 'Brother Saul, the Lord
Jesus, who appeared to you on your way here, has sent me so that

you may regain your sight and be filled with the Holy Spirit'" (9:17). Saul's sight is restored and he is baptized. It is again the Holy Spirit who enters the scene as the story of Paul and his mission gets under way. Ananias was sent so that Paul might receive the Spirit. Peter had already been filled with the Spirit and now Paul as well. The church throughout Judea, Galilee, and Samaria is at peace and lives "in the comfort of the Holy Spirit" (9:31).

We then come to the story of Cornelius (Acts 10:1–48), the first Gentile convert. The honors go to Peter, although Paul will become the apostle to the Gentiles. The experience is one of the more significant learning experiences for Peter and fundamental for the future of the church. Cornelius, a Roman centurion, sent three men to Joppa to find Peter. The Spirit, of course, was the force behind the scenes. "The Spirit said to him [Peter], 'Look, three men are searching for you. Now get up, go down, and go with them without hesitation'" (10:19). Peter must now struggle with a mission to Gentiles. Could they too be called by the God of Israel to receive the gift of the Spirit, the same gift as that bestowed upon his fellow Israelites?

Peter begins to understand: "I truly understand that God shows no partiality, but in every nation anyone who fears him and does what is right is acceptable to him" (Acts 10:34–35). The Spirit does not necessarily respect humanly constructed barriers within humankind, whether religious or otherwise. God calls all people of good will. "While Peter was still speaking, the Holy Spirit fell upon all who heard the word" (10:44). Here the reception of the Spirit followed upon neither baptism nor laying on of hands, but subsequent to preaching and hearing the Word. "The circumcised believers who had come with Peter were astounded that the gift of the Holy Spirit had been poured out even on the Gentiles…" (10:45). This is what Peter had learned. Just as Jesus had once said, "Not even in Israel have I found such faith" (Matt 8:10), so Peter and his companions are discovering that faith and the Spirit are not confined to those whom we define as appropriate recipients.

Thus Peter, realizing that Gentiles had received the very same gift that he had received, cannot show partiality. "Then Peter said, 'Can anyone withhold the water for baptizing these people who have received the Holy Spirit just as we have?'" (10:47). The lesson learned remained with Peter. Defending himself upon his return to Jerusalem, he repeats: "The Spirit told me to go with them and not to make a distinction between them and us" (11:12). "The Holy Spirit fell upon them just as it had upon us at the beginning" (11:15). "If then God gave them the same gift that he gave us when we believed in the Lord Jesus Christ, who was I that I could hinder God?" (11:17). To this same argument Peter returned later when Paul and Barnabas came to defend a mission to the Gentiles at the council of elders in Jerusalem. Peter ended the debate, "God, who knows the human heart, testified to them by giving them the Holy Spirit, just as he did to us; and in cleansing their hearts by faith he has made no distinction between them and us" (15:8–9).

Meanwhile, in Antioch, where the followers of Jesus first came to be called Christians (11:26), the Holy Spirit instructed (13:2) them that Barnabas, "a good man, full of the Holy Spirit and of faith" (11:24), and Saul, "also known as Paul, filled with the Holy Spirit" (13:9; 20:22–23), were to be set apart for "the work to which I [the Holy Spirit] have called them" (13:2). "So, being sent out by the Holy Spirit, they went down to Seleucia; and from there they sailed to Cyprus" (13:4). Paul is later described as "a captive to the Spirit" (20:22). The early church, in its fragile origins, was a work of the Holy Spirit who was there at every turn, guiding every event.

The *Ecclesia* as Mystery and Grace

How might we talk about this continuing outpouring of Spirit as church today? The Latin word for church is *ecclesia*, the Greek or New Testament word is *ekklēsia*, and this is a translation of the Hebrew word *qahal*, which refers in the Hebrew Scriptures to the assembly or gathering of Israel. The *ecclesia* is the Christian assembly. Paul speaks about the *ekklēsia theou* or church of God.[3]

The church at its most fundamental is *mysterium*. It participates in the mystery of Christ, the mystery of the triune God, the mystery of God as Spirit present to people. This "mystery of the church" was a concept central to the ecclesiology of the Second Vatican Council.[4] It manifests the influence of Yves Congar.[5] The church is first of all the mystery of grace, the mystery of the Holy Spirit.

Grace, in Latin *gratia*, in Greek *charis*, etymologically goes back to the Sanskrit *gir*, a hymn of praise. Grace is first of all Uncreated Grace, the Holy Spirit who is grace itself. Roger Haight writes, "Grace is God as Spirit poured out anew through Jesus and dwelling in human hearts (Rom 5:5)."[6] The church ultimately is a field of grace, the sphere of influence of the Holy Spirit. As Irenaeus (ca. 135–ca. 200) said in the second century, "Where the church is, there is the Spirit of God; and where the Spirit of God is, there is the church, and every kind of grace" (*Adversus Haereses* 3.24.1).

The Holy Spirit is both *the soul of the soul* and *the soul of the church*. Augustine spoke of the Spirit in this latter way. "What the soul is to the body, the Holy Spirit is to the body of Christ, which is the church" (*Sermo 266 in Pent* chap. 4).[7] Thomas Aquinas referred to the Holy Spirit as the heart of the church.[8] It is through the Holy Spirit that all Spirit-animated persons are interconnected into a living spiritual network. The one and only Holy Spirit is ultimately in one sense the soul of each. The Holy Spirit ties us into being one, diverse though we may be. Although we spoke in chapter 1 of the human spirit as sometimes described as the soul of the soul, it is the Holy Spirit in union with the human spirit who is ultimately the human person's deepest center. The human spirit is more like the obediential potency for the Holy Spirit or gift of grace. It is in this sense that grace is often described as our "second nature" and the Holy Spirit as the vital principle of both the soul and the church.[9]

One of the primary works of the Holy Spirit is deification. The church is the milieu in which this deification takes place. Grace is nothing other than a participation in the divine nature. Uncreated grace is the Holy Spirit, and we participate in this life-giving uncreated grace through the Holy Spirit's indwelling. This participation in the life of the Spirit can be habitual and sanctifying (or *gratia gratum faciens*,[10] grace that makes us pleasing to God). Through this grace, that is to say, through the presence of the Holy Spirit as given to us, we become friends of God, children of God, heirs of God, co-heirs with Christ, pleasing to God, intimately united to God, temples of the Trinity sharing in the divine triune life. The Holy Spirit becomes in one sense our truest self.

The church at its source is an invisible sphere of grace, the sphere of influence of the Holy Spirit, the "milieu" of the Spirit, or the divine milieu, to use an expression of Teilhard de Chardin.[11] Nor does the history of the Spirit, and therefore the history of the church, begin at Pentecost, but rather goes back in time.[12] Augustine had noted that in one sense the church began with Abel.

> We are, therefore, all members of the body of Christ, not only we who are here, but all Christians spread through-out the earth, not only those who exist at the present time, and what shall I say here?, but also all those who, from the time of the just man Abel, have existed and will exist until the end of this world...all the just who pass through this life, and all those who exist now...and all those who are to be born in the future; all form the one body of Jesus Christ.... (Augustine, *Sermo*, 341.11–13)[13]

The *Ecclesia* as Charismatic and Pneumatic Community

The church has an inner invisible dimension but is also visible as a charismatic community. Spirit breaks through into our created, human, and material world. Just as the Word takes on flesh in and through incarnation, so the Spirit as animator enters into the very depths of history. The church as "mystery" and its "institutionaliza-tion" are distinguishable but inseparable. The invisible church and visible church are like soul and body. The church is the embodiment

41

of the risen Christ. This is one of Paul's great images for the church (see 1 Cor 10; 12; Rom 12; Eph 4).

The Holy Spirit breaks into a community of believers through interacting and interdependent charisms or graces. Michael Fahey defines charism as "a gift or ability conveyed to an individual within the Christian community enabling the person to fulfill a specific service, either over a long period of time or in a relatively short period of time."[14] In First Corinthians, Romans, and Ephesians, Paul acknowledges the reality of *charismata* at work, that is to say, charisms, the Holy Spirit. A diversity of charisms makes the church to be church.

There are charisms of speech (prophecy, teaching, encouraging [Rom 12:6–7], utterance of wisdom, utterance of knowledge, prophecy, tongues, kinds of tongues, and interpretation of tongues [1 Cor 12:8–10, 28–30]) and charisms of action (service, sharing, caring, leading, acts of mercy [Rom 12:7–8], healing and miraculous activities, helpful deeds, and giving guidance [1 Cor 12:9–10, 28–30]).[15] No one has all of them. Nor are the Pauline lists intended to be exhaustive. Each charism is a manifestation of the Spirit. Each charism is the visibilization of grace *(charis)*. The body of Christ for Paul is a community of charisms—an orchestration of the varied gifts of the Spirit. The church is a *koinōnia pneumatos* (2 Cor 13:13–14; Phil 2:1), a spiritual fellowship or participation in the Spirit. Each member of the body participates in the life of the Spirit. "To each is given the manifestation of the Spirit for the common good" (1 Cor 12:7). These charisms are not *gratia gratum faciens* but *gratiae gratis datae* (graces freely given for the benefit of others and of the community as a whole).[16]

The *Ecclesia* as Structured and Evangelical

The Holy Spirit not only animates the church and gives its members varied charisms for the sake of the community, but the Holy Spirit helps to structure the church and its charismatic gifts. If the church is first of all the invisible reality of the Spirit as

Uncreated Grace, and then this Grace made visible, embodied, and manifest in the many *gratiae gratis datae*, the grace of the Holy Spirit is also made visible through structures of leadership and service.[17]

It is not our intention here to outline the emergence and evolution of the structures by which the early Christian communities were organized, but simply to acknowledge that structure is inherent in the life of the *ecclesia*. Varied forms and patterns emerged under the guidance of the Holy Spirit. This movement toward order was a work of the Holy Spirit as well as historically conditioned. Both order and adaptation were ways in which the Spirit worked, and these are not opposed to each other.[18] Early patterns of leadership and ministry can be found in the letters of Paul and the Acts of the Apostles as well as in the pastoral letters to Timothy and Titus. The postresurrection Jesus movement had to adapt and undergo transformation. Changes and developments were dependent on the nature of the communities—their needs, tensions, social contexts, Jewish or Gentile character—and the vision of their founders. These adaptations emerged under the guidance of the Holy Spirit. By the time of the pastoral letters, the first letter of Clement, and the second century, the church had moved toward increasing order.

The church in its own way manifests a fundamental principle of all complex systems: there is always a delicate balance between order and disorder, and a move too far in one direction or the other leads either to stagnation or to anarchy.[19] A complex system, which is what the visible church of God is, requires both structure and adaptability—both of which are manifest in the working of the Holy Spirit within the early Christian movement. Some structures may have been innovative, but they emerged under the impulse of the Spirit. Some ministries, such as apostle, prophet, and teacher, were more enduring. Eventually there were elders and overseers, or *presbyteroi* and *episkopoi*. Authority and leadership were necessary.

Although the church is *both* charismatic *and* structured, both charisms and structures are subordinate to the gospel. The *ecclesia* is structured but evangelical. According to James D. G. Dunn, Paul is the one who coined the word *gospel* (*euangelion*, good news) as a description of his own proclamation about Jesus.[20] Sixty of the seventy-six occurrences of the word in the New Testament are Pauline. It was due to the influence of Paul that the word came into use in Mark (1:1, 14, 15; 8:35; 10:29; 13:10; 14:9) and through Mark to the Synoptic tradition. Then the term came to refer to the written Gospels.

When people hear the word *gospel*, they ordinarily think of the four Gospels, that is, gospel as a literary genre. But these four have come to be called Gospels because they contain "the gospel of Jesus Christ," that is, the good news of the life, death, and resurrection of Jesus Christ. This is a deeper level at which the word *gospel* is to be understood—the gospel of Jesus Christ, but recorded according to Matthew, Mark, Luke, and John. At still another level, however, we can distinguish the gospel of Jesus Christ understood as the gospel about Jesus Christ (Jesus Christ as the object of the preaching) from the gospel of Jesus Christ understood as the good news *that* Jesus preached. This latter is "the gospel of God."[21] According to Mark, after John the baptizer was arrested, Jesus returned to Galilee proclaiming the gospel of God (Mark 1:14). Thus, there are three levels at which we can understand the word *gospel*: a literary form (the four Gospels); the story of Jesus as the Christ of God (the gospel about Jesus); and the God whom Jesus proclaimed (the gospel of God). Ultimately, the gospel *is* God—God experienced and proclaimed as good news, God as revealed in Jesus Christ, God as Spirit present as power to God's people.

One cannot live for the sake of the gospel, however, without living as church. The gospel requires church. *Church* here does not refer to any particular way of being structured but to communities of the faithful among the followers of Christ. Church implies both people and structures. The gospel is not lived in isolation. Any movement eventually requires structure, rituals, and institutional forms if the cause is to go on. In other words, one cannot live the gospel completely unchurched. The Holy Spirit, who is the source of the gospel, is also the source of the church.

Nevertheless, the church as structured is always inadequate to the gospel. There is always "more" to the gospel than the church can express. People of the gospel will frequently be disappointed with church at the same time that they see the need for church. The church remains human and only approximates or attains intermittently what the gospel calls forth. The church may even grieve the Holy Spirit (Eph 4:30).

In this reciprocal relation between gospel and church, it is the church that is judged in the light of the gospel and not the other way around. The church is evangelical in its very nature. The gospel remains the norm in terms of which the *ecclesia* understands itself. No church is apostolic that is not also evangelical. The church, as visible, is both charismatic and structured, but both charisms and structures must serve the gospel. The church is accountable to the Spirit, not the Spirit to the church.[22] In the Book of Revelation, the word goes out to seven churches in Asia Minor: Ephesus, Smyrna, Pergamum, Thyatira, Sardis, Philadelphia, Laodicea. Each message is followed by the admonition, "Let anyone who has an ear listen to what the Spirit is saying to the churches" (2:7, 11, 17, 29; 3:6, 13, 22). The authority behind the church is that of the Spirit.

There are thus three primary aspects to *ecclesia:* (1) church as the invisible workings of the Holy Spirit who is the soul of the church, which is as inclusive and universal in its scope as is the Spirit; (2) the church as visible and charismatic, with the Holy Spirit's breaking into a community through charisms, which at its core is a pneumatic community that acknowledges Jesus as Lord and whose members participate in the life of the Spirit; and (3) the church as visible and structured with patterns of ministry and leadership that are also gifts of the Spirit and are enduring as well as innovative, manifesting order as well as adaptability. The *charisma* and the structures are both pneumatic and complementary. Leadership is a gift, and the structures of leadership must evolve to meet the needs of the *ecclesia*.

Ecclesia as *Communio* and *Sacramentum*

"Communion" and "sacrament" were less prominent terms in the Second Vatican Council's Dogmatic Constitution on the Church, *Lumen Gentium*, than "people of God" and "body of Christ." These terms were nevertheless prevalent ways of speaking and have become even more prominent since the council. *Communio* carries with it the twofold aspect of our participation in the life of the Spirit ("the communion of the Holy Spirit" [2 Cor 13:13]) as well as our interconnectedness with one another ("members one of another" [Rom 12:5]).[23] We share communion with the Father, through the Son, in the Spirit as a community of believers. The church is a communion of communities, a communion of basic Christian communities, of local churches, and of various traditions of faith and worship. Communion with God, fellowship, *koinōnia*, community of the faithful: these are the ideas contained within the concept of *communio*. The starting point for understanding the communion that we all share is our participation in the divine triune life. This fellowship with God is realized among us through the Spirit and is the foundation for the life of the *ecclesia*.

For Walter Kasper, *communio* includes (1) fellowship with God as the foundation; (2) participation in the life of God through word and sacrament; (3) a unity among local churches; and (4) the participation and coresponsibility of the faithful, the *communio fidelium*.[24] Thus, the concept of *communio* holds together the church as the invisible mystery of grace; the church as gifted by the Spirit who is visibly manifest in charisms, ministries, preaching, and sacraments; as well as the church as structured, both hierarchically and collegially, for the sake of its unity and diversity.

An equally satisfying concept for holding together the invisible reality of grace that the church most fundamentally is, as well as its visible socio-juridical character, is that of the church as sacrament. This theme is present in the early theology of Edward Schillebeeckx, for whom Jesus Christ is the primordial sacrament.[25] Christ is the sacrament of God.[26] The church, then, is *the* sacrament of the risen

Christ.[27] The seven sacraments of the Catholic tradition are understood as ecclesial actions of the church. Sacramentality ties the people of God into communion with God and allows the invisible to be made visible.

The impetus today behind the church's understanding of itself as sacrament, however, lies in the frequent references to the church as sacrament in the documents of the Second Vatican Council: in the Dogmatic Constitution on the Church (*Lumen Gentium* 1, 9, and 48); the Constitution on the Liturgy (*Sacrosanctum Concilium* 5 and 26); the Pastoral Constitution on the Church in the Modern World (*Gaudium et Spes* 42 and 45); and the Decree on Missions (*Ad Gentes* 1 and 5). Although used in various ways, the most common is that of referring to the church as a sacrament of salvation (*Lumen Gentium* 48). The church is *the* sacrament of the risen Christ and of salvation that comes through Christ. The church has its visible, tangible aspect as well as the invisible *res* or reality: the living risen Christ, the Uncreated Grace that is the Holy Spirit.

At one end, the church is the Holy Spirit's sphere of influence, as deep and inclusive as the Spirit herself. In that sense, Israel as God's people is already the church. The church as Augustine understood it goes back to Abel. The church is inclusive of all religious traditions wherein the Holy Spirit is at work. The church is deeper and wider than we may think. But on the other end, the visible church, structured as it must be, and fragmented as it may be, is also church, the working of the Holy Spirit. The "institutionalization" itself is a magnificent work of the Spirit, even if the way the church is structured at any one period of history or the way authority is exercised is not the only option available to it. The Spirit blows where he will. But the visible church remains our access to the invisible life of the Spirit. The church is the sacrament par excellence of the risen Christ, who is for Christians the primordial sacrament of God, and ordinarily we come to God through Christ in the power of the Spirit at work in the *ecclesia*.

Holy Spirit: Source of Unity, Source of Diversity

Pope John Paul II wrote, "One and the same Spirit is always the dynamic principle of diversity and unity in the Church."[28] The Book of Revelation describes diversity gathered into unity at the end times:

> I looked, and there was a great multitude that no one could count, from every nation, from all tribes and peoples and languages, standing before the throne and before the Lamb, robed in white, with palm branches in their hands. They cried out with a loud voice saying, "Salvation belongs to our God who is seated on the throne, and to the Lamb!" (Rev 7:9–10)

Diversity has been with the followers of Christ from the beginning. The Twelve were recruited or called from varied backgrounds (Matt 10:2–4; Mark 3:14–19; Luke 6:12–16). The first Pentecost was made manifest in many languages (Acts 2:4–6). The Christian movement soon comprised both Christian Jews and Gentiles. In the New Testament itself the Pauline churches, the church of Jerusalem, and the Johannine community were distinctive. The New Testament manifests a significant diversity as well as a fundamental unity.[29] Note the difference in emphasis between two well known texts:

> What good is it, my brothers and sisters, if you say you have faith but do not have works? Can faith save you? If a brother or sister is naked and lacks daily food, and one of you says to them, "Go in peace; keep warm and eat your fill," and yet you do not supply their bodily needs, what is the good of that? So faith by itself, if it has no works, is dead. But someone will say, "You have faith and I have works." Show me your faith apart from your works, and I by my works will show you my faith...." (Jas 2:14–18)

> We ourselves are Jews by birth and not Gentile sinners;
> yet we know that a person is justified not by the works of
> the law but through faith in Jesus Christ. And we have
> come to believe in Christ Jesus, so that we might be jus-
> tified by faith in Christ, and not by doing the works of
> the law, because no one will be justified by the works of
> the law. (Gal 2:15–16)

These two theologies, those of James and Paul, are not irreconcilable, but they do manifest two contrasting emphases.

Diversity continued to manifest itself in every century of
church life. Not only were there Jewish and Gentile Christians, but
eventually both Greek-speaking and Latin-speaking churches, or
the Greek East and Latin West, Hellenistic and Latin theologies,
Orthodoxy and Catholicism. Later came the theologies of the
Reformation. The Christian tradition is pluriform, and its plurifor-
mity is a work of the Holy Spirit. Ernst Cassirer addresses this
point:

> In all human activities we find a fundamental polarity,
> which may be described in various ways. We may speak of
> a tension between stabilization and evolution, between a
> tendency that leads to fixed and stable forms of life and
> another tendency to break up this rigid scheme....In all
> this we feel very distinctly the presence of two different
> tendencies—the one leading to conservation, the other to
> the renovation and rejuvenation....[30]

Both tendencies are essential to human life and culture—the one of
rejuvenation, innovation, and creativity and the other of conservation, stabilization, and consolidation. These tendencies may cause
conflict or tension, but such conflicts can be constructive. The contemporary sciences of complexity have noted the same phenomenon, that both order and chaos are constituents of a dynamic
system.[31] Valuing one at the expense of the other leads either to stagnation, rigidity, and fixed forms, or to complete chaos and collapse.

A living system is a delicate balance not achieved once and for all. That balance must be regained or reestablished continuously if the system is to thrive. The church itself is such a complex system, and the Holy Spirit is the source of the movement toward renovation as well as the movement toward conservation.

In response to a question following a lecture, Karl Rahner replied, "Some people may be given the charism to be an accelerator and others the charism to be a brake." Here he uses the metaphor of an automobile in contrast to Paul's metaphor of the body. In both cases, however, it takes many parts. An accelerator may never understand why there needs to be a brake, and vice versa, and yet both are essential. As Ralph Powell, a Dominican philosopher friend of mine, once said, "It's hard to see the whole picture when you're inside the frame." It is hard to see that others, whose directions and styles may be other than mine, are also acting under the influence of the Holy Spirit. Yet the Holy Spirit, who sees the whole picture, undergirds both tendencies.

One Spirit, One Body, Many Members

The great New Testament images for diversity in unity are the Pauline image of the body in First Corinthians and Romans; the Johannine image of the vine and branches; and Jesus' prayer "That they may all be one" (John 15:1–12; 17:20–21). In First Corinthians, Paul enumerates a variety of gifts present in the *ecclesia*. "Now there are varieties of gifts, but the same Spirit; and there are varieties of services, but the same Lord; and there are varieties of activities, but it is the same God who activates all of them in everyone. To each is given the manifestation of the Spirit for the common good" (1 Cor 12:4–7). Though there are many gifts, many ministries, many activities, there is one Lord and one Spirit. Each "gift" is a manifestation of the Spirit given for the good of the community.

Just as there are many gifts within the body, there are many members. All the members, though many, are one.

> For just as the body is one and has many members, and
> all the members of the body, though many, are one body,
> so it is with Christ. For in the one Spirit we were all bap-
> tized into one body—Jews or Greeks, slaves or free—and
> we were all made to drink of one Spirit. (1 Cor 12:12–13)

There are both individual members, interconnected and interdependent, and at the same time one body, an organic unity. Each
part contributes to the whole.

> Indeed, the body does not consist of one member but of
> many. If the foot would say, "Because I am not a hand, I
> do not belong to the body," that would not make it any
> less a part of the body....If all were a single member,
> where would the body be? As it is, there are many mem-
> bers, yet one body. The eye cannot say to the hand, "I
> have no need of you," nor again the head to the feet, "I
> have no need of you."...Now you are the body of Christ
> and individually members of it. (1 Cor 12:14–26)

In Romans, Paul uses the same metaphor of the body: "For as
in one body we have many members, and not all the members have
the same function, so we, who are many, are one body in Christ,
and individually we are members one of another" (Rom 12:4–5).
Not only are we members of one body, we are also members of one
another. Such is the interconnected whole that we form in Christ.
We are related not only to the head of the body but to each member. There is in the body, as in the Trinity itself, a kind of *perichoresis.*[32] Where one of us is, there all the others are. I am not who
I am by myself alone.

Charity, Love, Spirit as Bond of Unity

The twelfth chapter of First Corinthians, Paul's discourse on
the body of Christ, is followed by his discourse on love in chapter

13. Likewise Romans 12:4–8, on Christ's body, is followed by verses 9–13 on love. The two themes are integrally linked. There is diversity within the body but love holds it together. Charity or love is *how* the body is held together. Paul is quite aware of the diversity in his communities, of the conflicts they have faced, the divisions that some of them experienced, and thus the importance of the bond of charity (1 Cor 13:1–13). Paul's tribute to love follows upon his discussion of spiritual gifts and charisms that make up a community, none of which compares to the gift of love. As Paul had said following his exposition on charisms, "I will show you a still more excellent way" (1 Cor 12:31), and he does indeed as he launches into "If I speak in tongues but do not have love…" (1 Cor 13:1). Love is the more excellent way: "the greatest of these is love" (1 Cor 13:13).

An axiom in the thought of Pierre Teilhard de Chardin is appropriate in this context: Union differentiates. Teilhard de Chardin (1881–1955) was a French paleontologist, synthetic thinker, and mystic. Evolution, for Teilhard, unfolds as a process of complexification accompanied by the rise of consciousness: increasing complexity, increasing consciousness. In this process there is both diversification and unification, and the two are not at cross purposes with each other. Love is the energy within this process, radial energy as Teilhard calls it, which is the cause of unity. "Love alone is capable of uniting living beings in such a way as to complete and fulfill them, for it alone takes them and joins them by what is deepest in themselves."[33]

> It is through love and within love that we must look for the deepening of our deepest self, in the life giving coming together of human kind. Love is the free and imaginative outpouring of the spirit over all unexplored paths. It links those who love in bonds that unite but do not confound.[34]

Love is an energy that unites while it differentiates.

O Holy Spirit, Life Divine,
heart and soul of the church,
gather your people together
in peace, harmony, and love.
O Uncreated Grace,
pour your grace out abundantly upon us.
Fill our hearts and souls, minds and bodies, and human
     spirits
with your love and joy.
Help each of us to put your gifts at the service of the
     community.
Help us to grow
in our lives of faith, hope, and love.
Come to the aid of your church
and sustain it in this hour of need.
Help us to love and respect one another.
Pour out your charismatic gifts upon your loved ones.
Lead us toward those structures,
human though they may be,
that will be of greatest service to the gospel.
Bless us, Holy Spirit, with the gift of charity.

Notes

1. I am going to follow here the theological account of Luke in the Acts of the Apostles, not presenting it as the historical record as such, in order to remain within Luke's theology of the Holy Spirit. For more critical and historical concerns, see Jerome Murphy-O'Connor, *Paul: A Critical Life* (Oxford: Clarendon Press, 1996); idem, *Paul: His Story* (Oxford: Oxford University Press, 2004); as well as critical commentaries on the Acts of the Apostles.

2. See the works by Murphy-O'Connor cited in the preceding note for a more critical and historical background to the mission and journeys of Paul.

3. 1 Cor 1:1; 10:32; 11:22; 15:9; 2 Cor 1:1; Gal 1:13; 1 Thess 1:1; 2 Thess 1:1.

4. For a brief analysis of the history of the schemas and revisions of *Lumen Gentium*, the Second Vatican Council's Dogmatic Constitution on the Church, see Herwi Rikhof, *The Concept of Church: A Methodological Inquiry into the Use of Metaphors in Ecclesiology* (London: Sheed & Ward, 1981), 11–66.

5. Yves Congar, *Esquisses du Mystère de l'Eglise* (Paris: Editions du Cerf, 1941; 2nd ed., 1953), in English translation as *The Mystery of the Church* (Baltimore: Helicou Press, 1960). Yves Congar, *Sainte Eglise* (Paris: Editions du Cerf, 1963), 21–44.

6. Roger Haight, "Sin and Grace," in *Systematic Theology: Roman Catholic Perspectives*, vol. 2, ed. Francis Schüssler Fiorenza and John P. Galvin (Minneapolis: Fortress Press, 1991), 112.

7. In Juan Arintero, *The Mystical Evolution in the Development and Vitality of the Church*, 2 vols., trans. Jordan Aumann (St. Louis: Herder, 1950), 1:185.

8. "The head has a manifest pre-eminence over the other exterior members; but the heart has a certain hidden influence. And hence the Holy Spirit is likened to the heart, since He invisibly quickens and unifies the Church..." (*Summa Theologiae*, III, 8, 1, ad 3). Also see *De Veritate* q. 29, a. 4, ad 7.

9. Arintero, *Mystical Evolution*, 1:20, 28, 36, 71–75; 2:448. Arintero was a Spanish Dominican and mystical theologian from the early part of the twentieth century.

10. See Thomas Aquinas, *Summa Theologiae*, I/II, q. 110–11.

11. Pierre Teilhard de Chardin, *The Divine Milieu*, trans. Bernard Wall (New York: Harper & Row, 1960).

12. See Kilian McDonnell, *The Other Hand of God: The Holy Spirit as the Universal Touch and Goal* (Collegeville, MN: Liturgical Press, 2003), 55–61.

13. *Patrologiae cursus completus: Series latina*, 221 vols. (Paris: J. P. Migne, 1844–64), 39:1499–1500. For translation, see J.-M. R. Tillard, *Church of Churches: The Ecclesiology of Communion* (Collegeville, MN: Liturgical Press, 1992), 20.

14. Michael Fahey, "Church," in *Systematic Theology: Roman Catholic Perspectives*, 2:39.

15. James D. G. Dunn, *The Theology of Paul the Apostle* (Grand Rapids: Eerdmans, 1998), 555–56.

16. See Thomas Aquinas, *Summa Theologiae*, I/II, q. 111, a. 1 and 4. English translation by the Fathers of the English Dominican Province, 3 vols. (New York: Benziger Brothers, Inc., 1947).

17. For a discussion of some of the issues concerning ministry and authority in the Pauline churches, see Dunn, *Theology of Paul the Apostle*, 565–98.

18. Yves Congar sees no opposition between the charismatic and institutional facets of the church (*The Word and the Spirit*, trans. David Smith [San Francisco: Harper & Row, 1986], 64) and speaks of "an understanding of the Church as a spiritual communion that has a social structure" (ibid., 55). For a balanced and yet critical perspective on this same topic, see Edward Schillebeeckx, *Church: The Human Story of God* (New York: Crossroad, 1990), 158–59.

19. On complexity theory, see Mitchell Waldrop, *Complexity: The Emerging Science at the Edge of Order and Chaos* (New York: Simon & Schuster, 1992).

20. Dunn, *Theology of Paul the Apostle*, 164–69, 572–74, 595.

21. 1 Thess 2:2, 8, 9; Rom 1:1; 15:16; 2 Cor 11:7; Mark 1:14. Paul refers to "the gospel of Christ" in Rom 15:19; 1 Cor 9:12; 2 Cor 2:12; 9:13; 10:14; Gal 1:7; Phil 1:27; 1 Thess 3:2; to the "gospel of his Son" in Rom 1:9; and to "the gospel of our Lord Jesus" in 2 Thess 1:8.

22. "From this there emerges one basic question. Is the Holy Spirit the endowment bequeathed by Christ to the Church, i.e., the *magisterium*, to administer His grace? In other words, is the Church subjected to God's grace, or is God's grace subjected to the activity of the clergy?" (Angelos J. Philippou, *The Orthodox Ethos* [Oxford: Holywell Press, 1964], 90).

23. On the ecclesiology of "communio," see Walter Kasper, *Theology and Church* (New York: Crossroad, 1989), 148–65; Tillard, *Church of Churches*, 1–74; Rikhof, *Concept of Church*, 55–60, 229–36.

24. Kasper, *Theology and Church*, 156.

25. Edward Schillebeeckx, *Christ the Sacrament of Encounter with God* (New York: Sheed & Ward, 1963), 13. On the church as sacrament, also see the essay by Walter Kasper, "The Church as a Sacrament of Salvation," in *Theology and Church*, 111–28. On Schillebeeckx, also see Erik Borgman, *Edward Schillebeeckx: A Theologian in His History* (New York: Continuum, 2003); and Mary Catherine Hilkert and Robert J. Schreiter, eds., *The Praxis of the Reign of God*, 2nd ed. (New York: Fordham University Press, 2002).

26. Schillebeeckx, *Christ the Sacrament*, 5–54.

27. Ibid., 55–109.

28. John Paul II, *Christifideles Laici*, apostolic exxhortation on the laity, #20, in *Origins* 18 (Feb. 9, 1989): 570.

29. See James D. G. Dunn, *The Unity and Diversity of the New Testament* (Philadelphia: Westminster Press, 1977).

30. Ernst Cassirer, *An Essay on Man: An Introduction to a Philosophy of Human Culture* (New Haven, CT: Yale University Press, 1944), 224 and 226.

31. See Waldrop, *Complexity*.

32. *Perichoresis*, the Greek equivalent of the Latin *circumincessio*, refers in trinitarian theology to the being-in-one-another or mutual indwelling of the three Persons of the Trinity within the one godhead.

33. Pierre Teilhard de Chardin, *The Phenomenon of Man*, trans. Bernard Wall (New York: Harper & Row, 1959), 265.

34. Pierre Teilhard de Chardin, "The Grand Option" (1939) in *Future of Man* (New York: Harper & Row, 1964), 55.

Chapter Four
THE DIVERSITY OF RELIGIONS

In the previous chapters our focus has been on the presence of the Holy Spirit within us personally as well as among us ecclesially. Does the diversity that flows from the Holy Spirit extend beyond the visible body of Christ? Are the many religious traditions of the world also manifestations of the Spirit? Is the whole picture even bigger than we might have imagined? Is it possible that the Holy Spirit is at work within the religious traditions of India and Africa, among Hindus and Buddhists, within Islam and Judaism? Making such a claim in the concrete for a particular religious tradition requires discernment, study, and experience in interfaith dialogue. In theory, however, theologically, is there anything to prevent us from understanding the diversity of religions as a work of the Spirit?

The Holy Spirit in the Gospel of John

When we turn to the Gospel of John, further images and names for the Holy Spirit emerge: the Spirit of truth, the Advocate or Comforter or Counselor, the Holy Breath. The Greek word for spirit is *pneuma*. The Hebrew word is *ruach*, which can also be translated as "breath" or "wind." Any translator of the Hebrew Bible needs to make a decision on how to translate based on the meaning of the text and the context. For example, the first two verses of the Book of Genesis speak of the spirit of God or of a mighty wind. The New Revised Standard Version translates the text as "In the beginning when God created the heavens and the earth, the earth was a formless void and darkness covered the face of the deep, while a wind from God swept over the face of the waters" (Gen 1:1–2). The *New American Bible* and the *New Jerusalem Bible* also speak of wind. Other translations, however, say "the spirit of God" (Revised English Bible) or "Spirit of God" (Revised Standard Version). It would even be possible to say "the breath of God."

The image of the Spirit as breath is conveyed in the Gospel of John in one of the postresurrection appearances: "When he had said this, he breathed on them and said to them, 'Receive the Holy Spirit'" (John 20:22), which could also be translated, "Receive the Holy Breath." The Johannine text recalls another text from Genesis where God breathed into *adam* the breath of life (Gen 2:7). The breath of God gives life; the Holy Breath gives eternal life. Gary D. Badcock writes:

> The special significance of spirit—or, more correctly, "breath"—in the vocabulary of the religions of the world appears to derive from the associations between breathing and living and between life and the sacred. In many languages, the words for life and breath are the same; and in the ancient cultures from which these languages derive, the sign that indicates the presence of life in animals such as ourselves is not the pulse or the brainwave, as in modern medicine, or even physical movement or consciousness, but more often than not the presence of breath. To have breath or spirit is quite simply to be alive, and to be alive is to be in receipt of that life from God.[1]

Some of the images for the Spirit connote great intimacy, such as the Spirit's pouring God's love into us (Rom 5:5), coming to us when we do not know how to pray (Rom 8:26), empowering us to say Abba (Rom 8:15), all Pauline ways of speaking; but also the breath of the risen Christ being breathed into us (John 22:22). "Wind" is an image with different connotations. Wind can be a gentle breeze on a warm evening; we are glad there's a wind tonight. Wind can also be destructive when it comes as a hurricane, a typhoon, or a tornado. The wind can blow us away or tear things down. Wind is not something we tame or domesticate. It is unpredictable, perhaps soothing, perhaps frightening. This is a quality of the Spirit that leads a friend of mine to speak of the Spirit as the trickster.

The significant text from the Gospel of John in this regard is that of Jesus' nighttime discourse with Nicodemus.

> Now there was a Pharisee named Nicodemus, a leader of the Jews. He came to Jesus by night and said to him, "Rabbi, we know that you are a teacher who has come from God; for no one can do these signs that you do apart from the presence of God." Jesus answered him, "Very truly, I tell you, no one can see the kingdom of God without being born from above." Nicodemus said to him, "How can anyone be born after having grown old? Can one enter a second time into the mother's womb and be born?" Jesus answered, "Very truly, I tell you, no one can enter the kingdom of God without being born of water and Spirit. What is born of the flesh is flesh, and what is born of the Spirit is spirit. Do not be astonished that I said to you, 'You must be born from above.' The wind blows where it chooses, and you hear the sound of it, but you do not know where it comes from or where it goes. So it is with everyone who is born of the Spirit." (John 3:1–8)

Jesus begins to instruct Nicodemus concerning the spiritual life. Eventually one must be born again, from above. Just as there is a physical birth, so there is a spiritual birth. Nicodemus seems unable to comprehend what Jesus is teaching. Jesus is talking about being born of the Spirit. People have often characterized the Gospel of John as having a high Christology. Jesus comes from above, not from below. But it is also true that the Gospel has an exalted anthropology. We, too, are to be born from above.

No one can belong to God without being born of water and Spirit. This second birth is that of baptism, but a baptism with the

Spirit. We may tend to put these two, "water and Spirit," on an equal footing, but the emphasis falls upon "*and* Spirit." The Jewish people and Nicodemus would have been familiar with water baptisms as practiced within Judaism at that time. Baptism was a water ritual. What is exceptional in Jesus' teaching is that no one can enter the reign of God without receiving a baptism of the Spirit. Spirit baptism is referred to earlier in the Gospel of John when John the baptizer indicates, "I baptize with water" (John 1:26) and elaborates further, "the one who sent me to baptize with water said to me, 'He on whom you see the Spirit descend and remain is the one who baptizes with the Holy Spirit'" (John 1:33). When Jesus speaks later to Nicodemus about being born from above, he refers to water *and the Spirit.*

Both Jesus and his baptism are distinguished by references to the Spirit. More important for our purpose is what Jesus says next in the discourse with Nicodemus: "The wind blows where it chooses, and you hear the sound of it, but you do not know where it comes from or where it goes. So it is with everyone who is born of the Spirit" (John 3:8). The ones who are born from above are those born of the Spirit. Jesus is the supreme exemplification of this being born of the Spirit. The Johannine Jesus makes an explicit connection between spirit and wind *(ruach).* The comparison of the Holy Spirit to wind is supposed to help Nicodemus and the reader understand what Jesus has been trying to teach.

Nicodemus does not yet know the Holy Spirit. He has not yet been baptized with the Spirit. He comes to Jesus by night to find out more about Jesus' teaching. Jesus tries to tell him about the Holy Spirit, about baptism in the Spirit, and about the Spirit's unpredictable freedom. Can you not see, Nicodemus? "Are you a teacher of Israel, and yet you do not understand these things?" (John 3:10). We are talking here about something new, Nicodemus, about the Spirit, who is not confined by the Law, not confined by anything we may have previously taught, not confined by whatever limitations we may wish to place on him from below. He comes from above, is subject to no one, blows where he wills, and is being offered to us.

This is the Spirit who gives eternal life. John the baptizer came to give testimony concerning Jesus (John 1:6–8), but Jesus had to die in order to send the Spirit (John 16:7). John is the precursor of Jesus and Jesus is in another way the precursor of the Spirit.

Jesus is the one who gives the Spirit without measure: "The one who comes from above is above all; the one who is of the earth belongs to the earth and speaks about earthly things....He whom God has sent speaks the words of God, for he gives the Spirit without measure" (John 3:31, 34). Jesus uses the image of a potentially comforting, potentially frightening wind to convey something to Nicodemus about the Spirit who is source of unity and source of diversity.

One Spirit, Many Religions

When it comes to the question of religion, we are aware of the need to speak in the plural. One God, many religions or religious traditions. For Christians this means one triune God, a God whose very being is community, and a plurality of religions intended to be not simply many but also one. What we think of as major religious traditions in the world are each plural in themselves. We may speak in the West of Hindus, but in reality there are Shaivites and Vishnaivites. Not all Buddhist traditions are the same, although they all claim access to the same Buddha. Judaism, Christianity, and Islam each comprise varied and often significantly diverse forms. What are we to say as Christians looking through Christian glasses at this extensive religious diversity in the world? Is only one an acceptable path to God? Are we all on a similar journey however we articulate our understanding of the means and ends along the way? Can we be friends, or must we be enemies? Can our faith embrace a wideness in God's providence that incorporates the many into a harmonious whole?

I write as a Roman Catholic Christian, knowing there is beauty and goodness and truth in all the major religious traditions of our world. As a person of the Christian faith, I necessarily speak the language of that faith tradition. I would like to be bi- or trilingual, religiously speaking, but my primary faith language remains Christian. When I confront the mystery of God and the religions of the world, it is easier for me to use my primary tongue. Do I see the other religions primarily as "other," or primarily as embodying deep spiritual traditions that come from the one and only Spirit? If the other religious traditions are manifestations of the same Holy Spirit who is at work in my own life and ecclesial community, but also "blows where he will" (John 3:8), then the other religions may be less "other" than we at first may think. The more I am at home with the Spirit, the less other religious traditions are alien to me. They fall within my embrace just as they fall within the embrace of God's Spirit. But is the Holy Spirit present outside the Christian traditions?

Catholic teaching answers yes to this question. Pope John Paul II was explicit in this regard. He wrote:

> What we have just said must also be applied—although in another way and with the due differences—to activity for coming closer together with the representatives of the non-Christian religions, an activity expressed through dialogue, contacts, prayer in common, investigation of the treasures of human spirituality, in which, as we know well, the members of these religions also are not lacking. Does it not sometimes happen that the firm belief of the followers of the non-Christian religions—a belief that is also an effect of the Spirit of truth operating outside the visible confines of the Mystical Body—can make Christians ashamed…? (*Redemptor Hominis* 6.3)[2]

> But as we follow this reason for the Jubilee, we cannot limit ourselves to the two thousand years which have passed since the birth of Christ. We need to go further back, to embrace the whole of the action of the Holy Spirit even before Christ—from the beginning, throughout the world, and especially in the economy of the Old Covenant….The Second Vatican Council, centered

primarily on the theme of the Church, reminds us of the Holy Spirit's activity also "outside the visible body of the Church." (*Dominum et Vivificantem* 53.2–3)[3]

As we entered the third Christian millennium, John Paul II suggested we go back prior to the Christian era in order to embrace the entirety of the action of the Holy Spirit, who was present and active in the world even before the coming of Christ, indeed active *throughout the world* and *since the beginning*. The Second Vatican Council already taught, John Paul II reminded us, that the Holy Spirit is active "outside" the visible church. In other words, the Holy Spirit's presence and activity cannot be confined to Christian church history and Christian churches.

Pope John Paul II was merely elaborating the teaching of the Second Vatican Council:

> The Catholic Church rejects nothing that is true and holy in these religions. She regards with sincere reverence those ways of conduct and of life, those precepts and teachings which, though differing in many aspects from the ones she holds and sets forth, nonetheless often reflect a ray of that Truth which enlightens all men. Indeed, she proclaims, and ever must proclaim Christ "the way, the truth, and the life" (John 14:6), in whom all may find the fullness of religious life, in whom God has reconciled all things to Himself.
>
> The Church, therefore, exhorts her children, that through dialogue and collaboration with the followers of other religions, carried out with prudence and love and in witness to the Christian faith and life, they recognize, preserve and promote the good things, spiritual and moral, as well as the socio-cultural values found among these people. (*Nostra Aetate* 2)[4]

The council recognized a dilemma but felt the need to affirm both sides of it: the presence of truth and holiness in other religions as well as the obligation to proclaim Christ. This tension between dialogue and proclamation remains in current teaching, sometimes one side of the dilemma emphasized and sometimes the other.[5] The universal presence of the Spirit throughout the world from the beginning does not negate Christ as a universal mediator between God and creation.

Some might suggest that the Spirit is present to non-Christians in spite of their religious traditions, but the council suggested something more in its references to social life and culture. John Paul II became more and more aware of the significance of culture in human life and thus the need for a respect for diverse cultures. In his message of January 1, 2001, for the celebration of the World Day of Peace, the pope reflected on "Dialogue Between Cultures for a Civilization of Love and Peace."[6]

> I therefore consider it urgent to invite believers in Christ, together with all men and women of good will, to reflect on the theme of dialogue between cultures and traditions. This dialogue is the obligatory path to the building of a reconciled world, a world able to look with serenity to its own future. (#3)

> Cultural diversity should therefore be understood within the broader horizon of the unity of the human race. In a real way, this unity constitutes the primordial historical and ontological datum in the light of which the profound meaning of cultural diversity can be grasped. In fact, only *an overall vision of both the elements of unity and the elements of diversity* makes it possible to understand and interpret the full truth of every human culture. (#7, emphasis added)

The importance of culture, he said, can hardly be overemphasized. The theme of unity and diversity applies to the cultures of the world as well. One cannot grasp the significance of respect for diverse cultures as well as their underlying unity without at the same time realizing the degree to which religion is the soul of a culture. One cannot affirm a culture and negate its soul. The unity and diversity of cultures are grounded in the unity and diversity of religions and the need for respect and dialogue among the latter as well.

John Paul II has also stated, "The Spirit's presence and activity affect not only the individuals but also society and history, peoples, cultures and religions" (*Redemptoris Missio* 28.3).[7] Undoubtedly the acknowledgment of value in other religious traditions and the recognition that salvation is available to their members while at the same time taking seriously the Christian mission to proclaim Christ to all nations raise theological questions that will be with Christians for some years to come.[8] But the fundamental affirmation of the Holy Spirit at work in those diverse cultures and religions is what is important. Among the religions of the world, the one Holy Spirit is again the source of both diversity and unity.

Jesus Christ, Mediator

Affirming the presence of the Holy Spirit in diverse religious traditions does not negate the traditional Christian belief in Jesus Christ as a unique mediator, but the understanding of this doctrine requires theological scrutiny. Both dialogue and evangelization are incumbent upon the church. The presence of the Holy Spirit outside the Christian church and the unique mediatorship of Jesus Christ must both be affirmed. John Paul II commented: "In the light of the economy of salvation, the Church sees no conflict between proclaiming Christ and engaging in interreligious dialogue" (*Redemptoris Missio* 55.2).

> The *diakonia* of the truth: This mission on the one hand makes the believing community a partner in humanity's shared struggle to arrive at truth; and on the other hand it obliges the believing community to proclaim the certitudes arrived at, albeit with a sense that every truth attained is but a step towards that fullness of truth which

will appear with the final Revelation of God: "For now we see in a mirror dimly, but then face to face. Now I know in part; then I shall understand fully" (1 Cor 13:12). (*Fides et Ratio* 2)[9]

Both interreligious dialogue and evangelization are at the service of truth. The search for truth is incumbent upon all the religions of the world and upon all humankind. It is a shared search. Both interreligious dialogue and the proclamation of Christ have truth as their goal. Each religious tradition contains truth; no one at this point in history contains all the truth; dialogue serves the purpose of sharing and clarifying truth. Nor is truth served by a refusal to share one's beliefs out of a false sense of respect for the other. The fullness of truth lies in the future. The final revelation lies ahead of us. We are all pilgrims along the way. Another Johannine image sees the Holy Spirit as the Spirit of Truth (John 14:17; 15:26; 16:13). The Holy Spirit will guide us to the fullness of truth.

In making this twofold affirmation of the church's faith in the Holy Spirit as acting outside the visible church and, at the same time, of Jesus Christ's unique role in human history as a universal mediator between God and creation, John Paul II was only accepting the twofold challenge of the Christian Scriptures: God makes salvation available to all, for there is one God who is the God of all; and Jesus Christ plays a unique role in the story of God's salvation (1 Tim 2:4–5).

This is not the place to develop a theology of the religions of the world.[10] Our purpose is to suggest that the theology of the Holy Spirit can be a starting point for such a theology. Other religious traditions may not speak in this way, for this is Christian language, but it is the language Christians have for affirming God's real presence and action in religion everywhere. The Holy Spirit is God, and the Holy Spirit is present outside the visible body of the church.

Reflecting on the breadth of the Spirit's presence, and yet believing in the uniqueness of Jesus Christ among God's saving actions, Christians need to be attentive as all people of good will journey together under the guidance of the Spirit to that fullness of truth that lies ahead of us. We cannot say in advance whether the truth present in other religious traditions is ultimately the same as ours, whether it complements ours, or whether it will simply help us to understand ours more deeply. The fullness of truth is not already in our grasp. Truth requires an attitude of humility, not only on the part of individuals but on the part of institutions and religious traditions. Dialogue does not have as its purpose the conversion of the other, but it can and should lead to our own continuing conversion. As Raimon Panikkar argues, there is no interreligious dialogue without intrareligious dialogue.[11] The church itself is in the process of growth; doctrine develops; we are not yet who we will be a millennium from now. We are still in the process of discovering the fullness of meaning in what we believe.

To speak about Jesus Christ as a unique mediator does not imply that we who believe in Jesus Christ already know all there is to know about the Christ, the *mysterium Christi* and the *totus Christus*. The whole Christ, the cosmic Christ, the christic principle within an evolving creation: we ourselves still have much to learn about the Christ. Everything that functions as mediator between God and creation is christic, is Christ, the only mediator. The Christ who is unique and universal mediator may not completely conform to Jesus as I envision him. It is not "my" Jesus, nor any church's Jesus, but the Spirit's Christ who is mediator, and there can be no conflict between that Spirit and that Christ. Thus Christ, to use Christian language again, is also present in the other religious traditions, and that is not said arrogantly or offensively but with respect. Christ would not be Christ if not omnipresent.

The Spirit and the Word act in unison. But who is this Christ who was there before the creation of the world, before the incarnation of the Word, and who will only be complete in a future eschatological coming? The Christians' Christ may often be too small. A sincere openness to dialogue and other faith traditions and a commitment to truth and Jesus Christ are not irreconcilable but essential. Dialogue and truth are companions, not enemies, as is true of the religions of the world.

No Salvation apart from the Spirit

We have probably heard the axiom, "No salvation outside the church," although the church now teaches clearly that there is salvation outside the church, depending of course on how one understands church.[12] If by church we mean the visible church or the Catholic Church as an institution, clearly there is salvation for those who are not members of the Christian church or churches. On the other hand, if we are speaking about the invisible church (if we can make that distinction) that is the Mystical Body of Christ in its fullness, the whole Christ, then of course it is different, since one may be a member of the body of Christ without explicit knowledge of that participation. If to be "in the Spirit" is to be "in Christ," then Christ is more coextensive with humanity and all of creation than we ordinarily imagine.

The teaching "No salvation outside the church" goes back to Cyprian of Carthage in the third century, and Cyprian did not have in mind those who never knew Christ. He had in mind baptized Christians who were heretical or schismatic; he wanted to impress upon them that there was no salvation without the church. This idea, in a more rigid sense than Cyprian had used it, eventually became a part of the teaching of the church. Pope Pius XII's letter to the archbishop of Boston concerning the unacceptable position of Father Leonard Feeney (1949) is pertinent. Pius XII did not deny the dogmatic character of the teaching but wrote, "This dogma is to be understood as the Church itself understands it."[13] As the church understands it today, of course, there is salvation outside the church. The confusion resulting from the development of the teaching and its interpretation led Yves Congar to qualify it significantly.[14] It cannot be interpreted literally and leads to misunderstanding unless one is familiar with the history of the doctrine.

The teaching was influenced in the course of history by new contexts, developments, and questions. Thomas Aquinas, recognizing the importance of faith and baptism for salvation, distinguished in the thirteenth century between implicit faith and explicit faith and also spoke about baptism by desire. Although Thomas himself believed in the importance of explicit faith (*Summa Theologiae*, II/II, 2, 7–8), he could still say, "they have implicit faith who believe in divine providence" (II/II, 2, 7, ad 3). In referring to those indicated in Hebrews 11:6 who simply believe that God is and that God rewards those who seek God, Thomas maintained that "all the articles of faith are contained implicitly in certain primary matters of faith, such as God's existence and His providence..." (II/II, 1, 7). Thomas thus opened a door to further inquiry. Likewise, baptism is necessary for salvation as is faith, but the sacrament is not wanting to someone who desires it (III, 68, 2), and that desire may even be implicit (III, 69, 4, ad 2). These distinctions helped the church come to grips with salvation for those without explicit faith or the sacrament of baptism. The Council of Trent later affirmed the theology of baptism by desire as part of church teaching.

Within a new context, that of the sixteenth century and the discovery by Europeans of a whole new world, Thomas's theology assisted theologians at the University of Salamanca in Spain as well as Bartolomé de las Casas in the Americas to refine the church's understanding in defending the rights of the indigenous. All of these developments contributed to the church's growing understanding of who can be saved and to the contemporary teaching of the church that in fact there is salvation outside the church.[15] We might add: "for those who at least implicitly desire the good that God wills for us" even if unaware of what that might explicitly be. Certainly this applies to all religious people of good will throughout the world.

The church today is becoming increasingly aware that it is spirituality and the Holy Spirit that are essential for salvation. We might therefore say today: No salvation apart from the Holy Spirit, outside the Spirit's sphere of influence. Salvation means "living in the Spirit," whether consciously or not. Baptism is a baptism with the Spirit. Perhaps we are being called today to the same conversion within our context that Peter was called to within his context, a conversion partially prompted by his experience of meeting Cornelius, a "pagan" but good and God-fearing. "Then Peter began to speak to them: 'I truly understand that God shows no partiality, but in every nation anyone who fears him and does what is right is acceptable to him'" (Acts 10:34).

We recall the words of Irenaeus: "Where the church is, there is the Spirit of God, and where the Spirit of God is, there is the church" (*Adversus Haereses* 3.24.1). Where the Spirit is, there is salvation and there is no salvation outside or apart from the Spirit. Yet the Spirit is the source of a great diversity of religions as well as their unifying, underlying common bond.

> *Holy God, Holy Mystery,*
> *Father, Son, and Spirit,*
> *may all the religious and spiritual traditions of the world*
> *live harmoniously with respect for one another.*
> *Heavenly Father,*
> *you have taught us that in your house*
> *there are many dwelling places (John 14:2).*
> *There are even more than we may have thought or*
> *imagined.*
> *Eternal Son, Risen Christ,*
> *you have revealed that in your Body there are many*
> *members (Rom 12:4–5).*
> *Your Body is not limited to those whom we might choose*
> *but rather comprises those whom you have chosen.*
> *Most Holy Spirit,*
> *source of unity, source of diversity (1 Cor 12:4, 11, 13),*
> *help us to appreciate what is distinctive*
> *about each human person, about each species, about each faith,*
> *and to recognize what we all have in common,*
> *that though many, we are one.*

Give us eyes that see, ears that hear, hearts that understand
that we are one as you are One.
All who journey in this life,
all who seek you with sincere hearts,
though our paths are many,
may our hearts be one.

Notes

1. Gary D. Badcock, *Light of Truth and Fire of Love: A Theology of the Holy Spirit* (Grand Rapids: Eerdmans, 1997), 10.

2. See also §§11, 12; available on the Vatican Web site at http://www.vatican.va/edocs/ENG0218/__P7.HTM.

3. Available on the Vatican Web site at http://www.vatican.va/holy_father/john_paul_ii/encyclicals/documents/hf_jp-ii_enc_18051986_dominum-et-vivificantem_en.html.

4. The Declaration on the Relation of the Church to Non-Christian Religions, altered for inclusive language. Available on the Vatican Web site at http://www.vatican.va/archive/hist_councils/ii_vatican_council/documents/vat-ii_decl_19651028_nostra-aetate_en.html. Also see the Dogmatic Constitution on the Church, *Lumen Gentium* 16: "Those also can attain to salvation who through no fault of their own do not know the Gospel of Christ or His Church, yet sincerely seek God and moved by grace strive by their deeds to do His will as it is known to them through the dictates of conscience. Nor does Divine Providence deny the helps necessary for salvation to those who, without blame on their part, have not yet arrived at an explicit knowledge of God and with His grace strive to live a good life. Whatever good or truth is found amongst them is looked upon by the Church as a preparation for the Gospel...." Available on the Vatican Web site at http://www.vatican.va/archive/hist_councils/ii_vatican_council/documents/vat-ii_const_19641121_lumen-gentium_en.html.

5. See, e.g., "The Attitude of the Church toward Followers of Other Religions, Reflections and Orientations on Dialogue and Mission," a document of the Secretariat for Non-Christians (May 10, 1984); and

"Dialogue and Proclamation, Reflection and Orientations on Interreligious Dialogue and the Proclamation of the Gospel of Jesus Christ," a joint document of the Pontifical Council for Interreligious Dialogue and the Congregation for Evangelization of Peoples (May 19, 1991), in *Interreligious Dialogue: The Official Teaching of the Catholic Church (1963–1995)*, ed. Francesco Gioia (Boston: Pauline Books and Media, 1997), 566–79, 608–42.

6. The text of the message and following quotations can be found on line at the Vatican Web site, www.vatican.va/holy_father/john_paul_ii/. Go to messages, then World Day for Peace, then January 1, 2001.

7. Available on the Vatican Web site at http://www.vatican.va/holy_father/john_paul_ii/encyclicals/documents/hf_jp-ii_enc_07121990_redemptoris-missio_en.html.

8. See Jacques Dupuis, *Toward a Christian Theology of Religious Pluralism* (Maryknoll, NY: Orbis Books, 1997); idem, *Christianity and the Religions: From Confrontation to Dialogue* (Maryknoll, NY: Orbis Books, 2001).

9. Available on the Vatican Web site at http://www.vatican.va/holy_father/john_paul_ii/encyclicals/documents/hf_jp-ii_enc_15101998_fides-et-ratio_en.html.

10. See especially Dupuis, *Toward a Christian Theology of Religious Pluralism*. Also Donald Goergen, "Dialogue and Truth," *Focus* 21 (2001): 96–112.

11. Raimon Panikkar, *The Intrareligious Dialogue*, rev. ed. (New York: Paulist Press, 1999).

12. Two excellent studies in this regard are Dupuis, *Toward a Christian Theology of Religious Pluralism;* and Francis Sullivan, *Salvation Outside the Church? Tracing the History of the Catholic Response* (New York: Paulist Press, 1992).

13. "Est tamen hoc dogma intelligendum eo sensu, quo id intelligit Ecclesia ipsa." In H. Denzinger-A. Schönmetzer, *Enchiridion Symbolorum Definitionum et Declarationum*, 33rd ed. (Freiburg im Breisgau: Herder, 1965), 770, #3866. Also see Dupuis, *Toward a Christian Theology of Religious Pluralism*, 99–100, 127–28.

14. Yves Congar, "No Salvation Outside the Church," in *The Wide World My Parish: Salvation and Its Problems* (Baltimore: Helicon Press, 1961), 93–154. For example, "Catholic theology has kept the formula 'Outside the Church...,' but it must be recognized that it is now given a sense very different from that of its originators, Origen and St. Cyprian" (p. 98).

15. That is, outside the visible church. Congar writes: "In the form of moral 'justness' and divine grace, such people have dispositions which can make them Christ's saved ones, members of his Body; but they do not belong effectively to that Body inasmuch as it is visible and recognizable on this earth, that is, identical with the Church. They are indeed in line with the life of the mystical Body, but they are not—yet—effectively within its visible unity" ("No Salvation," 102–3). Also, "In loving Amida, the Buddhist who is invincibly ignorant of the true God is in reality honouring him" (p. 127). We might phrase these insights differently today. Congar was writing them in 1959.

Chapter Five
WORD AND SACRAMENT

In the church our invisible fellowship with the Holy Spirit is made visible. Jesus Christ, as sacrament of God, was conceived through the power of the Spirit. The church, as sacrament of Christ, was given birth through acts of the Holy Spirit. Each individual sacrament of the church is a manifestation of that power of the Spirit.

The Holy Spirit and Eucharist

The sacrament of the church par excellence is the Eucharist. In the Eucharist we come together as church. The church is the assembling of a eucharistic community. Where the Eucharist is, there is the church, and where the church is, there is the Spirit of the risen Christ. The church celebrates the Eucharist and in celebrating makes the church visible.

A key to understanding the Eucharist is an instruction contained in the Lucan and Pauline traditions and repeated in the church's great Eucharistic Prayer: "Do this in remembrance of me" (Luke 22:19; 1 Cor 11:24, 25). The Eucharist is remembering, *anamnesis*, a memorial in which Christians recall the life, death, and resurrection of Jesus. The Holy Spirit is the key to the church's collective memory.[1] The Holy Spirit is also the source of the church's prayer, its worship, its liturgy. An awareness of the Holy Spirit is heightened in the church's great Eucharistic Prayers in what is known as the *epiclesis*, a prayer invoking the Holy Spirit.

"Eucharist" can refer to (1) the entire action of the assembly gathered together to remember and give God thanks and praise;

(2) the Eucharistic Prayer or prayer of thanksgiving, the *anaphora*, which forms the core of the liturgy of the Eucharist; or (3) the "eucharistified" bread and wine, the body and blood of Christ, which we receive.[2] It is the Eucharistic Prayer as a whole that is central. We assemble to pray the prayer, and through praying the prayer to give God thanks, and in return to receive once again the risen Christ's offering of himself to us as a spiritual food and drink. Although it would be tempting to go further into the origin, development, and theology of the Eucharist,[3] we must limit ourselves here to the realization that there would be no Eucharist in any of three senses above apart from the Spirit. The Spirit calls us together, empowers us to pray, and transforms the holy gifts.

The epiclesis is the invocation of the Holy Spirit during the praying of the Eucharistic Prayer.[4] There are actually two epicleses, or two parts, the consecratory epiclesis before the account of the institution of the Eucharist ("Let your Spirit come upon these gifts to make them holy, so that they may become for us the body and blood of our Lord Jesus Christ") and an epiclesis after the account asking that the sacrament bear fruit in unity among us ("May all of us who share in the body and blood of Christ be brought together in unity by the Holy Spirit").[5] It is the second (invoking the Father to send the Holy Spirit on us) that is the more original.[6] Edward Kilmartin highlights the importance of this second epiclesis: "The Eucharistic Prayer provides a global and dynamic vision of this ecclesiastical mystery which requires identifying the epiclesis of transformation of the participants as the key to the ultimate meaning of the eucharistic celebration."[7]

Although there has been dispute about the consecratory function of the words of institution vis-à-vis that of the epiclesis, particularly between the Latin West emphasizing the narrative of institution and the Greek East, emphasizing the epiclesis,[8] the difficulty can be resolved if we realize that it is not a question of either/or. The difficulty comes if we isolate either the words of institution or the epiclesis from the Eucharistic Prayer as a whole. It is the whole prayer that is the prayer of the church, with its institution narrative and twofold epiclesis. It is the whole prayer that the church prays and in it the Holy Spirit is essential if the Eucharist is to bear fruit among us.

Christian Initiation

Full participation in the Christian Eucharist follows only upon initiation into a Christian community of faith. Christian baptism is a baptism in the Spirit. Early in the Gospel of John, Jesus' baptism is characterized in that way: "this is he who baptizes with the Holy Spirit" (1:33). The Gospel of Mark states the same: "I have baptized you with water, but he will baptize you with the Holy Spirit" (1:8).

Confirmation, or chrismation, is then an anointing with the Spirit whom we have already received. Confirmation is conferred by the laying on of hands and an anointing with chrism, a holy oil, which is accompanied in the current revised rites of Christian initiation by the words: "Be sealed with the Gift of the Holy Spirit."[9] This rite of chrismation, or sacrament of confirmation, is really the final stage of baptism, even if separated from it in time, as suggested in the Rite of Christian Initiation of Adults and as celebrated during the Easter Vigil, when chrismation follows immediately upon baptism. In the Catholic tradition, both Christian baptism and confirmation are sacraments of the Holy Spirit, but the Holy Spirit is emphasized in different ways in each of them.

Baptism is an initiatory celebration acknowledging the gift of the Spirit. The words accompanying the anointing in confirmation suggest a sealing of that gift. The idea of the gift being sealed, confirmed, ratified has its orgins in Scripture: "But it is God who establishes us [Silvanus, Timothy, Paul] with you in Christ and has anointed us, by putting his seal on us and giving us his Spirit in our hearts as a first installment" (2 Cor 1:21–22). The Spirit is given in installments, not necessarily all at once. Even though the gift has been given, it is being given continually, poured out not once and for all but in accord with our capacity to receive.

There seems to be more to the gift of the Holy Spirit than we acquire in baptism. In baptism the Holy Spirit is given to us as our inheritance as we become sons and daughters of God (Rom 8:17), but is given also as a pledge of more to come. Now we have only the firstfruits of the Spirit (Rom 8:23). Indeed, throughout our lives the Spirit remains a pledge of more to come (Eph 1:13–14). There are stages in our succumbing to or acquiring the gift of the Spirit.

In the history of the sacrament, the "sealing" of the gift was its confirmation by the bishop. Confirmation as a ritual separate from baptism did not exist before the third century. The name was first used in the fifth century. A theology accompanying this separate confirmation existed by the end of the ninth century. Between the ninth and thirteenth centuries the custom of episcopal confirmation spread throughout Europe. Priests had been given permission to anoint children they baptized with chrism, but these baptisms were later to be confirmed by the bishop and the laying on of hands.

Confirmation in particular has come to be associated with the Holy Spirit and with Pentecost, as baptism is associated with Easter, the paschal mystery, and the risen Christ.[10] Christians are baptized into the death and resurrection of Christ, during which ritual they receive the gift of the Spirit, but the giving of this gift is highlighted with the chrismation or holy anointing. Confirmation celebrates this gift of the Spirit. Our attention is called to it, just as at Pentecost our attention is called to the Spirit, not necessarily away from the risen Christ but to another facet of the mystery.

Easter cannot be understood apart from Pentecost. These events are one mystery and are joined together liturgically as one season. What Easter inaugurates, Pentecost confirms. Likewise baptism inaugurates our life in the Spirit, but the rite of chrismation confirms it. With confirmation we take our life in the Spirit courageously and prophetically out into the world as the disciples were able to do after Pentecost. Just as Easter and Pentecost are one feast even if distinct, so baptism and confirmation are one even if distinguished, as christology and pneumatology are inseparable.

There is no Christ story apart from the Spirit, and no one can narrate a history of the Spirit without reference to Christ. They have set their seals on each other forever.

The Spirit and the Word

The expression "Word of God" has three distinct although interrelated referents: (1) the eternal Word, which was with God in the beginning, and which is God, the second *hypostasis* of the sacred Trinity; (2) the incarnate Word, Jesus of Nazareth, the crucified, risen, and exalted Christ; and (3) the Word of God in Sacred Scripture. It is the latter to which we refer here. We have seen how integrally involved the Spirit is with the incarnate Word, which incarnation came to be through the power of the Spirit. The Word and the Spirit are integrally connected in the triune life of God as well. God's Word is also present within Sacred Scripture and in the sacred writings of many religious traditions. The Hebrew prophets manifested their authority by saying, "This is the word of the LORD" (Isa 1:10; Jer 1:4, 11, 13; 2:1, 4; Ezek 1:3; 12:1; Hos 1:1; 4:1; Amos 1:2, among many others). Scripture is God's word within human words. Just as the Spirit is the source of the liturgical and sacramental life of the *ecclesia*, so the Spirit is the source of its scriptures.

The Catholic Mass comprises both a Liturgy of the Word and the Liturgy of the Eucharist. The celebration of God's Word contributes to the "remembering." Do this in remembrance of me (Luke 22:19; 1 Cor 11:24, 25). The Christian Scriptures came to be as *memoria Jesu* under the influence of the Spirit. They are part of the *anamnesis*, or collective memory, of the church. They are read and celebrated as God's Word present and active through the power of the Spirit. The indwelling Spirit opens our minds, hearts, souls, and human spirits to hear what God is saying, and it is through inspiration (*inspirare*, to breath into) by the Spirit that the human words transmit divine speech.

The *General Instruction of the Roman Missal* of Paul VI states: "Although the Mass is made up of the liturgy of the word and the liturgy of the eucharist, the two parts are so closely connected as to form one act of worship" (#8). "In the readings, explained by the homily, God speaks to his people of redemption and salvation and nourishes their spirit: Christ is present among the faithful through his word" (#33). "In the readings the treasures of the Bible are opened to the people: this is the table of God's word" (#34). The eucharistic celebration comprises two liturgies, one focused on the Word and one focused on the Eucharistic Prayer. God's Word is also presented as the table of the Lord, where we are nourished and fed.

The risen Christ is really present to people in both Word and sacrament. The Holy Spirit is also really present in both. Yves Congar observed that there is "a real presence" associated with the Word and a sacramentality to the Word.[11] Just as there is no Eucharist apart from an epiclesis, so there are no scriptures apart from the inspiration by that same Spirit. Congar suggests that preaching needs to be accompanied by an epiclesis as well: "All preaching should moreover be preceded and accompanied by an invocation of the Spirit, in other words, by an epiclesis."[12]

It is the Holy Spirit who stands behind the coming to be of God's Word as a written word. "All scripture is inspired by God and is useful for teaching, for reproof, for correction, and for training in righteousness, so that everyone who belongs to God may be proficient, equipped for every good work" (2 Tim 3:16–17). We spoke about the Hebrew word for spirit, *ruach*, which can be translated as wind or breath as well as spirit. The Holy Breath breathes life and truth into the holy writings and they are filled with the breath of the Lord.

This relationship between the Spirit and breath is manifest in Thomas Aquinas's speaking of the Holy Spirit within the Trinity as spiration.[13] The Second Person of the Trinity is the only-begotten one who proceeds from the Father by a process of generation. The Third Person is the spirated one; its specific mode of coming forth from the Father is that of being the divine breath. If the first procession leads to the Eternal Word, the spiration of the Third Person leads to the Holy Spirit.

Inspiration everywhere is a work of the Spirit of God, God breathing life into not only the sacred writings of varied religious traditions but also poetry, art, music, and drama as well. Art, poetry, literature, drama, music, theater, as well as religious and philosophical writings along with scientific discoveries have their origins in the Spirit. Although inspiration as such is not limited to Sacred Scripture,[14] scripture holds a special place among the works of the Spirit.

"It is, I believe, poetry, art and music," George Steiner writes, "which relate us most directly to that in being which is not ours."[15] In other words, poetry, art, and music carry within them intimations of the transcendent. There is a real presence within them. The poem or painting or symphony is a manifestation of the Spirit. Some works of art manifest the Spirit more than others. An egalitarian understanding does not work. Steiner writes, "Given a free vote, the bulk of humankind will choose football, the soap opera or bingo over Aeschylus." Democracy is at odds with canonicity. Not anything and everything qualify as great literature, great art, or great music. Not everything gives equal access to the divine. Steiner continues, "It is in music and through music that we are most immediately in the presence of the logically, of the verbally inexpressible but wholly palpable energy in being that communicates to our senses and to our reflection what little we can grasp of the naked wonder of life."[16]

What is specifically called biblical inspiration in the Christian tradition manifests the conviction that the authors of the books of the Bible thought and wrote under divine influence through a charismatic outpouring of the Holy Spirit. Inspiration takes a variety of analogous forms: thinking, speaking, writing can all be inspired. Although biblical inspiration denotes a movement to write, it is the whole process by which the author's work comes to be that is under God's influence.

Inspiration may even be a collective or social phenomenon; an entire group is guided, enlightened, inspired, even if only one is the channel for the inspiration to take shape or form. Pierre Benoit, the

French Dominican biblical scholar, wrote: "For instance, the question is asked: Who enjoyed scriptural inspiration: the last editor of the biblical text, or also those who preceded him? Does not the answer become clear once it is realized that the text is the result of a long history directed throughout by the Holy Spirit?"[17]

We are quite aware today that behind the biblical text lies an oral tradition that was also inspired. Scripture and tradition are works of the same Spirit. There is an apostolic tradition as well as sacred texts.

> ...having noted the continuous action of the Holy Spirit who was not satisfied merely to move a number of authors to write, but rather began by bringing heroes to life and inspiring prophets and apostles to speak, who, in brief, directed the whole history of salvation before committing it to the books which he transmitted to the Church, shall we break abruptly and say, now that the work is accomplished, the Holy Spirit rests and inspiration is a charism of the past at least on the Church's social plane? Does he not preside over the researches of the Fathers, of the doctors and theologians, over the deliberations of Councils, and the dogmatic decisions of the Magisterium, in order to guarantee the results?[18]

The Holy Spirit continues to work today through a wide variety of channels even though the canon of Scripture retains a privileged place as God's Word. Nevertheless, that written word is part of a larger, wider picture.

> Seen in this broad perspective, scriptural inspiration ceases to be an isolated and, as it were, exceptional phenomenon. It takes its place at the center of a great current of the Breath of God passing through the history of salvation from beginning to end—from the Spirit who stirred the primordial waters to the Spirit who will perpetuate souls and bodies in the final manifestation.[19]

Word and sacrament are not exceptional as God's presence in the universe but supreme exemplifications of that universal presence.

God's Word not only is a written word but must be proclaimed. Proclamation, preaching, evangelization, and catechesis are all part of the "great current of the Breath of God passing through the history of salvation." Not all preaching is inspiring, but effective preaching is a work of the Spirit—the Spirit at work in the Word, in the preaching itself, and in the hearers of the Word. Interpretation itself is a charism. In the art of preaching, through the power of the Spirit, the sacred text illuminates the lives we are living and our social concerns.[20]

Evangelization is principally a work of the Holy Spirit according to Pope Paul VI:

> Evangelization will never be possible without the action of the Holy Spirit....Techniques of evangelization are good, but even the most advanced ones could not replace the gentle action of the Spirit....It must be said that the Holy Spirit is the principal agent of evangelization: it is he who impels each individual to proclaim the Gospel, and it is he who in the depths of consciences causes the word of salvation to be accepted and understood. (*Evangelii Nuntiandi* 75).[21]

Evangelization can have a bad sound to it and so must be distinguished from proselytizing. The primary form of evangelization is the witness of one's life. For those called to a Christian way of life, it will mean the formation of Christian communities that are the basis for mission in the world and the inculturation of the gospel. First comes genuine conversion, then formation in community, and finally a sense of mission on behalf of justice and peace in the world.[22]

Forgiveness and Hope

The words of Scripture and the teachings of Jesus can almost be reduced to two essential ingredients of life: forgiveness and hope. Give us enough food, clothing, and shelter to live. Forgive us our sins as we forgive those of others. These are two of the basic petitions in what we know as the Lord's Prayer. Forgiveness and hope are both works of the Spirit.

In the Gospel of John the Spirit is associated with forgiveness. "When he had said this, he breathed on them and said to them, 'Receive the Holy Spirit. If you forgive the sins of any, they are forgiven them; if you retain the sins of any, they are retained'" (John 20:22–23). The mission of the Spirit is seen here as one of forgiveness. In the rites of the Catholic Church, in the Sacrament of Reconciliation, at the time for absolution, the priest prays: "God, the Father of mercies, through the death and resurrection of his Son has reconciled the world to himself and sent the Holy Spirit among us for the forgiveness of sins...."[23] The Holy Spirit has been given in order to effect forgiveness through the ministry of the *ecclesia*.

The prophets were ultimately preachers of hope. The gift of prophecy and the gift of the Spirit are practically synonymous in the scriptures. The prophets helped Israel to sustain its hope: what at first was hope with respect to the near future, then a hope for the distant future, and finally eschatological hope.[24] The history of Israel is a history of a people's hope.

Paul's letter to the Romans describes Abraham as "hoping against hope" (4:18). Paul continues:

> Now hope that is seen is not hope. For who hopes for what is seen? But if we hope for what we do not see, we wait for it with patience. Likewise the Spirit helps us in our weakness; for we do not know how to pray as we ought, but that very Spirit intercedes with sighs too deep for words. (Rom 8:24–26)

Hope is a gift of the Spirit who comes to us in our weaknesses. "May the God of hope fill you with all joy and peace in believing, so that you may abound in hope by the power of the Holy Spirit" (Rom 15:13).

Our hope is ultimately for God; it is God whom we seek. At the deepest level of our innermost spirit we hope for divine and eternal life, for everlasting happiness. Christians place their hope in Christ, for through Christ we come to the Father. But we come to Christ in the power of the Spirit. Our return to God begins with life in the Spirit, with the gift of the Spirit, with baptism in the Spirit. Thomas Aquinas spoke about hope as leaning on God (*Summa Theologiae*, II/II, q. 17, a. 1 & 2).

The church celebrates both reconciliation and healing in the sacrament of the anointing of the sick. Body, mind, heart, soul, and human spirit are all integral to our being whole. Nor am I ever whole by myself alone. Humanity itself must be healed for me to be fully healed, and I must be healed for humanity to be fully healed. During the rite of the anointing of the sick in the Catholic Church, the priest prays: "Through this holy anointing may the Lord in his love and mercy help you with the grace of the Holy Spirit."[25]

The Holy Spirit is present as power in both the Word of God and the sacraments of the church.[26] In Paul, the Holy Spirit is associated with power (Rom 15:13; 1 Cor 2:4). When the Word is proclaimed, both in its proclamation and in its hearing, the Holy Spirit is present to proclaimer and hearer. In the celebration of the sacraments, the Holy Spirit is present, given in baptism, sealed with confirmation, invoked in the Eucharistic Prayer, called upon in the anointing of the sick, and acknowledged as the power of forgiveness in the sacrament of reconciliation. In Word and sacrament the church makes visible the invisible Spirit.

Word and sacrament do not confine the presence of the Holy Spirit in the church but rather manifest that Spirit. Just as the visible church itself is not a delimitation of the action of the invisible Spirit, so proclamation and celebration do not limit the Spirit to those events but rather make known through those events the universality of the Spirit. A sacramental vision invites us to see through the visible to the invisible, to recognize spirit at work within matter, to see our created world as a diaphanousness of the divine.

The Holy Spirit is God breaking through into the world. Whether in our own personal lives, or in our ecclesial lives, or in the world or creation itself, the Holy Spirit is the breakthrough of God into our midst. God may break into our lives in rather dramatic ways or in very ordinary ways, but Word and sacrament acknowledge this breaking into our midst on the part of God. Where the Word is proclaimed, the bread broken, or the cup shared, there is God once again in our midst in tangible, visible, and audible form. The formless has taken on form to conform to our hearing, seeing, touch, smell, or taste so that we might know who God is as the One-Who-Is-With-Us.[27] This is the good news that the *ecclesia* celebrates in its sacramental life. Our God is not a God who is ultimately and utterly Other, but rather one who as Spirit is intimately present.

Holy Spirit, Gift of God,
friend of our souls, the power of love,
heal us, strengthen us, enlighten us.
Make me receptive, Most Holy Spirit, to your divine
  presence.
Bring the Word of God to life within me.
Through your power
help me to recognize your presence in our world.
Help me to believe.
Give me hope.
Teach me to love.
Reconcile all peoples with one another.
Stir up forgiveness and the capacity to love
in my own heart, soul, and human spirit.
Bring me fervent to your holy sacraments.
Anoint me in my innermost spirit with the oil of gladness.
Make me grateful for the abundant blessings that you have
  bestowed.

Notes

1. Edward J. Kilmartin emphasized the role of the Holy Spirit in the liturgical memory of the church. See Jerome M. Hall, *We Have the Mind of Christ: The Holy Spirit and Liturgical Memory in the Thought of Edward J. Kilmartin* (Collegeville, MN: Liturgical Press, 2001), 109–16, 122–24, 140–48.

2. "Body of Christ" can refer to (1) the flesh and blood of Jesus of Nazareth, the body of the earthly Jesus, as well as the transformed pneumatic body of the risen Christ; (2) the community of the faithful or people of God who are also the body of Christ; or (3) the eucharistified bread or sacramental body of Christ.

3. See Enrico Mazza, *The Celebration of the Eucharist: The Origin of the Rite and the Development of Its Interpretaion* (Collegeville, MN: Liturgical Press, 1999).

4. On the role of the Holy Spirit and the eucharistic epiclesis, see Yves Congar, *I Believe in the Holy Spirit*, trans. David Smith, 3 vols. (New York: Seabury Press, 1983), 3:228–74.

5. These texts are from the second Eucharistic Prayer of the Roman Catholic Church, from the revised rites approved by Pope Paul VI. This second Eucharistic Prayer in the Missal of Paul VI, however, derives from the anaphoral text in the *Apostolic Tradition* attributed to Hippolytus. These two eucharistic epicleses can be found in other Eucharistic Prayers as well, e.g., the third Eucharistic Prayer in the Missal of Paul VI ("And so, Father, we bring you these gifts. We ask you to make them holy by the power of your Spirit, that they may become the body and blood of your Son, our Lord Jesus Christ, at whose command we celebrate this Eucharist," and "Grant that we, who are nourished by his body and blood, may be filled with his Holy Spirit, and become one body, one spirit in Christ"). It is noteworthy, however, that the ancient Roman Canon, the first Eucharistic Prayer, which acquired its essential form in the fourth century and remained the only Eucharistic Prayer in the Latin church until the Second Vatican Council, does not include an explicit epiclesis.

6. Mazza, *Celebration of the Eucharist*, 56–59, 292–94.

7. Edward J. Kilmartin, *The Eucharist in the West*, ed. Robert J. Daly (Collegeville, MN: Liturgical Press, 1999), 355.

8. See Congar, *I Believe in the Holy Spirit*, 3:228–41; also Mazza, *Celebration of the Eucharist*, 251–95; Hall, *We Have the Mind of Christ*, 7–72, 164–66. It is also interesting to note that the *anaphora*, or Eucharistic Prayer, of Addai and Mari, recognized as valid by Rome, does not include the words of institution. See Robert Taft, "Mass Without the Consecration?" *America* 188 (May 12, 2003): 7–11.

9. See the Rite of Confirmation, in *The Rites of the Catholic Church as Revised by Decree of the Second Vatican Council and Published by Authority of Pope Paul VI* (New York: Pueblo, 1976), 296, 301, 310, 319. On the sacrament of confirmation, also see Gerard Austin, *Anointing with the Spirit: The Rite of Confirmation* (New York: Pueblo, 1985).

10. Congar, *I Believe in the Holy Spirit*, 3:219. Edward Schillebeeckx, *Christ the Sacrament of Encounter with God*, trans. Cornelius Ernst (New York: Sheed & Ward, 1963), 197–210.

11. Yves Congar, *The Word and the Spirit*, trans David Smith (San Francisco: Harper & Row, 1986), 25. Also see Paul Janowiak, *The Holy Preaching: The Sacramentality of the Word in the Liturgical Assembly* (Collegeville, MN: Liturgical Press, 2000); and Mary Catherine Hilkert, *Naming Grace: Preaching and the Sacramental Imagination* (New York: Continuum, 1997).

12. Congar, *Word and the Spirit*, 23.

13. *Summa Theologiae*, I, q. 27, a. 4, ad 3: "Hence the procession which is not generation has remained without a special name; but it can be called spiration, as it is the procession of the Spirit."

14. "Inspiration" can be used theologically in both a strict sense and a wider sense. In the wider sense, it is used in reference to the Holy Spirit's presence in great works of art as well as in the sacred writings of the world's great religious traditions. They, too, have their source in the Holy Spirit. In the stricter sense, inspiration is reserved for the church's canonical books, which are accepted as inspired in a special way and are a unique work of the Spirit, whose breath is nevertheless broader than those texts alone.

15. George Steiner, *Real Presences* (Chicago: University of Chicago Press, 1989), 226.

16. Ibid., 67, 32, 216–17.

17. Pierre Benoit, *Aspects of Biblical Inspiration* (Chicago: Priory Press, 1965), 24–25.

18. Ibid., 31–32.

19. Ibid., 34.

20. See Bruce Chilton, *A Galilean Rabbi and His Bible: Jesus' Use of the Interpreted Scripture of his Time* (Wilmington, DE: Michael Glazier, 1984).

21. Pope Paul VI, *Evangelii Nuntiandi*, apostolic exhortation on evangelization in the modern world (Washington, DC: United States Catholic Conference, 1975).

22. See Helen Marie Raycraft, OP, *Seeds of Hope: Hispanic Spirituality in the Basic Ecclesial Communities* (Austin, TX: Dominican Missionary Preaching Team, 1994).

23. *Rites of the Catholic Church*, 362–63, 372–73.

24. See Donald Goergen, *The Mission and Ministry of Jesus* (Wilmington, DE: Michael Glazier, 1986; reprint, Eugene, OR: Wipf & Stock, 1992), 68–83.

25. *Rites of the Catholic Church*, 587, 603.

26. One could have included here as well references to the Holy Spirit in the rite of Christian marriage and in the ordination rites. The Holy Spirit is integral to both a theology of marriage and a theology of orders.

27. Donald Goergen, *Jesus, Son of God, Son of Mary, Immanuel* (Collegeville, MN: Liturgical Press, Michael Glazier, 1995; reprint, Eugene, OR: Wipf & Stock, 1995), 40–53.

Chapter Six
THE SPIRIT IN AN
EVOLVING UNIVERSE

The Spirit dwells within the depths of the human spirit, in the inner recesses of the soul, transforming and sanctifying us. The Spirit works within community, the *ecclesia*, as the soul of the church, building up the body of Christ. What about the Spirit's cosmic activity?

The "Within" and the "Without"

A central fact about ourselves as well as the cosmos, or perhaps a central intuition, according to Pierre Teilhard de Chardin, is that there are two sides to the universe. There is a "within" and a "without," interiority and exteriority, inner space and outer space. There is not a "without" without a "within," nor a "within" without a "without." We are not only physical, embodied beings. We have depth; we have soul. Teilhard de Chardin describes a personal experience of this depth.

> And so, for the first time in my life perhaps (although I am supposed to meditate every day!), I took the lamp and, leaving the zone of everyday occupations and relationships where everything seems clear, I went down into my inmost self, to the deep abyss whence I feel dimly that my power of action emanates. But as I moved further and further away from the conventional certainties by which social life is superficially illuminated, I became aware that I was losing contact with myself. At

each step of the descent a new person was disclosed within me of whose name I was no longer sure, and who no longer obeyed me. And when I had to stop my exploration because the path faded from beneath my steps, I found a bottomless abyss at my feet, and out of it came— arising I know not from where—the current which I dare to call *my* life.[1]

Teilhard also intuited or postulated a psychic, interior "within," not only for ourselves but for our universe: "Things have their *within*."[2] The human phenomenon is a key to unlocking the mystery of the universe. What makes its appearance somewhere in the universe has a history, a past, before it became observable, obvious. Evolution means that what has come to be has come to be by way of birth from what was there before.[3]

The "within" is also identified for Teilhard with "consciousness," which in a rudimentary or advanced form permeates the whole universe.[4] Teilhard's observation about the double aspect of the universe is affirmed also by Ken Wilber, for whom there is also a within and a without and for whom the within is also synonymous with consciousness.[5] This twofold aspect of the universe raises for Teilhard the necessity of two forms of energy, which he calls tangential and radial. [6]

There is no concept more familiar to us than that of spiritual energy, yet there is none that is more opaque scientifically. On the one hand the objective reality of psychical effort and work is so well established that the whole of ethics rests on it and, on the other hand, the nature of this inner power is so intangible that the whole description of the universe in mechanical terms has had no need to take account of it, but has been successfully completed in deliberate disregard of its reality.[7]

Ultimately energy is one; yet there are two forms of energy, one associated more with the "within" and the other more with the "without." Tangential energy, associated more with the without of things, is energy as generally understood in modern science. It links or binds together things of the same order of complexity. Radial ("axial" or "centric") energy, on the other hand, associated more with the within, draws things forward toward greater complexity and higher stages of consciousness. The latter is the energy behind the evolution of the universe. Radial energy moves the universe in the direction of the less probable, namely, to higher, more complex, and more centered forms of consciousness.

This radial energy undergirding the creative evolutionary process, or the process of an evolutionary creation, is, simply put, love: "Considered in its full biological reality, love—that is to say the affinity of being with being—is not peculiar to humanity. It is a general property of all life and as such it embraces, in its varieties and degrees, all the forms successively adopted by organised matter."[8] Teilhard names the spiritual energy underlying the evolution of the universe love, the source of the universe's unity and diversity. This sounds an awful lot like the Spirit, who theologically is named Love and who is the source of unity and diversity, now perceived at cosmic—macrocosmic and microcosmic—levels. Is the radial energy of which Teilhard speaks the Holy Spirit, or at least an energy radiating from the Holy Spirit?[9]

The Spirit of Evolution

Teilhard himself seldom mentions the Holy Spirit. He was writing for a scientific world as well as to avoid censorship of his vision. He was not writing a theological treatise but giving witness to a personal, cosmic, and mystical vision in which God and the world, Christianity and evolution, religion and science are perceived as partners rather than in opposition.[10] To say, therefore, that he does not name the Holy Spirit frequently in his writings is not to deny the presence of the Spirit. Ultimately the energy of the universe is the Holy Spirit, radial energy, love.

Teilhard manifests this awareness of the Spirit in one of his last great essays, "The Heart of Matter," written in 1950.[11] Without explicitly naming it Holy Spirit, he writes, "Spirit was by no means the enemy or the opposite pole of the Tangibility which I was seeking to attain: rather was it its very heart."[12] Spirit is the heart of matter. Emile Rideau, in his extensive study of Teilhard's thought, writes:

> Finally, it might seem surprising that the Person of the Holy Spirit is not mentioned in Teilhard's writings. The reality, however, of his action is always present in it, at different levels: it is from the Spirit that the spiritual energy at the heart of matter and life proceeds, and the energy that later, in the course of man's history, brings persons together. And this energy is a love, light, and fire, which constitutes the divine ambience in which all things and all souls dwell. This love proceeds in its entirety from Christ....For Teilhard, then, it is indeed the spirit—not "the spirit of philosophers and scientists," but the Holy Spirit, the Spirit of Christ, who is active in history and in the world until they achieve their fulfillment.[13]

There is not only a cosmic Christ but a cosmic Spirit who indwells the universe.

Although Teilhard does not refer so explicitly to the Holy Spirit, the image of fire had great significance for him,[14] which is associated in the Lucan writings with the Holy Spirit. Teilhard writes: "The day will come when, after harnessing space, the winds, the tides, gravitation, we shall harness for God the energies of love. And, on that day, for the second time in the history of the world, humanity will have discovered fire."[15] Traditionally the Holy Spirit has been seen as kindling in our hearts the fire of love. Teilhard also had a devotion to the Sacred Heart.[16] The "heart of Christ" in Teilhard is associated with fire: "Christ. His Heart. A Fire: a fire with the power to penetrate all things—and which was now gradually spreading unchecked."[17] Teilhard's devotion to the heart of Jesus and his association of heart with love and fire may also explain the few references to Spirit that would have those same associations. For in some sense the Spirit can be seen as the heart of Jesus. Thomas Aquinas had associated the Spirit with the heart of the church, as we have already indicated.[18]

Teilhard's references to the Spirit, spirit, and fire are particularly prominent in his "Mass on the World" (1923).[19] Fire is addressed as "blazing Spirit," is perceived as penetrating the earth from within, and is recognized as having come down into the heart of the world to absorb us. He writes: "How strange, my God, are the processes your Spirit initiates!"[20] In a trinitarian way, he writes:

> In the beginning was *Power*, intelligent, loving, energizing. In the beginning was the *Word*, supremely capable of mastering and moulding whatever might come into being in the world of matter. In the beginning there were not coldness and darkness: there was the *Fire*.[21]

An early essay, "The Mystical Milieu" (1917),[22] prefiguring *The Divine Milieu* (1927), emphasized similar themes. The universe is ablaze! "In very truth, it is God, and God alone whose Spirit stirs up the whole mass of the universe in ferment."[23]

At the heart of Teilhard's universe is movement. The universe is not a cosmos but a cosmogenesis. It is in the process of coming to be, not yet finished. This cosmogenesis is also biogenesis and anthropogenesis and, for Teilhard, christogenesis. Evolution is both matter and spirit, not in opposition to each other, but the evolution of spirit-matter. There is evolution at the level of the "within" and at the level of the "without." It is psychogenesis and, with the emergence of the human, noogenesis as well: Matter–Life–Thought; cosmos–biosphere–noosphere—and also theosphere. God and the universe, religion and science, are not at odds. God is the God of evolution.[24] God created the world evolutively.

From the perspective of the without, the universe is evolving. Looking at it from within, it is being created. Evolution is simply God's way of creating the universe. It is an evolving creation as well as a creative evolution. Just as the within and the without manifest a double aspect to the universe, so do creation and evolution. God remains the creator of an evolving universe, and evolution is how God's creative activity appears to human investigation. There is an evolution of both matter and spirit. They go hand in hand. But Teilhard gives a primacy to spirit. At the heart of the human phenomenon is the reality of spirit, indeed the reality of the Holy Spirit, and the God of evolution, the ultimate evolver of the world, is the Holy Spirit, the breath that breathes, the wind that blows, the power of love.

Although Teilhard speaks about the evolution of the within, the primacy of spirit, the phenomenon of spirituality, the future of humankind as ultra-human,[25] others like Sri Aurobindo (1872–1950) in India and Ken Wilber have explored the evolution of consciousness with greater precision. Our purpose here is not to explore this evolution of human consciousness but simply to take note of it. The human spirit has had a prehistory and has as well a future, whether we speak in terms of Teilhard's ultra-human or Aurobindo's Supermind, without identifying the two as synonymous.[26]

The Law of Complexity-Consciousness

For Teilhard, evolution is a process of complexification, unification, and centration, resulting in higher and higher levels of consciousness. Atoms unite to form molecules and molecules unite to form megamolecular substances. Cells emerge and become multicellular organisms. So it is with personality development. Individuals mature and integrate more and more into themselves. A challenge, especially at the higher levels of cosmic evolution, is whether unity can be achieved without destroying the identity or individuality of the elements united. This is where Teilhard contributes his essential axiom: true union differentiates.[27] How do we account for this phenomenon of a differentiating creative union? Love is the energy underlying the process.[28]

Ken Wilber comments on Teilhard's law of complexity-consciousness:

Greater depth, greater interiority, greater consciousness. Teilhard expressed this in his "law of complexity and consciousness"—namely, the more of the former, the more of the latter. Since, as we already saw, evolution tends in the direction of the greater complexity, it amounts to the same thing to say that it tends in the direction of greater consciousness (again, depth = consciousness).[29]

Likewise, the emerging sciences of complexity are studying the phenomenon of complexification.[30] Complex systems are disorderly but not chaotic; they manifest order within disorder; they operate in a zone between stagnation and anarchy. They are not just complicated but organized. At new levels of complexity, new properties appear, a threshold is reached, a phase transition takes place, and something new emerges. Complex systems are adaptive, flexible, and learn from feedback. Adaptability, not stability, is their goal. Evolution gives rise to the novel.

> ...healthy economies and healthy societies alike have to keep order and chaos in balance—and not just a wishy-washy, average, middle-of-the-road kind of balance, either. Like a living cell, they have to regulate themselves with a dense web of feedbacks and regulation at the same time that they leave plenty of room for creativity, change, and response to new conditions....[31]

Here within the sciences of complexity and emergent evolution lie the workings of the Holy Spirit, the source of unity and diversity in church, world, and cosmos. The Spirit is the energy underlying evolution's unification, diversification, complexification, and development of consciousness; the cosmos's innermost pull and push toward adaptability, balance, creativity, and emergent structures supporting ever more and more advanced levels of interiority, depth, and consciousness. The Holy Spirit is a force at work in the universe as well as among the religions of the world and in our own personal lives.

Individuality and Society

Besides the contrast between the inseparable "without" and "within," complexity and consciousness, there is also in Teilhard the contrast between individuality and society, another distinguishable but inseparable duality. Teilhard takes seriously the importance of individuality: "Each person, though enveloped within the same universe as all others, presents an independent centre of perspective and activity for the universe."[32] "Thus socialization, whose hour seems to have sounded for Humankind, does not by any means signify the end of the Era of the Individual upon earth, but far more its beginning."[33]

Equally important are the society, culture, milieu in which individuality takes shape and develops. To be a person is to be an individual in society. True individuality develops in the direction of personhood, that is in relationship to others. A person *qua* person is a center of a network of relationships that each one of us is. I am not who I am apart from others. My "individuality" and "the other" are both poles of an individual person's development.

> [Egoism's] only mistake, but a fatal one, is *to confuse individuality with personality*. In trying to separate itself as much as possible from others, the element individualises itself; but in doing so it becomes retrograde and seeks to drag the world backwards towards plurality and into matter. In fact it diminishes itself and loses itself. To be fully ourselves it is in the opposite direction, in the direction of convergence with all the rest, that we must advance— towards the "other." The goal of ourselves, the acme of our originality, is not our individuality but our person, and according to the evolutionary structure of the world, we can only find our person by uniting together....The true ego grows in inverse proportion to "egoism."[34]

The significance Teilhard attaches to the social phenomenon is evidenced by the frequency in his writings of words such as amorization, convergence, noogenesis, socialization, totalization, unanimization, and universalization.

The Four Quadrants or Dimensions

If we put Teilhard's "within" and "without" together with his "individual" and "social" poles, we come to the four quadrants of which Ken Wilber speaks.[35] There is the "without" of the individual (e.g., physicality, behaviors); the "within" of the individual (e.g., intrapsychic life, values); the "without" of a society (e.g., social systems, nation-states); and the "within" of a society (e.g., culture, shared values). Wilber writes, "In evolution in general, and human evolution in particular, we are tracing *four different strands*, each of which is intimately related and indeed dependent upon all the others, but none of which can be reduced to the others. The four strands are the interior and the exterior of the individual and the social."[36]

Societies have their withins just as individual persons do. In distinguishing the social from the cultural, Wilber gives the following example:

> Imagine you go to a foreign country where you do not speak the language. As soon as you arrive in that country, you are *in* the social system, or the actual material components of the country. You are *in* that country. People around you are speaking a foreign language, which you do not understand, but the physically spoken words hit your ears just like they do anybody else's; you and the natives are both immersed in the *identical* physical vibrations of the social system. But you don't understand a word. You are in the social system, but you are *not* in the worldview, you are not in the culture. You hear only the exteriors, you do not understand the interior meaning. All the social signifiers impinge on you, but none of the

cultural signifieds come up. You are an insider to the social system but an outsider to the culture.[37]

If culture is in one sense the heart of a society[38] and religion the soul of a culture, then religion, and thus the religions, function at the level of a society's and culture's "within." The religions themselves have their own "withouts," their external forms, structures, and rituals. But as religion manifests the interiority of cultures, so spirituality or mysticism is the innermost interiority of religion. Just as the human spirit is the innermost core of the human person, so societies and cultures have an innermost core as well. Religion is the soul of culture, and spirituality the soul of religion. As is the case with the human spirit, so with the cosmos, universe, and social systems. At their innermost core is the Holy Spirit.

Religion and Spirituality

There is more to spirituality than the practices of religion. There is more to religion than spirituality. They overlap but do not coincide.[39] Both, however, are concerned with the deepest and highest reality, with spirit, with the divine, with God. Religion is a manifestation of spirit, and spirit is made present through the religions of the world. Religion has an exterior, institutional, visible side to it, and this side comprises varied religious traditions and scriptures. Religion is expressed in myth and ritual. The history of religions and the phenomenon of religion parallel and overlap but are not identified with the history of spirituality.

Spirituality, however, is the heart and soul of religion. Spirituality concerns itself with ultimate reality, the holy mystery, the ground of being, infinity, eternity, transcendence, Presence— the invisible interiority of the world. Spirit opens onto an abyss (Abyss) that, on the one hand, is endless and formless and, on the other, takes the shape and forms of religion. Not everything religious is spiritual, but much that is religious *is* spiritual. Not everything that is spiritual is religious, but much that is spiritual *is* religious. They are distinguishable but not separable. Ordinarily one enters the world of spirit through religion and the religions of the world.

Teilhard de Chardin saw both the necessity and the limits of religion. "Contemporary humanity has passed through a period of great illusion in imagining that, having attained a better knowledge of itself and the world, there is no more need for religion."[40] At the same time, "we must, *with all that is human in us*, re-think our religion."[41] The true function of religion is to sustain and spur on the process of evolution, to affirm a future for this earth, to give humankind hope.[42] "Religion, if true, can have no other effect than to perfect the humanity in humankind."[43] For Teilhard, religion and spirit are both essential to the future of evolution. This does not mean that one should refrain from the critique of religion,[44] but one should suggest that religion in the future is not to be discarded but to be transformed.

The Evolution of Christ and the Christ of Evolution

For Teilhard, at the heart of evolution or cosmogenesis is the Christ of evolution or christogenesis. But the cosmic Christ, the universal Christ, the total Christ of whom Teilhard spoke is a Christ that is not yet fully formed. The "whole Christ" is not to be identified with Christianity in its present stage of development. For Teilhard, Christ is the completion of creation, but it is equally true that creation is the completion of Christ.[45] "The total Christ is consummated and may be attained only at the term of universal evolution."[46] Thus, the whole Christ, the fullness of Christ, the *plēroma* is something that we still await. Christ does not come to completion before the universe does, since in the end it is the whole cosmos that is the body of Christ.

The dialogue among religions raises the question: Who is Jesus Christ? Not simply the question, Who do you say that *Jesus* is? (Mark 8:29), but, What do we mean by "the Christ"? Jesus

Christ ordinarily refers to Jesus of Nazareth, the earthly historical Jesus, whose life, mission, ministry, and death have been the object of historiographical scrutiny for centuries now. Jesus Christ is *that* Jesus, who lived and walked and talked among us. But "Jesus Christ" also refers to the risen Jesus, the risen Christ, the only Christ there is, "Jesus Christ, our Lord" (Acts 2:36; Phil 2:11). This is the selfsame Jesus to be sure. There is only one Jesus Christ, the crucified *and* risen one. Yet the denotation, point of reference, and meaning are not always the same. We are saying more when we say "risen Christ" than when we say "Jesus of Nazareth."

"Jesus Christ" also means the incarnate Word. Yet Christ can also refer to the pre-incarnate Word, the eternal Son who was with the Father in the beginning. We are familiar with the prologue to the Gospel of John (1:1–18), but the letter to the Colossians suggests a preexistent *Christ* (1:15–20).[47] The words "Jesus Christ" are polyvalent, multileveled, with layers of meaning, all rich and suggestive: Jesus Christ who was, who is, and who is to come, the Alpha and Omega (Rev 1:8), not only the pre-incarnate Christ but also the One who is to come. Even here, with all this meaning, we still have not called to mind the whole Christ, the *totum Christum* (Paul, Augustine), for what is Christ without his members? Jesus is not who he is by himself alone. His singularity is not isolated, disconnected individuality. Jesus Christ also refers to this total Christ, cosmic Christ, the Christ of creation, the universal Christ, in whom and through whom God will be all in all, who will hand everything over to the Father (1 Cor 15:24–28), who is incomplete apart from his members.[48]

"Jesus Christ" are not words that have only one meaning. Ultimately they mean the Christ, Jesus of Nazareth, but the whole Christ, head and members, the incomplete Christ who is still in the process of coming to completion because his body is not yet fully formed, the Christ in whom those who are not explicitly Christian have their place and space, the mystical Christ, the *mysterium christi*, before whom we stand in awe, the one who invites us into the very mystery of God and makes us sharers in the divine life.

The Christian's Christ can sometimes be too small. There is more to Christ than we may have thus far appropriated. Our own christification, our own conversion, is not complete. We know Christ in spirit and truth, but there is always more. Not simply, Do I believe in Jesus Christ? but Who is the Christ in whom I believe? The Spirit will guide us into the fullness of truth (John 16:12–13).

> *Holy Spirit, cosmic Spirit,*
> *infinite energy deep within the universe,*
> *power of love, source of our universe's creative evolution and its*
>   *manifold forms,*
> *Spirit of evolution, soul of the cosmos,*
> *heart of matter, lover of diversity,*
> *principle of our unity, pure indwelling consciousness,*
> *animator of religions and cultures,*
> *Spirit of Christ,*
> *energizer, evolver, holy breath, blazing fire,*
> *fill us with your life,*
> *re-create us as your people,*
> *pour yourself out upon our world,*
> *renew the face of the earth.*

Notes

1. Pierre Teilhard de Chardin, *The Divine Milieu* (1927), trans. Bernard Wall (New York: Harper & Row, 1960), 48.

2. Pierre Teilhard de Chardin, *The Phenomenon of Man* (1940/1947), trans. Bernard Wall (New York: Harper & Row, 1959), 54.

3. Pierre Teilhard de Chardin, "The Phyletic Structure of the Human Group" (1951), in *The Appearance of Man* (New York: Harper & Row, 1965), 136; see also *Phenomenon of Man*, 53–74.

4. Teilhard de Chardin, *Phenomenon of Man*, 57.

5. See Ken Wilber, *Sex, Ecology, Spirituality: The Spirit of Evolution* (Boston: Shambhala Publications, 1995), 109–52.

6. Teilhard de Chardin, *Phenomenon of Man*, 62–66.

7. Ibid., 62.

8. Ibid., 264. Translation adjusted for inclusive language. Also see Pierre Teilhard de Chardin, *The Activation of Energy* (New York: Harcourt Brace Jovanovich, 1970), 70–71, 118–20.

9. Paul Pearsall (*The Heart's Code* [New York: Broadway Books, 1998]) speaks about "L" energy, a vital life force, and writes: "So pervasive is 'L' energy that indigenous peoples and ancient religious systems have given it over one hundred different names and base their healing systems on it. In India and Tibet, this energy is called 'prana'. Polynesians call it 'mana', and the Sufis called it 'baraka'. Jews in the cabalistic tradition call it 'yesod', the Iroquois call it 'orendam', the Ituraea pygmies call it 'megbe', and Christians call it the 'Holy Spirit'" (59). Whether all these refer to the same reality may be a question, but positing such a fundamental energy and associating it with love and the Holy Spirit are of interest. Also, *ruach*, the Hebrew word for spirit, as we have seen, is associated with energy. Its Semitic root *ruh* in cognate languages signifies "to breathe" and "to blow." In its original meaning it suggested "air being in motion," wind, breath, but commonly carried the meaning of "energy" because wind and breathing connote energy. See R. Birch Hoyle, "Spirit," in *Encyclopaedia of Religion and Ethics*, ed. James Hastings (New York: Charles Scribner's Sons, 1968), 11:784–803.

10. For a Christian theological interpretation of an evolving universe, see Karl Schmitz-Moormann, *Theology of Creation in an Evolutionary World* (Cleveland: Pilgrim Press, 1997).

11. Pierre Teilhard de Chardin, "The Heart of Matter" (1950), in *The Heart of Matter* (New York: Harcourt Brace Jovanovich, 1978), 15–79.

12. Ibid., 28.

13. Emile Rideau, *The Thought of Teilhard de Chardin* (New York: Harper & Row, 1967), 169.

14. Ibid., 30, 214, 287–88 n. 24, 615 n. 131.

15. Pierre Teilhard de Chardin, "The Evolution of Chastity" (1934), in *Toward the Future* (New York: Harcourt Brace Jovanovich, 1975), 86–87, adjusted for inclusive language. Also "space" in the quotation is in the original text "ether." See note, p. 86.

16. See Teilhard de Chardin, "Heart of Matter," esp. 39–58.

17. Ibid., 47.

18. Thomas Aquinas, *Summa Theologiae*, III, 8, 1, ad 3. Also see *De Veritate* q. 29, a. 4, ad 7.

19. Pierre Teilhard de Chardin, "The Mass on the World" (1923), in *Hymn of the Universe* (New York: Harper & Row, 1965), 19–37.

20. Ibid., 22, 23, 29, 34.

21. Ibid., 21.

22. Pierre Teilhard de Chardin, "The Mystical Milieu" (1917), in *Writings in Time of War* (New York: Harper & Row, 1968), 117–49.

23. Ibid., 129, 130.

24. Pierre Teilhard de Chardin, "The God of Evolution" (1953), in *Christianity and Evolution* (New York: Harcourt Brace Jovanovich, 1971), 237–43. On science and religion, see Ken Wilber, *The Marriage of Sense and Soul: Integrating Science and Religion* (New York: Random House, 1998).

25. See especially Pierre Teilhard de Chardin, "The Spirit of the Earth" (1931), "The Phenomenon of Spirituality" (1937), and "Human Energy" (1937), in *Human Energy* (New York: Harcourt Brace Jovanovich, 1970).

26. For studies contrasting Teilhard de Chardin and Sri Aurobindo, see Jan Feys, *The Philosophy of Evolution in Sri Aurobindo and Teilhard de Chardin* (Calcutta: Firma K.L. Mukhopadhyay, 1973); and K. D. Sethna, *The Spirituality of the Future: A Search apropos of R.C. Zaehner's Study in Sri Aurobindo and Teilhard de Chardin* (London: Associated University Press, 1981).

27. There are numerous references in Teilhard's writings to this axiom; see, e.g., *The Future of Man* (New York: Harper & Row, 1964), 53, 55, 302; *Human Energy*, 144, 149, 152; *Science and Christ* (New York: Harper & Row, 1968), 136–37, 174–86.

28. Pierre Teilhard de Chardin, "The Grand Option" (1939), in *Future of Man*, 55. Also see *Phenomenon of Man*, 264–67; *Science and Christ*, 160; and *Future of Man*, 91–92.

29. Wilber, *Sex, Ecology, Spirituality*, 113.

30. See M. Mitchell Waldrop, *Complexity: The Emerging Science at the Edge of Order and Chaos* (New York: Simon & Schuster, 1992).

31. Ibid., 294.

32. Teilhard de Chardin, *Divine Milieu*, 122. Translation adjusted for inclusive language.

33. Pierre Teilhard de Chardin, "The Grand Option" (1939), in *Future of Man*, 54. Translation adjusted for inclusive language.

34. Teilhard de Chardin, *Phenomenon of Man*, 263.

35. Wilber, *Sex, Ecology, Spirituality*, 109–52.

36. Ibid., 120.

37. Ibid., 125. Emphases in original.

38. See chapter 4 for the emphasis John Paul II placed on the importance of culture.

39. See Sandra M. Schneiders, "Religion vs. Spirituality: A Contemporary Conundrum," *Spiritus* 3 (2003): 163–85.

40. Teilhard de Chardin, "Spirit of the Earth" (1931), in *Human Energy*, 43. Translation adjusted for inclusive language.

41. Teilhard de Chardin, "Some Reflections on the Conversion of the World" (1936), in *Science and Christ*, 126.

42. *Human Energy*, 44; *Science and Christ*, 122–23; *Divine Milieu*, 134–35.

43. Pierre Teilhard de Chardin, "The Mysticism of Science" (1939) in *Human Energy*, 178. Translation adjusted for inclusive language.

44. There have been many modern critiques of religion, including modern secular cultures' indifference as well as hostility toward religion. Nonetheless, religion remains humanity's primary access to S/spirit. This does not discount the need for serious reform and even transformation among the religions of the world. For Sri Aurobindo's affirmation as well as critique of religion, see *The Human Cycle* (Pondicherry, India: Sri Aurobindo Ashram, 1970), 162–70, as well as the entire essay. Also see Ken Wilber, *One Taste: Daily Reflections on Integral Spirituality* (Boston:

Shambhala Publications, 2000), 25–35. James Carroll has written, "The evidence suggests that religion is ambiguous, a source of consolation, hope and compassion but also intolerance, contempt and even violence" (review of *The Heart of Islam* by Seyyed Hossein Nasr, *The New York Times Book Review* [Sept. 8, 2002]: 13). Religion needs to be challenged and critiqued as well as respected and valued. Also see Charles Kimball, *When Religion Becomes Evil* (San Francisco: HarperSanFrancisco, 2002).

45. See especially Teilhard's last essay, "The Christic" (1955), in *Heart of Matter,* 80–102.

46. "How I Believe" (1934), in *Christianity and Evolution,* 129.

47. The preexistent Christ and the preexistent Logos are in fact the same, but the use of preexistent Christ indicates again the manifold richness of meaning in the expression "Christ."

48. "Yet this, also, must be held, marvellous though it may seem: Christ has need of his members" (Pius XII, *Mystici Corporis Christi* [1943] 44, in *The Papal Encyclicals,* ed. Claudia Carlen, 5 vols. [Wilmington, NC: McGrath, 1981], 4:37–63).

Chapter Seven
IN THE MIDST OF THE WORLD

The Spirit of God has been present to creation from the beginning of time. The Spirit is divine energy deep within God's evolving creation, the source of its creative evolution, its increasing complexity, its growth in consciousness, its unity, its diversity. This creative Spirit breaks through from within creation, not only as the energy of evolution but as the indwelling Spirit within each of us, as St. Paul so emphasized, and also as the heart and soul of ecclesial life, as Paul also understood. This Holy Spirit comes like breath, like wind, like fire, to which both Luke and the Gospel of John testify. There is no reason to limit the outpouring of God's Spirit, no reason to suggest that this one, holy, universal Spirit does not break through in manifold ways into the workings of the world itself—from within creation and throughout all of history.

The Holy Spirit and Creation

In Christian theology, it is the Trinity, the triune God, who creates the heavens and the earth. At times, however, creation is attributed more to one Person of the Trinity than to the others. In the Apostles' Creed and the Nicene-Constantinopolitan Creed we profess belief in God, the Father Almighty, Creator of heaven and earth. In the prologue to the Gospel of John, however, it is the Second Person through whom all things come to be (John 1:1–3). On the other hand, a well-known medieval Latin hymn of unknown authorship but usually attributed to Rabanus Maurus (776–856) proclaims:

> Veni, creator Spiritus,
> Mentes tuorum visita;
> Imple superna gratia
> Quae tu creasti pectora....[1]

In Genesis, the Creator Spirit, the divine *ruach* (spirit, wind, breath), is associated with all that comes to be (Gen 1:1–2). The association between the Spirit and creation is reflected also in the Psalms (e.g., Ps 104:27–30). In the *Summa contra Gentiles*, Thomas Aquinas referred to the Holy Spirit as "the principle of the creation of things."[2]

We pray in the Nicene-Constantinopolitan Creed: "I believe in the Holy Spirit, the Lord, the giver of life" (*to zōopoioun*, "the life-giver," is the Greek word in John 6:63). The breath of God is a life-giving breath, and all living things depend for their existence on this Holy Breath. God breathes and we are created. "If God should take back his spirit to himself, and gather to himself his breath, all flesh would perish together, and all mortals return to dust" (Job 34:14–15).

As is true in the church and among the various religious traditions, the Holy Spirit is the source of unity and diversity in creation as well. Let us ponder the unity. If I were to ask what is the most precious gift God has given us, we could respond in varied ways. As I consider the question today, I would say: the gift of being itself, just being: to be. Otherwise there would be no other gifts, there would be no one to receive them. What greater gift could there be than the act of being itself?

I begin to realize that this is a gift that I share with every other creature in the heavens or on the earth, whether mineral, plant, or animal, with the sands on the shore of the sea as well as with the waters of the sea itself. Each of us has been given its own act of being. If I have deep respect for that gift, if I am aware of the giftedness of that creative act, then I must hold in awe that gift wherever it is manifest. We are all one in that we all share the gift of being itself. The wonder is that each of us *is*, indeed that any of us is.

Our love for all creation, for all creatures, our respect for the earth, our love of neighbor, our awe before the evolving and expanding universe, all these are grounded in a heightened awareness that each one of them IS, that each is a creation, a creature of God's making, something or someone that shares with us the ineffable act of existence. To fail to love, to respect, to appreciate any other is to fail to see and appreciate the fact that I myself am. It is to have lost the wonder of my own being. We stand in awe before the amazing fact that we are, aware that every other creature shares in common with me the fact of being.

We are held together as a cosmos by the Spirit. Apart from the Spirit there would be absolute chaos. The Spirit is the ultimate unifying energy underlying the universe. But the Spirit is also the source of the cosmos's lavish diversity and complexity—its cosmic diversity, its biodiversity, its human diversity, its religious diversity—its cultures, genders, races; its quarks, protons, neutrons, electrons, atoms; its one hundred billion galaxies, each with its one hundred billion stars. Creation itself awaits redemption being worked out by the Spirit (Rom 8:22).

The material world is a manifestation of God and the grandeur of God. This was Paul's understanding. "Ever since the creation of the world his eternal power and divine nature, invisible though they are, have been understood and seen through the things he has made" (Rom 1:20). Creation is already revelation. For Swami Abhishiktananda, Henri Le Saux (1910–73), the French Benedictine monk who came to India in 1948 to live a contemplative life, this Pauline text discloses the cosmic presence of God. "The mystery of creation and the universe is the primary revelation of the divine glory."[3] Creation itself is the first proclamation. Humankind is not something other than creation but, rather, creation at a more evolved stage. All faiths and religious traditions are also God's creations. Creation is one, albeit diverse, revealing the unity and differentiation within the Godhead itself. The Creator Spirit gives birth to diversity and holds together in unity God's evolving and expanding cosmos.

The Holy Spirit and Prophecy

The Creator Spirit, the Holy Breath, is the principle and source of life. Likewise the Holy Breath inspires, as we have noted, scripture, tradition, sacred writings, art, dance, music, poetry, science, and the imagination. The Holy Spirit is also the source of prophecy. A prophet is the Spirit speaking, one who has inhaled the breath of the Lord. In the Judeo-Christian tradition, being anointed by the Spirit and a prophetic vocation are almost synonymous. A prophet belongs to the Spirit, has turned his or her life over to the Spirit, or has had it overtaken by the Spirit. A prophet is someone possessed by the Spirit, a possession of the Spirit, one who can say, "It is now not I but the Spirit who lives in me."

Being an instrument of the Spirit affects one's consciousness. As evolution is a rise of consciousness, prophets stand out as "ahead of their time," voices crying in the wilderness. Empowered by the Spirit, they are literally ahead of time, calling us toward a future that we will shape. A prophetic consciousness is both a God-consciousness and a social consciousness. The prophet is someone aligned with God who speaks God's word, lives God's life, and is God's messenger. But a God-consciousness is always social consciousness. God's word is a word for us, God's world, this people at this period of history. The prophet is radically aware of the disjunction between the world as it is and the world as it is intended to be. The prophet is one who lives with this experience of contrast between God's dream for creation and the excess of suffering and injustice in the world.[4]

Prophecy is a charism, a gift of the Spirit, manifest in Israelite and Judean history, in the early Christian movement, and throughout history. Paul speaks of it as a charism active within his Christian communities (1 Cor 12:10). There are contemporary prophets as well. The paradigmatic prophet in the West is the Hebrew prophet. Abraham Heschel's description remains classic: "The prophet is not a mouthpiece, but a person; not an instrument, but a partner, an associate of God."[5]

The prophet is a human being who lives in the presence of God but also in the world of history. The prophet lives God's life and God's word in this world. The prophet is a bridge, one who has passed over to the other shore and yet remains on this side with us. When Samuel anointed Saul ruler over Israel, he said to Saul, "The spirit of the LORD will possess you" (1 Sam 10:6, 10). When Samuel later anointed David, "The spirit of the LORD came mightily upon David from that day forward" (1 Sam 16:13). When the mantle of prophecy is to be passed from Elijah to Elisha, Elisha's final request of Elijah is, "Please let me inherit a double share of your spirit" (2 Kgs 2:9). Once Elijah is taken away, the company of prophets proclaim, "The spirit of Elijah rests on Elisha" (2 Kgs 2:15).

In the Book of Isaiah, the Spirit is associated with God's servants, with prophecy, and with the thirst for justice. About the king to come, a future messiah, Isaiah writes, "The spirit of the LORD shall rest on him" (Isa 11:2), and continues to delineate the "gifts of the Spirit" that will be given him (Isa 11:2). The great theme of the servant in the Hebrew Scriptures is condensed within the four servant poems in Second Isaiah (Isa 42:1–4; 49:1–6; 50:4–11; 52:13–53:12).[6] In the first of these, the Lord proclaims, "Here is my servant, whom I uphold, my chosen, in whom my soul delights; I have put my spirit upon him; he will bring forth justice to the nations" (Isa 42:1). God's servant as depicted here is given the gift of the Spirit with the mission of justice for the world. In Third Isaiah (61:1–2), in the text that we saw previously as Jesus' text for his first preaching in the synagogue in Nazareth (Luke 4:16–20), the Spirit of the Lord anoints the one chosen for a mission of justice and solidarity with the poor.

Micah associates the Spirit with power as well as with justice: "But as for me, I am filled with power, with the spirit of the LORD, and with justice and might" (Mic 3:8). Hosea equates a prophet with a person of the spirit (Hos 9:7). Ezekiel was aware of the spirit's entering him: "O mortal, stand up on your feet, and I will speak with you. And when he spoke to me, a spirit entered into me and set me on my feet; and I heard him speaking to me"

(Ezek 2:1–2). "The spirit lifted me up and bore me away" (Ezek 3:14). Numerous texts from the Hebrew prophets proclaiming God's love for justice can be cited (Isa 1:11–17; 1:23; 2:4; 3:12–15; 5:1–7; 10:1–2; 32:6–7; 42:1–7; Jer 5:28; 7:5–7; 22:13–17; Hos 6:5–6; Amos 2:6–7; 4:1; 5:7–12; 5:21–24; 8:4–7; Mic 6:8; Hab 2:5; Zech 7:9, among others).

Three Isaian texts referred to above (11:1ff.; 42:1ff., 61:1ff.) speak not only about justice but also about mercy and knowledge of God and the interconnection of all three.[7] True knowledge of God is reflected in doing justice and living lives of compassion. Not to be compassionate, not to thirst for justice is not to know God. To care about God is to care for God's people. Love of God and love of neighbor are already intimately connected in the Hebrew Scriptures. The Torah, itself a work of the Spirit, reveals God's solidarity with the weak and disadvantaged: strangers, widows, orphans, the poor (Exod 22:21–25; 23:6–9).

Where there is compassion for the poor, there God's Spirit can be found. The Spirit creates a realm in which the vulnerable are protected, the disadvantaged made safe, and human life valued. The prophet lives in this "realm of the Spirit," denouncing oppression, announcing peace. The prophet's concern is discerning truth from falsehood. Isaiah as well as other prophets spoke the truth and spoke it clearly.

> Wash yourselves; make yourselves clean;
> remove the evil of your doings from before my eyes;
> cease to do evil, learn to do good, seek justice, rescue the
> oppressed,
> defend the orphan, plead for the widow. (Isa 1:16–17)

What is God's dream for creation? "In days to come…they shall beat their swords into plowshares, and their spears into pruning hooks; nation shall not lift up sword against nation, neither shall they learn war any more" (Isa 2:2–4).

Nor is prophecy confined to the past or to the Hebrew prophets. Yves Congar wrote: "Does the charism of prophecy still exist nowadays? Has it continued in the Church? Is it to be found outside its visible boundaries? My answer is certainly 'yes'...."[8]

The Holy Spirit and Wisdom

Prophecy and wisdom manifested distinguishable traditions in the history of Israel and Judah and gave rise to both a prophetic literature and a distinctive wisdom literature.[9] Wisdom tended to be a reflection on experience in contrast to the prophet's more immediate "word of the LORD." Such experience was exemplified in different kinds of wisdom: a knowledge of nature; a popular, practical, proverbial understanding of life; wisdom pertinent to juridical and political affairs of state; a family wisdom; reflective, speculative, intellectual, and skeptical wisdom. The gift of prophecy was distinct from that of the sage (Jer 18:18). Yet both prophecy and wisdom are associated with the Spirit; both are gifts of the Spirit. Both are also concerned with God's justice.

The psalmist sings: "Where can I go from your spirit? Or where can I flee from your presence?" (Ps 139:7). Psalm 51 reveals the close connection between the human spirit and the holy spirit.

> Create in me a clean heart, O God,
>   and put a new and right spirit within me.
> Do not cast me away from your presence,
>   and do not take your holy spirit from me.
> Restore to me the joy of your salvation,
>   and sustain in me a willing spirit. (Ps 51:10–12)

The Book of Wisdom itself, probably composed during the latter part of the first century BC and thus coming late in the wisdom literature, is explicit about wisdom and spirit.

> Therefore I prayed, and understanding was given to me;
> I called on God, and the spirit of wisdom came to me.
> I preferred her to scepters and thrones,
> and I accounted wealth as nothing in comparison with her.
>   (Wis 7:7–8)

The wise, like the prophets, speak out on behalf of justice, the poor, the widow, and the orphan (Ps 82:3–4; Prov 14:31; 15:25; 19:17; 22:9; Sir 4:1–10; 34:21–27).

- "Those who oppress the poor insult their Maker, but those who are kind to the needy honor him." (Prov 14:31)

- "Give justice to the weak and the orphan; maintain the right of the lowly and the destitute." (Ps 82:3)

- "My child, do not cheat the poor of their living, and do not keep needy eyes waiting. Do not grieve the hungry, or anger one in need. Do not add to the troubles of the desperate, or delay giving to the needy. Do not reject a suppliant in distress, or turn your face away from the poor." (Sir 4:1–4)

The psalms refer frequently and variously to the poor, the afflicted, the needy, the oppressed, and the weak (Ps 9:12, 18; 10:2, 9, 17; 14:6; 18:27; 22:26; 25:9; 34:2; 37:11; 40:17; 41:1; 68:10; 69:33; 70:5; 72:2, 4, 13; 74:19; 82:3–4; 86:1; 109:22; 147:6; 149:4).[10]

Just as prophecy is not confined to Israel, nor only to ancient times, neither is wisdom. Hebrew wisdom especially manifests interaction with Israel's neighbors. Wisdom is international and multicultural. Egyptian parallels manifest a concern for the poor similar to that of the Hebrew psalms. A prayer to Amon reads, "Amon, incline your ear to one who stands alone in court, who is poor, but whose enemy is mighty."[11] The role of the king in protecting the weak is emphasized also in Mesopotamian and Egyptian literature.[12]

Some of the early Christian theologians, notably Justin Martyr and Clement of Alexandria, saw God's Word as present not only in Christ but also in the Hebrew prophets and Greek philosophers.[13] Justin mentions Heraclitus, Socrates, Plato, and the Stoics in particular, as well as Elijah and others, including poets. Indeed, seeds of the Word have been implanted in all of us. Clement of Alexandria speaks even more strongly. The truths of philosophy are forms of prophecy. The Greek philosophers were inspired in a way analogous to that of the Hebrew prophets, even if not to the same degree. Clement mentions explicitly Homer, Pythagoras, and Plato as well as others, but for the real masters of philosophy we must go back even further. The Greeks are only children in the pursuit of truth, which pursuit is even more ancient. Philosophy's exponents include the Egyptians, the Persians, and the traditions of India, and Clement even makes explicit reference to the Buddha. The Spirit blows where it will, and wisdom is not confined to the Hebraic and Christian traditions.

The word *philosophy* itself comes from two Greek words (*philos* and *sophia*) meaning friend or lover of wisdom. The first to use the term and to call himself a philosopher was Pythagoras. Originally someone was considered wise who could give good advice in practical affairs, a prudent person. The term was soon transferred to speculative affairs and the understanding of ultimate reality. For the Greeks, wisdom belonged primarily to the gods, but seekers of wisdom, the philosophers, shared in wisdom, although imperfectly. The pursuit of wisdom among the Greeks became a profession whose principal characteristic was dedication to its pursuit as a way of life. There are seekers after wisdom in all cultures at all times. Wisdom and understanding and knowledge are all seen as works of the Spirit (Isa 11:2). In the New Testament, in the Johannine tradition, the Spirit is the Spirit of Truth (John 14:17; 15:26; 16:13).

The Holy Spirit and History

The Creator Spirit was with the cosmos in its beginning and remains with it in its continuing emergent evolution. The Spirit gives birth to life, living organisms in all their variety with their various destinies, and the Spirit gives birth to human life wherein evolution becomes self-aware. The Spirit thus continues to break through from within history itself. The history of the Hebrew people gives us history in capsule form, a close look, like putting history under a microscope. The Spirit is present not only among the prophets and sages, outstanding charismatic and heroic figures, but in the unfolding of everyday life.

> The LORD spoke to Moses: See, I have called by name Bezalel, son of Uri son of Hur, of the tribe of Judah: and I have filled him with the spirit of God, with ability, intelligence, and knowledge in every kind of craft, to devise artistic designs, to work in gold, silver, and bronze, in cutting stones for setting, and in carving wood, in every kind of craft. Moreover, I have appointed with him Oholiab, son of Ahisamach, of the tribe of Dan; and I have given skill to all the skillful, so that they may make all that I have commanded you: the tent of meeting, and the ark of the covenant, and the mercy seat that is on it, and all the furnishings of the tent.... (Exod 31:1–11)

God gives his Spirit to all those whose work is necessary for God's work to get done, for God's dream to come true. Bezalel and Oholiab are endowed with God's Spirit, which is associated with ability, intelligence, knowledge, craftsmanship, artistic design, metal works, wood carving, and everything else that one might want to include. The daily life of Bezalel may have looked like someone doing ordinary manual work, but in the eyes of God it was all a work of the Spirit of God. The story is a continuing story of the Holy Spirit. The Spirit of God is with Balaam (Num 24:2), Joshua (Num 27:18; Deut 34:9), Othniel (Judg 3:10), Gideon (Judg 6:34), Jephthah (Judg 11:29), Samson (Judg 13:25; 14:6; 14:19; 15:14), Saul (1 Sam 10:6; 10:10; 11:6), David (1 Sam 16:13), and so on. History is perceived as one continuing work of the Spirit of God, as is creation itself.

It is not simply that the Spirit acts in history, however, but that she acts there with power, on behalf of a people, empowering them. The first unambiguous manifestation of the Spirit in the Hebrew Scriptures comes with the judges and their charismatic leadership: Othniel, Gideon, Jephthah, Samson. Of these stories Michael Welker writes:

The accounts tell us that in situations of this sort, God's Spirit brought deliverance. This deliverance does not happen all at once. It does not happen in an unambiguously miraculous way. The presumably first reliable testimonies to the action of God's Spirit report instead an *unexpected, unforeseeable renewal of the people's unanimity and capacity for action, a renewal of the people's power of resistance in the midst of universal despair, and a resulting change of fate.* The renewal and restoration of the capacity for action and the power of resistance is traced back to a specific human being. *God's Spirit* is said to have *come upon* this person. In situations of distress, God's Spirit lays hold of or comes upon a specific human being. The person succeeds in restoring loyalty, solidarity, and the capacity for communal action among the people. Israel shakes off the yoke of oppression; Israel withstands the threat; the people defend themselves, liberate themselves, dispose of imminent danger, and escape distress.[14]

At times we are prone to affirm God's historical actions but limit them to a sacred history as if there were two histories: salvation history, the story of God's saving actions on behalf of God's people, and the more universal human history devoid of God's sovereignty and presence. But there is only one human history, all of which belongs to God, and a closer look at the history of the Jewish or Christian peoples, or Muslim, Buddhist, or Hindu peoples, all these "sacred histories" are only history in concentrated form. What we find there, we find elsewhere, namely, God's Spirit present and active.

We come to understand what God is doing, what God is revealing, through our focus on God's acts in the Bible, but the Bible reveals a God who acts outside biblical history as well, a God of the nations, a God whose arena is the whole world. The Book of Wisdom gives witness to the Spirit's universality:

For you love all things that exist,
and detest none of the things that you have made,
for you would not have made anything if you had hated it.
How would anything have endured if you had not willed it?
Or how would anything not called forth by you have been
    preserved?
You spare all things, for they are yours, O LORD, you who
    love the living.
For your immortal spirit is in all things. (Wis 11:24–12:1)

The Spirit is not confined by space or time. All history is sacred. All peoples are chosen. Salvation history is not a part of human history, the part that God privileges, but is rather all of history as well as prehistory.

We now see more clearly the Holy Spirit's ever-expanding spheres of influence. The Holy Spirit is intimately present and indwells the human person, whose own innermost human spirit is the point of contact between spirit and Spirit. In the past, when we have thought of the Holy Spirit, it was often within this circle of the human person's interiority. As important as this is, the Spirit is not only the soul of our souls but also the one who builds community among us. The Holy Spirit is the soul of the church whose sphere of influence is the invisible church.

Yet the Holy Spirit's unifying and diversifying presence is not limited to ecclesial or Christian communities or Judeo-Christian histories. There is also a church outside the church, church in a less formal or structural sense, but nevertheless church in the sense of the visible presence of the invisible Spirit. The Holy Spirit is present in other religious traditions and histories. Even though the spiritual languages of other religious traditions are distinct and thus they may not describe their animating creative source as God's Spirit, nevertheless, using Christian language, it is God's Holy Spirit who pours itself out as spirit into the religions of the world. Religion in particular is the Spirit's access to the world and the world's access to the Spirit. There are ever widening concentric, interconnected circles in a spiral moving upward and forward.

Nor is the Spirit's presence confined to specifically "religious" spheres. Just as there are personal as well as ecclesial "presences," so the Spirit is present "in the world," in the *saeculum*, in seemingly secular or not demonstrably religious ways, in human movements that may not have their origins within the church or a religious tradition but are clearly "of the Spirit." This openness toward spirit in the world is reflected in the Second Vatican Council's Pastoral Constitution on the Church in the Modern World (*Gaudium et Spes*, 1965): "The people of God believes that it is led by the Spirit of the Lord who fills the whole world" (11).

Nor is the Spirit's action confined to an earlier period of history. The Spirit is not someone who acted once upon a time but has never been heard from again. In our own times we can point to dramatic inbreakings of the Holy Spirit: the Second Vatican Council itself (1963–65), the second General Conference of Latin American Bishops at Medellín, Colombia (1968), John Paul II's multifaith gatherings in Assisi to pray for peace (1986, 2002), the collapse of the oppressive Soviet system and of apartheid in South Africa. We can point to people of the Spirit like John Woolman (1720–72), Harriet Tubman (1820?–1913), Rose Hawthorne (1851–1926), Mohandas Gandhi (1869–1948), Pierre Teilhard de Chardin (1881–1955), Pope John XXIII (1881–1963), Edith Stein (1891–1942) Dorothy Day (1897–1980), Dietrich Bonhoeffer (1906–45), Bede Griffiths (1906–94), Mother Teresa (1910–97), Etty Hillesum (1914–43), Thomas Merton (1915–68), Oscar Romero (1917–80), Flannery O'Connor (1925–64), Joseph Bernardin (1928–96), Martin Luther King, Jr. (1929–68), Thea Bowman (1937–90), Pierre Claverie (1938–96), Maura Clarke, Ita Ford, Dorothy Kazel, Jean Donovan (d. 1980), Nelson Mandela (b. 1918), Jean Vanier (b. 1928), the Dalai Lama (b. 1935), and many others. There have also been great twentieth-century movements: the civil rights movement, the women's movement, gay liberation, and other actions on behalf of human rights. These are the workings of the Holy Spirit.

With any movement, as it unfolds, there is a mixture of what is "of the Spirit" and what is not. In their origins, however, movements struggling to establish justice, human dignity, and equality for gay and lesbian men and women; for all women of any class, race, or culture; and for African Americans in the aftermath of the history of slavery in North America as well as for the victims of that system elsewhere in the world—these movements are of the Holy Spirit. Sometimes the Spirit utilizes a religious conscience and sensibility and at other times acts from within a worldly context on behalf of the freedom and dignity of all. Selma and Montgomery, Alabama, were works of the Holy Spirit, as was Martin Luther King's "I Have a Dream" speech.

Among the antecedents of the twentieth-century women's movement in the United States were prophets like Elizabeth Cady Stanton and Susan B. Anthony and mobilization on behalf of universal suffrage and the women's right to vote. The women's movement has gone through several stages, phases, or waves, and there is no one feminism that speaks for all women. Asian, African, Latin American, European, and North American feminist theologies vary and have different emphases. The fact that a theology is feminist or womanist does not mean that it is true in an unqualified sense. Each facet of a movement and each spokesperson for it need to be weighed, and discernment is necessary. But at its core and in its origins, the women's movement was and is a manifestation of the Spirit in our own times.

The same can be said about the struggle for dignity by gay men and women. God desires their humane treatment as God's very own images. The gay men who took a stand at the Stonewall Inn in New York's Greenwich Village on June 28, 1969, were courageous, prophetic, and filled with the Spirit. Again this does not mean that everything that is promoted as liberation comes from the Spirit. Discernment becomes crucial.

Early Christian monasticism was a movement of the Spirit, but not everything in the history of monasticism can be credited to the Spirit. It gave rise to corruption and wealth as well as to spiritual awakenings and homes for those seeking God. So we can look at the gay liberation movement today and say both that it was inspired by the Spirit and yet that discernment, discretion, and wisdom are required in order to know what now is "of the Spirit" and what may not be. But the reality is that the Spirit is alive and at work today as in times past and at work in the world as well as among the religions, in the churches, and in our personal lives. Where there is the pursuit of justice, the offer of mercy, a seeking of the one true God, there is the Spirit of the God who acts in the world on behalf of justice and liberation from oppression.

Muhammad, Prophet of the One God to the Arab Peoples

In the West, when we think of prophets, we ordinarily think of the classical prophets of Israel and Judah. We may or may not include Jesus among the prophets, but Christians recognize prophets within the early Christian communities established by Paul. Yet true prophecy is not something confined to the Judeo-Christian tradition. Muhammad, the messenger of al-Llah (or Allah) and prophet of Islam, was also a true prophet. A prophet is first and foremost a man or woman of the Spirit, someone called by God (in Arabic *al-Llah*), someone who speaks al-Llah's word. There is ample testimony of all these in the life of Muhammad.[15] In the Qur'an (or Koran) Muhammad is called the unlettered prophet. The illiteracy serves to highlight the astonishing poetic character of the inspiration. Muhammad did not see himself as a prophet to the nations but rather as al-Llah's messenger to the Arab peoples. Muslims have never made the claim for Muhammad that Christians have made about Jesus, namely, that he is the Son of God. Their claim is that he is God's messenger and prophet—one might add, like Moses and Elijah, men called by God at a particular moment in history to speak God's word to a particular people—granted that there is a universality in the message as well. "Muhammad is naught but a Messenger, Messengers have passed away before him" (Sura 3:138).

One can point to features that are far less than admirable in the life of Muhammad, but again Muslims have never claimed that kind of perfection for Muhammad, nor has God required it of his messengers. Muhammad is a human being, a human prophet. We know more about the life of Muhammad than about many of the Hebrew prophets. One can liken him to someone like David, clearly called by God but hardly to be emulated in all things, yet someone whose poetic voice has spoken God's praise through the ages. According to the text, even Moses doubted God's word and was therefore kept from entering the promised land.

Muhammad received his prophetic call when he was forty.

> Did He [the Lord] not find thee an orphan, and shelter
>   thee?
> Did He not find thee erring, and guide thee?
> Did He not find thee needy, and suffice thee? (Sura 93)

On the seventeenth night of the month of Ramadan, about the year 610, Muhammad ibn Abdallah, an Arab Meccan merchant, while on retreat in a mountain cave, was abruptly awakened from sleep enveloped by the divine presence, which he later described as an angel, which ordered him to recite. The Qur'an means the Recitation. Fleeing in fear, he had another vision identified as the angel Gabriel. Muhammad had received a prophetic call.

Like so many of God's agents, Muhammad was an unlikely prospect. Hebrew prophets, beginning with Moses and Aaron, protested their lack of qualifications, although few went so far as Jonah to avoid the prophetic vocation. God calls whom God chooses, and the evidence is that God's Spirit was at work in Muhammad. The primary religious experience in his life was the Night Journey and Ascension. In the year 620, again seemingly awakened by Gabriel from sleep, he was transported through the night to Jerusalem. On the Temple Mount he was greeted by Abraham, Moses, Jesus, and other prophetic figures. Then a ladder appeared, and Muhammad and Gabriel began the ascent through the seven heavens to the very throne of God. This was the most powerful mystical experience in Muhammad's life.

Muhammad's political accomplishments also give witness to God's presence at work within him, from the victory whereby he was able to establish his authority over Mecca to the eventual unification of the tribes of Arabia and the construction of an Arab society based on God's word. He was both prophet and poet, and the beauty of the recited Arabic of the Qur'an has been acknowledged. It was given as God's word and intended for recitation.

The *umma*, the emerging community of muslims, was based not on kinship but on the recognition that there is but one God (al'Llah). This kind of community was a new political as well as religious reality. Surrender of one's life to God (al'Llah) is what makes one a *muslim* who practices *islam*. A *muslim* is literally "one who surrenders."

> The Arabic root *S-L-M* carried the connotation of being in that state of wholeness or balance that results from having all of one's relationships and priorities in order. That state is called *SaLaM* (related to the Hebrew *shalom*). Now when a person pursues that state in relation to God, it means attributing to God and to none else what belongs to God, and that is the root meaning of *iSLaM*. One who achieves that state of propriety in relation to God is a *muSLiM;* literally "one who brings about a state of *SaLaM*"...[16]

The doctrine of one God and one's right relationship to that one God is the heart and soul of Islam. "I bear witness that there is no god but al-Llah" is a part of the Muslim profession of faith, the *shahada*. There is one God, God (*al-Llah*), the compassionate (*al-Rahman*), the merciful (*al-Rahim*), whom alone we serve, and Muhammad is God's messenger, the apostle of al-Llah. This one God, of course, is the same God worshiped by Jews and Christians. "Allah" (al-Llah) is simply the Arabic word for "the God." At first al-Llah was seen as the Arabs' high God, but not the only god, and thus Muhammad had to lead the people into the awareness that there is only one God, al-Llah and no other. Arabs who converted to Christianity called their God al-Llah as well; it was their name or word for the one God.

Muslims accept Jesus of Nazareth as well as the prophets of Israel and Judah as prophets of the one God. They do not recognize Jesus as a uniquely begotten Son of God. Christians accept the Hebrew prophets as part of their own history. The Hebrew Scriptures have become the Christians' First Testament. Many Jewish people accept Jesus as a Jewish prophet, although they do not accept the Christians' interpretation of him. We cannot deny the prophetic character of Muhammad's life and work, although he was seen as a prophet primarily to his own peoples, which is how he saw himself. He intended the Qur'an to be recited as God's word among the Arab peoples. This does not mean that Christians and Jewish people need to accept everything in the teachings of Muhammad, just as Muslims do not accept everything in the teachings of Judaism and Christianity. But Muhammad, as a descendant of Abraham through his wife Hagar and their son Ishmael, ought to be seen in the line of the Spirit-anointed charismatic people that we trace back to the judges of Israel and the likes of Gibeon, Deborah, and Samson.

The Spirit of Truth

As we look back at the breadth and depth of God's activity *ad extra* as Spirit, we become increasingly aware of how wide and deep that action really is. We can easily be inclined to confine and limit the Spirit, yet the Gospel of John understands the Spirit both as a wind that blows where it will (John 3:8) and as the Spirit of Truth (John 14:17, 15:26, 16:13).

Thomas Hopko highlighted the close connection between truth and the Spirit in the theology of the Christian East.[17] The meaning of Christian freedom, its relationship to authority, and their relationship to truth "is basically a problem of the Holy

Spirit."[18] A "forgetfulness of the Holy Spirit" leads us to seek security in external guarantees for truth.

> The only authority for truth, if we might use the term "authority" in this way, is the Holy Spirit. He is the Spirit of Truth who proceeds from God, who brings to remembrance all that Christ has said, who teaches all things and guides into all the truth. The Spirit alone is the sole existing criterion for truth, its only guarantee....Neither hierarch nor magisterium, council or decree, the Book or the multitude of books which may have the gift of serving to manifest Christ in the Spirit can ever pretend to jurisdiction over this divine Spirit who is "sovereignly free" and who, in the freedom of his holiness, imparts freedom to human persons to know the truth, and to "know that they know" by no other criterion than that of the certain conviction of the Spirit within them.[19]

The crisis facing the church today is not so much a crisis of authority as a crisis of spirit.[20] The challenge facing the church is one of spirituality.

Václav Havel (b. 1936), Czech playwright, dissident, and later president, reflected frequently in his writing on truth, the power of truth, evasive thinking, ideology, and what it means *to live in the truth*.[21] Evasive thinking and ideology facilitate one's living within a lie, to use Havel's expression. Ideology for Havel, however, was not simply a Soviet phenomenon.

> I am taken aback by the extent to which so many Westerners are addicted to ideology, much more than we who live in a system which is ideological through and through. Those perennial reflections about whom this or that view serves or abets, what political tendency it reinforces or weakens! Which idea can or cannot be misused by someone! That endless, exhausting examination of this or that attitude, opinion, or person to determine

whether they are rightist or leftist, left of center or right of center, right of the left or left of the right! As if the proper pigeonhole were more important than the substance of an opinion![22]

In contrast, however, is the option for living within the truth. "If the main pillar of the system is living a lie, then it is not surprising that the fundamental threat to it is living the truth."[23] One cannot negate the power of truth, the power of the Spirit, the power of love, as a power more powerful than the power of evil. The continuing search for truth and to be true to oneself are manifestations of the Spirit in our own times.

> *O Spirit of Truth, Spirit of the Living God,*
> *Creator Spirit, Lord of history,*
> *Spirit of prophecy, Spirit of wisdom,*
> *re-create us in the image of the living and triune God,*
> *redirect history once again toward its predestined goal of all*
>   *becoming one,*
> *reveal your divine presence at the heart of the universe*
> *and at work in our world,*
> *bring justice to the poor, freedom to the oppressed, and*
>   *dignity to all,*
> *raise up again in our land prophetic voices and give us ears to*
>   *hear,*
> *teach us to be wise and grant us discerning hearts,*
> *lead us with strength to live always in your Truth.*

Notes

1. Literally translated: "Come, creator Spirit, / Visit the minds/souls of your people; / Fill with grace from on high / The hearts which you have created."

2. Thomas Aquinas, *Summa Contra Gentiles (On the Truth of the Catholic Faith)*, IV, 21 (Garden City, NY: Doubleday, 1957), 120.

3. Abhishiktananda, *Prayer*, a new edition translated from the French (Delhi: ISPCK, 1999), 22.

4. On the experience of contrast, see Edward Schillebeeckx, *God Among Us: The Gospel Proclaimed* (New York: Crossroad, 1983), 32–44, 88–90; and idem, *Christ: The Experience of Jesus as Lord* (New York: Seabury Press, 1980), 694–700.

5. For a fuller description, see Abraham Heschel, *The Prophets* (New York: Harper & Row, 1962), 25–26.

6. Donald J. Goergen, *The Death and Resurrection of Jesus* (Collegeville, MN: Liturgical Press, Michael Glazier; reprint, Eugene, OR: Wipf & Stock, 1988), 40–61.

7. See Michael Welker, *God the Spirit* (Minneapolis: Fortress Press, 1994), 108–82.

8. Yves Congar, *The Word and the Spirit* (San Francisco: Harper & Row, 1986), 66–67.

9. See James L. Crenshaw, *Old Testament Wisdom* (Atlanta: John Knox Press, 1981); R. B. Y. Scott, *The Way of Wisdom in the Old Testament* (New York: Macmillan, 1971); R. N. Whybray, *The Intellectual Tradition in the Old Testament* (New York: de Gruyter, 1974), among many other studies.

10. See Hans-Joachim Kraus, *Theology of the Psalms* (Minneapolis: Augsburg, 1986), 150–54.

11. Ibid., 151.

12. F. Charles Fensham, "Widow, Orphan, and the Poor in Ancient Near Eastern Legal and Wisdom Literature," in *Studies in Ancient Israelite Wisdom*, ed. James L. Crenshaw (New York: Ktav, 1976), 161–71.

13. Jean Daniélou, *Gospel Message and Hellenistic Culture* (Philadelphia: Westminster Press, 1973), 39–105.

14. Welker, *God the Spirit*, 53 (emphasis in the original).

15. A sympathetic, readable, and scholarly biography is Karen Armstrong's *Muhammad: A Biography of the Prophet* (San Francisco: HarperSanFrancisco, 1993).

16. John Renard, *Responses to 101 Questions on Islam* (New York: Paulist Press, 1998), 35–36.

17. Thomas Hopko, "Holy Spirit in Orthodox Theology and Life," *Commonweal* (Nov. 8, 1968): 186–91.

18. Ibid., 189.

19. Ibid.

20. Ibid., 190.

21. See Václav Havel, *Open Letters, Selected Writings (1965–1990)* (New York: Vintage Books, 1992), esp. "On Evasive Thinking" (pp. 10–24); "The Power of the Powerless" (pp. 125–214); and "Anatomy of a Reticence" (pp. 291–322).

22. Ibid., 305–6.

23. Ibid., 148.

Chapter Eight
DISCERNING THE SPIRIT

The ability to discern the presence of the Holy Spirit is an art and a gift. St. Paul sees discernment as a particular charism: "To each is given the manifestation of the Spirit for the common good. To one is given through the Spirit the utterance of wisdom...to another prophecy, to another the discernment of spirits" (1 Cor 12:4–11). Not everyone has the gift for discernment. The First Letter of John, nevertheless, encourages all followers of Jesus to test the spirits: "Beloved, do not believe every spirit, but test the spirits to see whether they are from God; for many false prophets have gone out into the world" (4:1).

Discernment is closely related to wisdom. Isaiah speaks of wisdom as one of the gifts of the Spirit (11:2). Solomon, the quintessential embodiment of wisdom in the Hebrew Scriptures, is depicted as having a discerning and wise heart and mind (1 Kgs 3:9–12). The Letter of James exhorts, "If any of you is lacking in wisdom, ask God, who gives to all generously and ungrudgingly, and it will be given you" (1:5). At times it appears as if wisdom, like discernment, is a gift given to some but not all; at other times it seems available to all.

St. Catherine of Siena (1347–80) taught that discernment or discretion *(discrezione)* was one of three principal virtues: charity, discernment, and humility. Charity is the tree, which must be rooted in the soil of humility, of which discernment is one of the branches.[1] Charity is both love for God and love for neighbor. The one cannot exist without the other. Humility is true self-knowledge, which also comprises two aspects: knowledge of self and of God within the self. Of all the virtues that spring forth from humility and charity, however, pride of place goes to discernment. It is essentially prudence in spiritual matters. For Thomas Aquinas, prudence was one of the core moral virtues; and prudence, wisdom, and discernment are closely related. Catherine taught fundamental principles for discernment, as St. Ignatius of Loyola (1491–1556) did later in his *Spiritual Exercises.*[2]

The foundational principle of all discernment, however, remains the biblical guideline: By their fruits, you shall know them (Matt 7:15–20). Later in the Gospel of Matthew, this principle is given flesh and blood: "Truly I tell you, just as you did it to one of the least of these who are members of my family, you did it to me" (Matt 25:35–40). St. Paul made it most clear in delineating to the Galatians things that can be perceived as coming from the Holy Spirit: "The fruit of the Spirit is love, joy, peace, patience, kindness, generosity, faithfulness, gentleness, and self-control" (Gal 5:22). By way of contrast, Paul also lists indications of the working of an evil spirit: "fornication, impurity, licentiousness, idolatry, sorcery, enmities, strife, jealousy, anger, quarrels, dissensions, factions, envy, drunkenness, carousing, and things like these" (Gal 5:19–21).

Personal Discernment and Spiritual Direction

Spiritual guidance comes from a wide variety of sources: the scriptures, liturgy, the fathers and mothers of the church, spiritual reading, the practice of meditation, the sacred writings of every religious tradition, the study of theology, as well as spiritual masters and guides. In the Christian tradition the Holy Spirit is the true director of one's interior life. The goal of spiritual guidance is to put someone in touch with the Spirit and to deepen one's awareness of the Spirit. A spiritual guide does not seek to solve someone's problem or to make decisions for them, or to have ready-made answers to life's questions. The goal of spiritual guidance is to put one in direct contact with the Spirit and to let the Spirit be the guide.

The prayer at the heart of spiritual direction is the prayer in the Letter to the Ephesians: May God grant that you be strengthened in your inner being with power through the Spirit (Eph 3:16). The Spirit working in us can accomplish far more than we can ask or imagine (Eph 3:20). It is to an awareness of the Spirit that spiritual guidance brings us. Thomas Aquinas enunciated a significant foundational principle in this regard: Reason does not suffice unless it receive the additional movements of the Holy Spirit (*Summa Theologiae*, I/II, q. 68, a. 2). As important as our rational faculties are in pursuing truth and holiness, in the end they are not sufficient by themselves alone to take us where we long to go. As in Dante's *Divine Comedy*, Beatrice is needed where Virgil cannot go (*Purgatorio*, canto 30).

Sri Aurobindo spoke of "two great psychological truths" with respect to an individual's interior life.[3] The first great truth is that the ego is not the true self; there is in the end only one Self of all. The second great truth is that individual persons are not only themselves but are in solidarity with all others. We might call these the twin principles of interiority and solidarity. The human person has depth (interiority) and breadth (solidarity). Discernment leads us into a greater and greater awareness of these two great psychological truths.

In the Christian mystical tradition, spiritual growth became focused on purification, enlightenment, and divine union. There are dangers on the path: the possibility of depression, the potential for a false self-centeredness, loss of balance. Prayer becomes difficult. John of the Cross spoke about both a dark night of the senses and one of the spirit.[4] Illumination was seen as accompanying the spiritual seeker as one's prayer becomes less discursive. Infused contemplation begins. It is recognized that it is no longer I, but Christ or the Spirit who lives in me. Silence becomes more relished. One longs to hear the voice of the divine Lover.[5] In the divine union there is a loss of self; there is now only the one Self. The Holy Spirit leads us into and through the purification of the ego, grants us illumination and suprarational understanding, and unites us with the one Self of all.

Discernment and Sociocultural Analysis

Discernment is often associated with that great psychological principle of interiority, but discernment in the Bible, both in the Hebrew Scriptures and in the New Testament, is often associated with that other great psychological principle of solidarity—the Spirit's presence in the world. How does one discern the action of the Holy Spirit in social, political, and economic contexts?

In previous references to the historical, prophetic, and sapiential traditions of Israel, as well as to the preaching and teaching of Jesus of Nazareth, we have seen that the Spirit stands in solidarity with poor, oppressed, and marginalized peoples. The Spirit acts on behalf of justice, liberation, life, mercy, and peace. "It seems plausible to conclude that the good Spirit is a Spirit who leads to the unity and community of a people or to the powerful, positive influence of an individual person. By contrast, the evil spirit leads to disintegration and destruction of a community."[6]

The Spirit is the spirit of truth (John 14:17; 15:26; 16:13), but there is also a spirit that lies, a mendacious spirit (1 Kgs 22:22–23), as reflected in the story of Ahab and the prophet Micaiah. Ahab, king of Israel, had decided to go to war and was attempting to secure the assistance of Jehoshaphat, the king of Judah, who was willing but asked that Ahab "inquire first for the word of the LORD" (1 Kgs 22:5). So the king of Israel gathered and consulted four hundred prophets, who authorized war in God's name. Jehoshaphat asked whether there were any other prophets, and Ahab indicated that there was a Micaiah who never prophesied favorably about the king. At Jehoshaphat's encouragement, Micaiah was consulted, already facing a formidable formed opinion.

The king's messenger says to Micaiah, "Look, the words of the prophets with one accord are favorable to the king; let your word be like the word of one of them, and speak favorably" (1 Kgs 22:13). In the end, however, Micaiah must speak the truth: "I saw all Israel scattered on the mountains, like sheep that have no shepherd" (1 Kgs 22:17). But how explain Micaiah's prophecy as contradicting that of four hundred prophets? Would not the four hundred be right? How could their consensus be wrong? Micaiah explains, although Ahab will not listen: "The LORD has put a lying spirit in the mouth of all these your prophets; the LORD has decreed disaster for you" (1 Kgs 22:22–23). The four hundred were clearly eager to be in favor with the ruling power rather than to hear the word of the Lord. They belonged not to the Lord but to the king. And thus a lying spirit had entered them as a group. But Micaiah, in order to be faithful to the Lord, had to go against the mainstream, the popular opinion, the consensus, the sense of the majority. He was not ready to add his opinion automatically in support of the prevailing opinion, but put their spirit to the test and found it not to be the spirit of truth.[7]

Within a social context there are three fundamental evil spirits: greed, power, and arrogance. Each of these can exist in isolation from the others, but they are particularly vicious when they come together. Greed or avarice or the love of money is found in all of us in some form. It becomes dangerous when allied with false, exploitative, and manipulative forms of power. For one then has the ability to act on one's greed, to seek its satiation. Otherwise greed may be personally destructive, but when accompanied by a power base or destructive power, it becomes socially destructive as well. Power is used against others rather than for others.

Arrogance is the sense of superiority that justifies one's acting on greed; it gives the sense of entitlement. This pattern can be seen in the historical exploitation of peoples, such as the European conquest of the indigenous peoples in the Americas. Whether disguised with other motives or not, greed (an economic factor) was the primary motivation for the *conquista*, which was accomplished by military power (might makes right) and justified by a sense of racial or religious superiority. Arrogance justifies the use of force to satisfy greed. It is easy for us to judge the past, but a discerning mind and heart sees the absence of God or presence of evil in similar contemporary contexts.

We do not always realize the degree to which our Western civilization has been constructed on a foundation of greed. This is not to deny tremendous human accomplishments, but rather to discern what in our Western world is the work of the Holy Spirit (basic human freedoms and an articulation of human rights, parliamentary forms of government, contributions in science, technology, art, literature, philosophy, and religion) and what is the work of evil spirits. We must acknowledge how our predominant and globally dominating economic practices are founded on one of the least noble aspects of humanity, our propensity toward greed. Early capitalism may have seen value in increased productivity and a competitive spirit, but today the market economy, multinational corporations, and consumer capitalism have become increasingly inhumane. In the Gospel of Matthew we read the blunt observation: "You cannot serve God and wealth" (6:24).

John Cassian (ca. 360–435), in his reflection on eight capital sins, observes how the scriptures speak about love of money as "the root of all evils" (1 Tim 6:10).[8] He observes that "this disease," which is "a slavery to idols," grows "more vehement as more money piles up." "For the madness of covetousness is that it always wants more than whatever a person can accumulate."[9] Greed, a sin against the Holy Spirit, manifests a tug between the Holy Spirit and the evil spirit within us as well as among us, among the nations of the world and within many economic systems.

Greed, by itself, is harmful to a person's or a group's soul. Combined with power, however, whether that of an individual or a group, greed becomes treacherous for society. For with power we have the ability to act on our greed and permit it to pursue our insatiable desires. Power, like money, is not in itself evil. It depends on the use we make of it. Money can be put to good use. Greed is money idolized, falsely valued for its own sake rather than for how it can serve the common good.

Similarly, there can be constructive forms of power as well as destructive ones. Rollo May distinguished between exploitative, manipulative, competitive, nutritive, and integrative forms of power.[10] There is the power of love, the power of truth, and the power of holiness. Ultimately all true power is the power of the

Spirit. Spirit and power are frequently associated in the scriptures. The Spirit is a power more powerful than the power of evil. But there are also false, distorted, destructive uses of power, power understood as coercion, power over or against others rather than for or with others. When a person or corporation or nation has available to it the potential for a misuse of power, or the use of false forms of power, combined with greed, the stage is set for human disaster. People will be sacrificed at the expense of an insatiable greed.

The misuse of power tends to disguise itself and justify itself. This is where "the lie," false speech, and the spirit of arrogance enter in. Arrogance is a spirit of superiority, of entitlement, of being above or beyond the law, of self-righteousness. It is the sin that puts us most at odds with God, that puts a block between God and us, the sin most clearly denounced by Jesus. It is a lying spirit that justifies our greed and violence. Arrogance deep down leads us to think of ourselves as more deserving than others.

Enthusiasm, Fanaticism, and the Spirit of Balance

"Spirit-filled" can suggest the irrational, the extraordinary, the ecstatic. There is a thin line between enthusiasm and fanaticism. Enthusiasts come in many shapes and forms, from "true believers" to "the committed," from "the uncompromising" to "the prophetic." Discernment is important in order to discover what is genuinely "of the Spirit" and what may be arising from our human needs, temperaments, or unresolved personal traumas. Not everything that is "deeply felt" is Spirit-filled. The Spirit is a spirit of balance and seldom found on the extremes. We all tend to veer off in one direction or another and need to be brought back not to a static state but to a dynamic equilibrium. The Spirit functions as the source of unity or order, but not a unity that is rigid nor an order that is stagnant. The Spirit does not create chaos without form. The Spirit creates a vital balance.

In considering the correlation between prophecy and teaching, James D. G. Dunn writes:

In short, the fact that Paul lists prophecy and teaching in close conjunction probably indicates that he saw the teaching function as an indispensable complement to prophecy. The normative role of the gospel and of the tradition common to all the churches would have provided an invaluable control on charismatic excess. Yet we should also recall that he ranked prophecy above teaching. Teaching, we may say, preserves continuity; but prophecy gives life. With teaching a community will not die; but without prophecy it will not live.[11]

In a similar vein, Dunn quotes Heinrich Greeven: "Prophecy without teaching degenerates into fanaticism, teaching without prophecy solidifies into law."[12] That is an issue for one discerning the Spirit: When does "charismatic" become "fanatic"? When does the enthusiast lose a sense of balance? When does single-mindedness become a closed mind? How do we stay in touch with both the heart of the matter and the complexity of factors in any context? All this indicates the need for a discerning mind, for there is no single answer for all times and all places. What may have proven wise in one context or period of history may not be the direction in which the Spirit takes us at another time or in another place.

In his reflection on First Corinthians 12–14, Dunn highlights three Pauline criteria for discerning spirits: the test of the gospel, the test of love, and the test of community benefit.[13] All gifts are given for the sake of the common good (1 Cor 12:7). "All things are lawful" is a slogan manifesting the Corinthians' sense of freedom in Christ, but Paul adds, "but not all things build up" (1 Cor 10:23). All is to be done with the consciousness of building up the community, not for individual gain. What builds up the community is a criterion for discerning the Spirit (1 Cor 14:3, 4, 5, 12, 17, 26). Whatever gifts I may have, if I do not have love, I am like a noisy gong or a clanging cymbal (1 Cor 13:1).

One of the important instruments for discernment is human reason itself, critical rationality, intelligence, and common sense.

The irrational is not to be identified with the prophetic. Ken Wilber has addressed a necessary distinction between the prerational and postrational.[14] Not all that is nonrational is superior to intelligence, as someone Spirit-sensitive might think. The Holy Spirit acts within and through human intellectual activity. Ronald Knox, in his classic study entitled *Enthusiasm*, indicated a variety of directions, some of them aberrations, that "enthusiasts" have taken.[15] There is something about common sense that rebels against fanaticism being identified with the Spirit.

The Christian tradition, following in the footsteps of Thomas Aquinas, has maintained *both* reason *and* revelation as sources of human wisdom.[16] It is in their interplay that one becomes wise and the Spirit's gift of wisdom increases. It is again a question of maintaining a vital balance. After millennia of struggle and pain to arrive at intelligence and reason, they ought not be dismissed easily. Neither must they become idols. The spiritual life rests upon a theology of grace. Thomas Aquinas maintained that grace builds on nature. Grace does not destroy nature but respects it. Both nature and grace, like reason and revelation, come from the one God. God does not create nature in order to send the Spirit to work against it. God sends the Spirit to complete, perfect, or divinize the created world and all creatures.

The Spirit's most intense presence to the world is most often between extremes. The Spirit is neither a rigorist nor a laxist, although each of those tendencies may be part of the truth about the cost of discipleship. The Spirit is neither fundamentalist nor secularist, neither antinomian nor moralistic, neither a legalist nor an anarchist. Yet neither is the Spirit totally absent from these historical realities. A tendency, concern, or value may become exaggerated and distorted. The Spirit tries to salvage the truth that is there. The secularist and the fundamentalist are counterparts; they mutually create each other. To exclude religion from public life is to give birth to religious movements in distorted forms. The fundamentalist's temptation is toward an earthly theocracy, and the secularist's is toward a religionless society.[17] But the Spirit points out that both religion and the *saeculum* are God's creations. It is not a question of either God or the world but of both God and the world. A distortion is often a question of emphasis, not a complete absence of spirit. As Ronald Knox wrote, "Let us note, from the first, that traditional Christianity is a balance of doctrines, and not merely of doctrines but of emphases. You must not exaggerate in either direction, or the balance is disturbed."[18]

This caution does not mean that there is no room for the visionary, the sage, the prophet, the charismatic, the ecstatic, the ascetic, the seeker, the sannyasin, the sadhuk, the monk, the nun, or the mystic; these are at the heart of every great religious tradition. "Blessed are the pure in heart, for they will see God" (Matt 5:8). Yet even here the Spirit pulls one in the direction of a balanced, holistic life, even as we acknowledge that some of the world's greatest saints may not have achieved what their period or another period of history might consider balance. They were, however, people who were transparent, through whom God broke through. In their search, grace broke through and transformed their human quest. In them we find God. They are men and women of the Spirit. Discernment suggests an ability to distinguish the quack, the lunatic, the self-absorbed, the cult leader from a true mystic.

The Gifts of the Spirit

Discernment means being attuned to the Holy Spirit, an ability to recognize the presence and workings of the Spirit whether in my own life, in the life of another, or in movements in the world. Wherever the Spirit is, there is giftedness. These gifts may be charismatic gifts given to a person for building up the *ecclesia* and for the sake of the common good (1 Cor 12:4–11, 27–31). Or they may be gifts that draw us more deeply, habitually, and personally into holiness and sanctity, such as faith, hope, and love (1 Cor 13:13). Or they may be gifts that manifest the fruit of living in the Spirit (Gal 5:22–23). Prayer itself is a work of the Holy Spirit (Rom 8:15–16, 26–27; 1 Cor 12: 3; Gal 4:6; Eph 6:18). There are also the classical gifts of the Spirit in the Christian tradition that go back to Isaiah's depiction of the manifestations of the Spirit in an ideal ruler or future messiah.

> A shoot shall come out from the stump of Jesse,
>   and a branch shall grow out of his roots.
> The spirit of the LORD shall rest on him,
>   the spirit of wisdom and understanding,
>   the spirit of counsel and of might,
>   the spirit of knowledge and the fear of the LORD.
> His delight shall be in the fear of the LORD. (Isa 11:1–3a)

This may have originally referred to the accession of a Judean king to his throne, someone like Hezekiah, but it then came to refer to a future ideal king, the coming messiah. The six gifts mentioned in Isaiah in the Hebrew Bible become seven in its Greek translation, the Septuagint, where "piety" is substituted for the first "fear of the LORD," giving us the classical seven gifts of the Spirit.

For Aquinas, the gifts are distinct from virtues but are given to us as aids to living a life of virtue.[19] The virtues take on a more "inspired" or perfected character through the action of the gifts (*Summa Theologiae*, I-II, 68, 1). In acquiring virtue, the human person is moved by human reason in accord with human nature. The gifts, however, manifest our "second nature," the gift of the Spirit itself. Aquinas takes note of the fact in Isaiah that they are not actually called gifts. The term employed is "spirit," the spirit of wisdom, the spirit of understanding (*Summa Theologiae*, I-II, 68, 1). They pertain to the action of the Spirit on our human spirits. They reflect a more direct action of the Holy Spirit in our human lives.

Aquinas's own theology of the gifts evolved to the point where he saw the gifts as necessary in the spiritual life (*Summa Theologiae*, I-II, 68, 2) and as operative in every graced person, even if imperceptibly so, for where the Spirit is, so there are the Spirit's gifts (I-II, 68, 3). The human person, without the divine assistance of these gifts, is unable to become all that God has predestined for us. The spiritual person becomes more and more under the influence of the

Spirit so that eventually it is the Spirit who is the source of our activities. The gifts dispose one to act in accord with the Spirit within (I-II, 68, 8). Although the gifts are more excellent than the virtues as such because of their *modus operandi*, they are not more perfect than *caritas*, the virtue of charity or love (I-II, 68, 5 and 8), which is the supreme goal (and one might say gift) of Christian life.

In the Catholic tradition, the sacrament most associated with the Holy Spirit is that of confirmation, although all the sacraments are "acts of the Holy Spirit." In the celebration of confirmation, during the rite of the laying on of hands, the bishop prays:

> Send your Holy Spirit upon them to be their Helper and
>   Guide.
> Give them the spirit of wisdom and understanding,
> the spirit of right judgment and courage,
> the spirit of knowledge and reverence.
> Fill them with the spirit of wonder and awe in your
>   presence.[20]

1. Fear of the Lord, Awe, Wonder

Fear of the Lord is in one sense the foundation and in another sense the culmination of life in the Spirit. In the Book of the Wisdom of Jesus, son of Sirach, fear of the Lord is described as the beginning of wisdom (1:14), the root of wisdom (1:20), the fullness of wisdom (1:16), the crown of wisdom (1:18), as well as wisdom itself (1:27). Fear of the Lord delights the heart (1:12). Those who fear the Lord will have a happy end (1:13). The psalmist writes in the same vein: "The fear of the LORD is the beginning of wisdom; all those who practice it have good understanding" (Ps 111:10). Fear of the Lord as a gift of the Spirit is clearly different from what we ordinarily think of as fear in a human context. How often do the Gospels not say, "Do not be afraid" (Matt 8:26; 10:28; 14:27; Mark 5:33; Luke 1:30; 2:10; 12:32; John 14:27), and the First Letter of

John teaches that perfect love casts out fear (4:18). But this human servile fear is not the fear that is a gift from the Spirit.

Thomas Aquinas distinguished different kinds or stages of fear (*Summa Theologiae*, II-II, q. 19, a. 2–9). Servile fear is a fear of punishment, and this is not a gift of the Spirit. Filial fear manifests a reverential attitude toward God, that of a loving child toward loving parents. This filial fear is a loving awe. Hence the rite of confirmation describes this gift not as fear but as a spirit of wonder and awe in God's presence. The gift of fear is manifest in wonder and awe at God's creation, at beauty in the universe, in gratuitous love and friendship. Fear of the Lord is an awareness of the awesomeness, the incomprehensibility, the majesty of the divine.

2. Piety, Reverence, Devotion

The word *pious* is rarely used in a complimentary way. It connotes a pretentious, sanctimonious attitude or excess of sentimentality. The gift, *pietas* in Latin, is more closely connected to ideas such as affection, compassion, conscientiousness, gentleness, gratitude, kindness, and loyalty. The pious person is devout in the best sense of that word—dedicated, faithful, a devotee. I think of the Hindu tradition of *bhakti*. The rite of confirmation uses the word *reverence*. "Devotion" is also a close parallel.[21]

Thomas Aquinas speaks of piety as "a filial affection towards God" (*Summa Theologiae*, II-II, q. 121, a. 1). Filial affection (piety) is not the same as filial fear (fear of the Lord). In the first gift, we let God be God, we recognize "the infinite qualitative difference" between God and ourselves, we stand in awe and wonder before God's presence. In the gift of piety, the gap between God and ourselves is narrowed. We experience the nearness and love of God. Our relationship with God becomes affectionate, familial, intimate. We experience God as friend. Fear of the Lord fills us with awe; piety prompts movements of affection. We "adhere to God"[22] in a new way, as friend to friend. We are not only servants of God, or daughters and sons of God, but we become friends of God through the gift of piety. Piety is filial but it is also friendship, as when we become friends with the mother or father whose daughters and sons we remain.

Piety puts us in touch with the maternal side of God, God as mother. As Julian of Norwich wrote, "As truly as God is our Father, so truly is God our Mother."[23] Pope John XXIII wrote in his journal, "It really looks as though God has lavished upon me his most tender and motherly care...."[24]

3. Courage, Fortitude, Strength

Commentators on Thomas Aquinas are always careful to distinguish the virtue of fortitude from the gift of fortitude—two distinct realities, the same name. As stated above, the gifts are not our natural, habitual, even if graced, human acts. A gift is a distinct grace that refines, perfects, and integrates more deeply our human ways of being, doing, and knowing. The gift enables us to surpass what our ordinary abilities might be capable of. The gift of courage is not recklessness but a holy courage grounded in reverence and love of God. In one sense it is the very power of God itself acting through us. We become instruments of the Holy Spirit in the world.

The gift of courage gives confidence, constancy, and endurance that manifest more than human forbearance. Lack of courage is manifested in lukewarmness and indifference, even in cynicism and resentment. Courage is not willfulness, a self-absorbed "I want what I want when I want it," a "nobody's going to tell me what to do" narcissism. Courage is not about me but about a deep connectedness with God. It is about being a channel of spiritual energy, about empowerment through surrender. There is no "ego," no false self, in the gift of courage. It is a gift given to facilitate realizing on earth God's intention for creation. A power more powerful than we has taken hold of us—the power of the Spirit, the power of love, the power of truth. The gift of courage is true freedom. It is manifest in the stories of women like Esther, Judith, and Susanna in the Hebrew Scriptures and deuterocanonical literature.

4. Counsel, Consultation, Collaboration

As we move from the gifts of awe, devotion, and strength to the gift of counsel, we move to a gift that facilitates or manifests an even greater connectivity among us. Whereas one can manifest courage by oneself alone—indeed it may often mean standing alone—the gift of counsel suggests interdependence, interrelatedness, and interconnectedness. Thomas Aquinas, in reference to the gift of counsel, speaks about "the research of reason" (*Summa Theologiae*, II-II, q. 52, a. 1). The word *research* suggests a deliberative component and *reason* suggests intelligence at work. We are reminded of the virtue of prudence or "good sense," to which Aquinas relates the gift of counsel. The rite of confirmation speaks of this gift as that of "right judgment." As a gift, again, it is a movement of the Holy Spirit taking us beyond where human common sense may go. Counsel is discernment and inquiry under the guidance of the Spirit. It suggests communication, consultation, and the seeking of advice.

John of St. Thomas, in his commentary on this gift, shows how essential the seeking of advice is. He writes:

> It is part of divine counsel to have recourse to others for advice, in matters beyond one's own capacity. For the Holy Spirit does not manifest his abundance to all in such a way that they do not need communication with others....Therefore, in matters from God not clearly heard or fully understood, it is necessary to consult others who are more enlightened.[25]

He also speaks about submitting oneself to the examination of wise and spiritual people.[26]

Counsel suggests the value of a spiritual community or network, such as *satsang* (the company of the holy) in the Hindu tradition or the Buddhist *sangha*—spiritual companionship and spiritual friendship. Those with whom we associate are a part of who we are, and we become like those with whom we connect. Thus, "community" is a dimension of the gift of counsel. At a wider level, counsel becomes collaboration and collegiality. There is a relationship between "counsel" and "council." The latter is calling together the elders or the wise for the sake of counsel. The great ecumenical councils of the church were manifestations of the Spirit and an outpouring of the gift of counsel. In these matters the Spirit is a spirit of collegiality.

5. Knowledge, Learning, Sacred Truth

Just as devotion builds on awe, and courage on devotion, and courage gives way to counsel, so counsel leads us to the gift of knowledge. Through consultation we learn. The last three gifts to be considered—knowledge, understanding, wisdom—likewise flow from one to the other. They are interconnected, one building on the other. One is tempted to see in them the medieval distinctions among *scientia* (knowledge), *intellectus* (understanding), and *sapientia* (wisdom). The higher contains the lower and goes beyond it. The gift of knowledge is not a gift for scholarship, although such a gift is not excluded and can prepare the way for the gift of knowledge. It is a gift for learning.

Learning is related to what the medievals called *sacra doctrina*, what we might translate as the holy teaching, the *dharma*, the tradition of the elders, sacred and saving truth. We are not simply talking about technical or intellectual knowledge as such. We are talking about spiritual and revealed truth that sets us free (John 8:32). In other words, we are talking about knowledge of God. It means knowing God and not just knowing about God. It means having met God—true *gnōsis*, if you will—personal knowledge. Aquinas speaks about the gift of knowledge as right judgment in discerning what is to be believed (*Summa Theologiae*, II-II, q. 9). The gift of counsel has already been described as right judgment, but here the judgment has to do with truths pertinent to salvation and is related to the life of faith.

6. Understanding, Insight, Vision

For Thomas Aquinas, both the gift of knowledge (*Summa Theologiae*, II-II, q. 9) and that of understanding (II-II, q. 8) pertain to faith. They strengthen or deepen faith. Faith seeks understanding *(fides quaerens intellectum)*. The gift of understanding *(intellectus)* is not the same as that of knowledge *(scientia)*, however. Aquinas gets at the meaning of understanding by going to its roots. The Latin *intelligere* (to understand) comes from *intus legere*, meaning to read inwardly, or from within, and hence refers to an interior kind of knowing, seeing the truth of things. To understand is to be a seer, one who sees.

Pierre Teilhard de Chardin entitled his prologue to *The Phenomenon of Man* "Voir" (to see or seeing), and writes: "This work may be summed up as an attempt *to see*....We might say that the whole of life lies in that verb..."[27] It has often been discussed whether Teilhard was more a scientist, a philosopher, or a theologian. In some sense, he was all three, but more than any of them he was a seer—one who had been given the gift for vision. This gift enables us to penetrate the depths of mystery, to take us as far as *intellectus* can before we acknowledge leaving it behind as we enter into what the intellect can only experience as darkness. We often like to say that seeing is believing, but for the person of faith it is rather stated that believing is seeing. Faith takes us beyond ordinary human knowledge.

Mohandas Gandhi's *satyagraha*,[28] Ramana Maharshi's path of self-enquiry,[29] and Sri Aurobindo Ghose's Integral Yoga[30]—great spiritual leaders in twentieth-century India—manifest an aspect of the gift of understanding *(intellectus)*. The same can be said for two Catholic Christian *sannyasi*, Dom Bede Griffiths (1906–93) and Dom Henri Le Saux, better known by his Hindu name, Abhishiktananda (1910–73).[31] Abhishiktananda wrote: "The life of prayer and contemplation is simply to realize God's presence in the depth of our being, in the depth of every being, and at the same time beyond all beings, beyond all that is within and all that is without."[32]

7. Wisdom and Love

We come now to what is often considered the most noble of the gifts, wisdom *(sapientia)*, and the most noble of the virtues, that of charity or love *(caritas)*, which Aquinas saw as interrelated, just as the gifts of knowledge and understanding are related to faith. Wisdom and love mutually perfect each other. We have already spoken about the Israelite and Judean sapiential traditions. Wisdom in pre-Christian Judaism was a way of speaking about God's nearness. Wisdom was highly exalted (Job 28:12–28; Prov 8:1–36; Sir 24:1–34; Wis 6:12–11:1). Wisdom was with God in the beginning.

> There is in her a spirit that is intelligent, holy, unique, manifold, subtle, mobile, clear, unpolluted, distinct, invulnerable, loving the good, keen, irresistible, beneficent, humane, steadfast, sure, free from anxiety, all-powerful, overseeing all, and penetrating through all spirits that are intelligent, pure, and altogether subtle. For wisdom is more mobile than any motion; because of her pureness she pervades and penetrates all things. For she is a breath of the power of God, and a pure emanation of the glory of the Almighty... (Wis 7:22–25)

In the New Testament, particularly in Paul, Jesus Christ is the supreme embodiment of wisdom (1 Cor 1:24, 30).[33] In time, however, in Christian tradition, wisdom became associated with Mary, the mother of Jesus, Mother of God, the seat of wisdom, the feminine face of God and primal maternal symbol in Christianity, to whom was attributed more and more the maternal qualities of God.[34]

Thomas Aquinas considered the gift of wisdom the highest or we might say deepest of the gifts (*Summa Theologiae*, II-II, q. 45). Wisdom as a gift, however, is distinct from the intellectual virtue associated with our human ways of knowing. John of St. Thomas explains the difference as well as any:

The formal nature by which wisdom knows the highest causes is an internal experience of God and divine things. It is a taste, love, delight, or internal contact, of the will with spiritual things. By reason of its union with spiritual truths the soul is, as it were, made connatural to things divine.[35]

In wisdom, the knower is one with the known in the very depths of his or her being. We see with the eyes of God because we are one with God. Wisdom is a mystical and loving knowledge beyond philosophy and speculative theology, which pursue knowledge of God in their own ways.[36]

For Aquinas, *caritas* and *sapientia* mutually reinforce each other. In the end they are not easy to distinguish. All the gifts of the Spirit for Aquinas come in stages; all are interconnected with each other, mutually strengthening one another; and all are ultimately held together or integrated in and through charity, for love of God is the source for them all (*Summa Theologiae*, I-II, q. 68, a. 5). Wisdom, then, is the contemplation of God, a loving gaze upon the divine, another kind of knowledge, not even best called knowledge, simply being wrapped up in things divine, in God herself, permeated through and through with the One, a unity of indistinction, to use Eckhart's way of seeing.[37] If the gift of knowledge is knowing, and the gift of understanding is seeing, then the gift of wisdom is loving. Understanding makes one a seer; wisdom makes one a sage. This is someone who has not only met God but is an instrument of God, someone who has acquired the Holy Spirit.

> *Most Holy Spirit,*
> *ignite the fire of love in our human spirits.*
> *Fill our souls, our communities, our churches, our world*
> *with those gifts that you so ordinarily bring:*
> *the gifts of peace, love, joy, kindness, goodness, faithfulness,*
> *patience, gentleness, and self-control.*

Help us to discern your presence in our world, in one another, and
   in our own lives.
Uproot our sins of greed and arrogance,
our misuse of power,
our egoism.
Replace all evil spirits with your divine presence, your loving grace,
   your gentle touch.
Keep us balanced in an unbalanced world.
Help us to use our reason
and teach us to think.
Continue to fill us with all the gifts you so generously give.

Notes

1. Catherine of Siena, *The Dialogue*, trans. Suzanne Noffke, Classics of Western Spirituality (New York: Paulist Press, 1980), 42. See Donald J. Goergen, *The Jesus of Christian History* (Collegeville, MN: Liturgical Press, 1992; reprint, Eugene, OR: Wipf & Stock, 1992), 180–203.

2. Catherine of Siena, *The Dialogue*, 39–45, 100–102, 113–16, 130–34, 193–204, among others (or chaps. 9–11, 49, 60, 69–72, 102–9); *The Spiritual Exercises of St. Ignatius*, trans. Louis J. Puhl (Chicago: Loyola University Press, 1951), ##313–36, pp. 141–50.

3. Sri Aurobindo, *The Human Cycle* (Pondicherry: Sri Aurobindo Ashram, 1977), 38–40.

4. See John of the Cross, *The Ascent of Mount Carmel* and *The Dark Night* in *The Collected Works of St. John of the Cross*, trans. K. Kavanaugh and O. Rodriguez (Washington, DC: Institute of Carmelite Studies, 1973).

5. See Teresa of Avila, *The Interior Castle*, Classics of Western Spirituality (New York: Paulist Press, 1979).

6. Michael Welker, *God the Spirit* (Minneapolis: Fortress Press, 1994), 85. Welker's theology of the Spirit is one that develops at greater length the social significance of the Spirit acting in the world.

7. Ibid., 86–96.

8. John Cassian, *The Institutes*, trans. Boniface Ramsey (New York: Newman Press, 2000), book 7, 169. Augustine likewise affirms that "greed is the root of all evils" in *The Trinity*, trans. Edmund Hill (Brooklyn, NY: New City Press, 1991), 330, referring also to 1 Tim 6:10.

9. John Cassian, *Institutes*, 171–72, 181.

10. Rollo May, *Power and Innocence: A Search for the Sources of Violence* (New York: W. W. Norton, 1972), 99–120. Donald Goergen, *The Power of Love* (Chicago: Thomas More Press, 1979), 234–66.

11. James D. G. Dunn, *The Theology of Paul the Apostle* (Grand Rapids: Eerdmans, 1998), 583.

12. Ibid. See H. Greeven, "Propheten, Lehrer, Vorsteher bei Paulus," *Zeitschrift für die neutestamentliche Wissenschaft* 44 (1952–53): 29.

13. Dunn, *Theology of Paul the Apostle*, 594–98.

14. See the "pre/trans fallacy" in Ken Wilber, *Sex, Ecology, Spirituality* (Boston: Shambhala, 1995), 205–8.

15. Ronald A. Knox, *Enthusiasm: A Chapter in the History of Religion* (Oxford: Clarendon Press, 1950).

16. Etienne Gilson, *Reason and Revelation in the Middle Ages* (New York: Charles Scribner's Sons, 1966).

17. See Karen Armstrong, *The Battle for God* (New York: Alfred A. Knopf, 2000).

18. Knox, *Enthusiasm*, 580.

19. Aquinas saw faith complemented and perfected by the gifts of understanding (*Summa Theologiae*, II-II, 8) and knowledge (II-II, 9); hope by the gift of fear of the Lord (II-II, 19); charity or love by the gift of wisdom (II-II, 45); prudence by the gift of counsel (II-II, 52); justice by the gift of piety (II-II, 121); fortitude by the gift of courage (II-II, 139); and temperance affected as well by the gift of fear of the Lord. Also see Christopher Kiesling, OP, "The Seven *Quiet* Gifts of the Holy Spirit," *Living Light* 23 (1986): 137–46; Bede Jarrett, *The Abiding Presence of the Holy Ghost in the Soul* (Westminster, MD: Newman Press, 1957); and Gerald Vann, *The Divine Pity* (Garden City, NY: Doubleday, 1961).

20. *The Rites of the Catholic Church* (New York: Pueblo Publishing Co., 1976), 309, 319, 104.

21. See Francis de Sales, *Introduction to the Devout Life* (New York: Doubleday, 1989); Thomas R. Kelly, *A Testament of Devotion* (San Francisco: HarperSanFrancisco, 1992).

22. John of St. Thomas, *The Gifts of the Holy Ghost*, trans. Dominic Hughes (New York: Sheed & Ward, 1951), 180 (John of St. Thomas's phrasing of Aquinas's understanding of the goal of the gift of piety).

23. Julian of Norwich, *Showings*, Classics of Western Spirituality (New York: Paulist Press, 1978), 295, 296; also see pp. 86–99.

24. Peter Hebblethwaite, *Pope John XXIII, Shepherd of the Modern World* (Garden City, NY: Doubleday, 1985), 36.

25. John of St. Thomas, *Gifts of the Holy Ghost*, 165.

26. Ibid., 170.

27. Pierre Teilhard de Chardin, *The Phenomenon of Man* (New York: Harper & Row, 1959), 31.

28. See Mohandas K. Gandhi, *An Autobiography: The Story of My Experiments with Truth* (Boston: Beacon Press, 1957). *Satyagraha* refers to the force of truth, truth-force: *Sat* = truth; *Agraha* = firmness.

29. Arthur Osborne, *Ramana Maharshi and the Path of Self-Knowledge* (London: Rider, 1970); *The Collected Works of Ramana Maharshi* (Tiruvannamalai: Sri Ramanasramam, 1996).

30. For biographies, consult Nirodbaran, *Sri Aurobindo for All Ages* (Pondicherry: Sri Aurobindo Ashram, 1990); or the lengthier A. B. Purani, *The Life of Sri Aurobindo* (Pondicherry: Sri Aurobindo Ashram, 1978).

31. Shirley du Boulay, *Beyond the Darkness: A Biography of Bede Griffiths* (New York: Doubleday, 1998), and *The Cave of the Heart: The Life of Swami Abhishiktananda* (Maryknoll, NY: Orbis Books, 2005).

32. Abhishiktananda, *Prayer*, new ed. translated from the French (Delhi: ISPCK, 1999), 5.

33. On wisdom both in pre-Christian Judaism and in St. Paul, see James D. G. Dunn, *Christology in the Making* (Philadelphia: Westminster Press, 1980), 163–212.

34. See Sally Cunneen, *In Search of Mary: The Woman and the Symbol* (New York: Ballantine Books, 1996); Jaroslav Pelikan, *Mary Though the Centuries: Her Place in the History of Culture* (New Haven, CT: Yale University Press, 1996).

35. John of St. Thomas, *Gifts of the Holy Ghost*, 125.

36. Ibid., 143.

37. Bernard McGinn, *The Mystical Thought of Meister Eckhart: The Man from Whom God Hid Nothing* (New York: Crossroad, 2001), 44–52, 75–100.

Chapter Nine
THE QUEST FOR THE TRUE SELF

The spiritual journey involves darkness as well as light, bewilderment as well as enlightenment, purification as well as illumination. The spiritual journey is in one sense a search for one's true self. It is not the I, the ego, the false self, but Christ, the Spirit, the true Self that is the source of abundant life (John 10:10).

The Hindu Doctrine of *Atman*

The human being in Hindu thought comprises Atman (or *Purusha*) and *Maya* (or *Prakriti*). The Hindu doctrine of Atman concerns one's deepest identity. Atman is most frequently translated as "Self," although sometimes as "Spirit." "Self" at times is also used to translate *Brahman*. Maya includes the body, senses, vital force, mind, understanding, and ego—most of what we in the West consider a human person to be. Atman is understood differently in the various philosophical systems in Hinduism.[1] In all the schools Atman is uncreated and eternal. In each perspective Atman is distinguished from ego, which we can refer to as the false self. In each view Atman survives physical death and becomes embodied more than once. The Katha Upanishad states, "Atman, the Spirit of vision, is never born and never dies. Before him there was nothing, and he is ONE for evermore. Never-born and eternal, beyond times gone or to come, he does not die when the body dies."[2]

Atman, the Self, lies unchanging behind the world of impermanence, the silent Witness, the innermost Self, pure spirit, unborn and uncreated. In the Katha Upanishad (III, 3–4) the metaphor of the chariot is employed. Atman is the lord or owner of the chariot. The body is the chariot itself. The higher intellect or intuitive awareness *(buddhi)* is the charioteer and the thinking function or mind is the reins or bridle.[3]

The pinnacle of Upanishadic wisdom is the realization that Atman is Brahman *(Tat Tvam Asi*, That thou art).[4] The macrocosmic Self (Brahman) and the microcosmic Self (Atman) are one and the same Self viewed under two aspects.[5] Atman is the inner Self; Brahman, the cosmic Self. The original meaning behind Atman is most probably "breath," which is why it came to signify the innermost core of something. *Prana* (breath) and *vayu* (wind) are two words associated with Atman or Brahman.[6] Prana, or breath, is the life-giving principle in all living creatures. It is the same as Vayu, the wind, which is the vital principle of the universe. Both *prana* and *vayu* are essential. We might note that both are translations of the Hebrew word *ruach*, or spirit. *Ruach* conveys air in motion—hence breath or wind, breathing or blowing.

The Indwelling Spirit

We have spoken about the intimate union between the Holy Spirit and the human spirit whereby we become temples of the Holy Spirit, who dwells within us. It is by the power of this Spirit that we become who God has created us to be: deified creatures, gods by grace, participants in the divine nature, our truest selves. This indwelling Spirit is the cause of our deification.[7] The Holy Spirit, who is uncreated grace itself, is received into the very soul of our souls, the core of our being, transforming and divinizing us. Grace is the beginning within us of the life of glory to come.[8] St. Paul calls the Holy Spirit the guarantee or pledge of our inheritance (2 Cor 1:22; 5:5; Eph 1:13–14). The First Letter of John states, "By this we know that he abides in us, by the Spirit that he has given us" (3:24).

We are God's daughters and sons, by grace to be sure, but nevertheless really "begotten by God." This is the effect of the Holy Spirit's indwelling. The Holy Spirit is a new principle of operation within us, the seed of a new life—a new self, if you will.[9] In his catechetical lectures on the Holy Spirit, St. Cyril of Jerusalem teaches:

> If fire, penetrating the mass of iron, sets the whole aflame, and what was cold becomes hot, and what was black becomes bright—if the body of fire penetrates the body of iron, why do you wonder, if the Holy Spirit enters into the inmost parts of the soul?[10]

We are permeated by the Spirit, who becomes, as it were, our new soul, the principle of our new life, the soul of our soul.[11] St. Augustine writes, "I shall say boldly but truly: There are two types of life; one of the body, the other of the soul. And as the soul is the life of the body, so God is the life of the soul."[12] As the soul is to the body, so the Holy Spirit is to the person who is living a life of grace.

Existentially, if we are living a spiritual life, the Holy Spirit is the principle of that life. Christian theology has referred to this life of grace as a second nature, but it is in one sense our first nature from a supernatural perspective, for it is the life to which we are called. Although grace is not our nature abstractly conceived, grace goes deeper than nature and is a second nature for one living the divine life and participating in the divine nature. The Holy Spirit indeed becomes our spirit. "Anyone united to the Lord becomes one spirit with him" (1 Cor 6:17).

We no longer live a purely natural life. It is now not I but the Spirit who lives within me. It is now not the "I" but the Spirit who is the source of my activities. It is now not the "I" that is my self, but the Spirit who is my deepest and truest Self. St. Paul writes, "Do you not know that your body is a temple of the Holy Spirit within you, which you have from God, and that you are not your own?" (1 Cor 6:19). Each of us is *hagiophoros*, a bearer of the Holy Spirit, as early Christians sometimes thought of themselves.[13]

The Indwelling Spirit as *Atman*

Arabinda Basu, a disciple of Sri Aurobindo at the Sri Aurobindo Ashram in Pondicherry, has written that there is no idea in Christian theology that parallels the concept of Atman.[14] Although it is true that one cannot equate concepts in diverse religious traditions as if they are synonymous or translatable as simple equivalents, one still searches for resemblances, or for what Raimon Panikkar has called homeomorphic equivalents.[15] What one religious tradition understands, experiences, and attempts to articulate may be found in another religious tradition but experienced or articulated differently, sometimes significantly so. So is there any counterpart in the Christian tradition to the Hindu doctrine of Atman? I think the answer is yes: the Holy Spirit *as* indwelling.

Now there is more to the Christian doctrine of the Holy Spirit than that of the indwelling, and there are aspects of the Hindu doctrine of Atman that we do not find in the Christian tradition. But if we search for resemblances or functional equivalents, what the Hindu experiences and articulates as Atman in the process of Self-realization is, from a Christian point of view, the Holy Spirit.[16] Texts from the Upanishads develop this thought:

> In the center of the castle of Brahman, our own body, there is a small shrine in the form of a lotus-flower, and within can be found a small space. We should find him who dwells there, and we should want to know him....The Spirit who is in the body does not grow old and does not die, and no one can ever kill the Spirit who is everlasting. This is the real castle of Brahman wherein dwells all the love of the universe. It is Atman, pure Spirit, beyond sorrow, old age, and death; beyond evil and hunger and thirst. It is Atman whose love is Truth, whose thoughts are Truth.[17]

Let us contemplate for a moment some impressions from this teaching. There is a small shrine within us in the form of a lotus flower. We can think back to our reflections on the human spirit in chapter 1. The language is reminiscent of Teresa of Avila's interior castle and the innermost dwelling place within it.[18] The impression is that of a Spirit indwelling us in the innermost recesses of our being. This Spirit does not grow old, indeed is everlasting. This is Atman, pure Spirit, who is Love and Truth.

Finding this Spirit within is like finding a treasure, a pearl beyond any price, the reign of God within. God dwells within this cave of the heart, within our innermost essence, within the ground of our soul. To live within this interior space is to live beyond time. This Spirit, this Inmost One, the source of joy, is *ananda* or pure delight, eternal life. This Spirit is the true Self. I repeat that I am not suggesting that the Holy Spirit in the Christian tradition and the Atman in Hindu thought are synonymous. Rather, I am suggesting that each has tapped experientially into the same reality: the indwelling Spirit.

The Spirit in the Hebrew Scriptures plays a role in history that we do not ascribe to Atman. The Spirit in history comes to us from the outside, rushing on us, resting on us, being poured out on us, anointing us prophets and kings, taking possession of us. The Spirit has a dynamism that underlies a Jewish or Christian interpretation of history. This same Holy Spirit is manifest in the charisms bestowed within the Pauline *ecclesia*. The Spirit has a historical and ecclesial as well as a cosmic role. This is the same Holy Spirit who indwells each of us who are in Christ. It is this indwelling Holy Spirit that is Atman. This Holy Spirit is conceived in personal terms in Christian thought and experience, but as we saw, Atman itself is conceived differently within various schools of Hindu thought, in some cases personally, in others not.

The Indwelling Spirit as True Self

Whatever the similarities or differences may be between the Hindu concept of Atman and the Christian understanding of the indwelling Holy Spirit, one gradually discovers within a Christian frame of reference that the Holy Spirit is one's true Self. This does not deny an ontological distinction between the Holy Spirit and the human spirit, which we have affirmed.[19] In the concrete realm of grace, however, existentially and experientially, the Holy Spirit has been given to us to be our Self. Christian life is a process of coming to this awareness and realization. The true Self is one's deepest identity. This Self does not emerge from within our created nature but is rather uncreated grace itself. The Holy Spirit becomes the source of our actions the more divinized or deified we become. Deification is not a concept but a reality. The more we realize the Spirit within us, the more we become who we are, namely, partakers of the divine nature where this "second nature" is existentially the source of actions.

Grace is a new life principle. If we are living in this "state of grace," the vital principle is no longer our "first nature" but our "second nature." We are new creatures, re-created, having come through a second birth. We are women and men in whom the Holy Spirit, respecting our human nature, builds upon that nature, not obliterating or destroying it but becoming the deepest source from which our activities flow. The Holy Spirit becomes the soul of our soul.[20] Is this not the sense of St. Augustine's analogy that the Holy Spirit is to the soul as the soul is to the body? The Holy Spirit is our True Self. Until we can let go of everything else, which is the process of detachment in the mystical life, and surrender to the Spirit, or realize that I am the Spirit (when there is no separate "I" but only the Spirit), we are not yet deiform, not yet our true Selves, but still our fallen false selves and egos.

St. Irenaeus seems to have identified the "spirit" naturally belonging to the human person with the Holy Spirit.[21] Angelos Philippou comments on Irenaeus:

> What is implied here is that as in the old creation the breath of life was the true essence of man [sic] (Genesis 2:7), so in the new creation it is the gift of the Holy Spirit which is the true essence of the life of the believer.[22]

Even earlier, Tatian (ca. 120), representative of the Syriac Christian tradition, held that the Holy Spirit belonged to the original state of humanity but that as a result of sin we were deprived of this original blessing. The new creation, however, is the restoration of this primeval unity of body-soul-Holy Spirit.[23] Of a later representative of that Syriac tradition, Aphraates (Aphrahat) of Syria (ca. 260–345), Tomás Spidlík writes: "In Aphraates of Syria, for example, the Spirit of Christ is given so abundantly that it becomes what is most spiritual in us, our true self."[24] The definition of a spiritual person includes the Holy Spirit, Spidlík observes.[25]

Theophane the Recluse (d. 1804), summarizing the spiritual tradition of the East, sees the spiritual life as consisting in the transformation of the human person into the sphere of the Spirit.[26] This S/spiritualization is what we were made for and is proper to our make-up as human beings. St. Paul's "Even though our outer nature is wasting away, our inner nature is being renewed day by day" (2 Cor 4:16) confirms this for Theophane. In a similar fashion, Abhishiktananda, commenting on 1 Corinthians 6:17 ("But anyone united to the Lord becomes one spirit with him"), writes:

> Whatever anyone does at this pre-eminent centre of his spirit shares in the power of the Spirit of God. At the centre of his being that person has in fact become one with the Spirit who dwells there.[27]

This S/spirit, if you will, the Self in us, is revealed in the Hebrew and Christian Scriptures. Not two, not one, not this, not that. It is the mystery at the core of our being—unnameable, ineffable, divine—the inmost being, the ground of the soul, the cave of the heart, the lotus of the heart, the secret place, the indwelling Holy Spirit of God, the Holy Breath, the true Self of all creatures. The psalmist speaks about "truth in the inward being" and "wisdom in my secret heart" (Ps 51:6). The prophet Ezekiel writes:

> A new heart I will give you, and a new spirit I will put within you; and I will remove from your body the heart

of stone and give you a heart of flesh. I will put my spirit within you, and make you follow my statutes and be careful to observe my ordinances. (Ezek 36:26–27)

And the letter to the Ephesians states as well:

Out of his infinite glory, may he give you the power through his Spirit for your hidden self to grow strong, so that Christ may live in your hearts through faith, and then, planted in love and built on love, you will with all the saints have strength to grasp the breadth and the length, the height and the depth; until, knowing the love of Christ, which is beyond all knowledge, you are filled with the utter fullness of God. (Eph 3:14–19 *[Jerusalem Bible]*)

Resisting the Spirit

It is possible not to know the Holy Spirit, even for those who have been baptized and received the gift of the Spirit. We recall Paul's experience as reported in the Acts of the Apostles: "While Apollos was in Corinth, Paul passed through the interior regions and came to Ephesus, where he found some disciples. He said to them, 'Did you receive the Holy Spirit when you became believers?' They replied, 'No, we have not even heard that there is a Holy Spirit'" (Acts 19:1–2).[28] Although today baptized Christians have heard of the Holy Spirit, it is not so clear that they know the Holy Spirit. What does it mean to know the Spirit? It must mean to have experienced the Spirit as an operative agent in my life and in the world.

Ignorance of the Holy Spirit is fraught with danger given the Spirit's central and essential role in personal, ecclesial, and social life. Yet it is possible to diminish or dismiss the Spirit. The New Testament speaks about "grieving the Spirit" and "suppressing the Spirit." The Letter to the Ephesians exhorts:

Let no evil come from out your mouths, but only what is useful for building up, as there is need, so that your words may give grace to those who hear. And do not grieve the Holy Spirit of God, with which you were marked with a seal for the day of redemption. Put away from you all bitterness and wrath and anger and wrangling and slander, together with all malice, and be kind to one another, tenderhearted, forgiving one another. (Eph 4:29–32)

As in Paul's Letter to the Galatians (5:16–26) as well as elsewhere in the Pauline writings (Rom 1:29–31; 1 Cor 6:9–10; 2 Cor 6:6–7; Col 3:8) we get a list of vices that are the works of an evil spirit and virtues that are the fruit of living in the Spirit. Paul writes in Galatians: "If we live by the Spirit, let us also be guided by the Spirit" (5:25).

All of this points out how it is possible to grieve the Holy Spirit, as the Letter to the Ephesians indicates. Undoubtedly our world, our church, and we ourselves can be a source of sadness for the Spirit. Our refusal of the Spirit causes sadness for the Spirit as well as for ourselves, even though we may not always know the cause of our sadness. "Do not grieve the Holy Spirit" (Eph 4:30). In the Hebrew Scriptures, Isaiah recognizes grief that Israel had brought to the Holy Spirit. In recalling God's gracious deeds and the favor bestowed on the house of Israel, Isaiah recalls the rebelliousness of the people in contrast to God's steadfast love (Isa 63:7–14). "They rebelled and grieved his holy spirit" (Isa 63:10). The Letter to the Hebrews warns us about "outraging the Spirit" (Heb 10:29). Besides grieving the Holy Spirit, there is the possibility of quenching, stifling, suppressing the Spirit.[29] Paul writes to the Thessalonians, "Do not quench the Spirit" (1 Thess 5: 19). The Greek word in the text, *shennymi*, can be translated as extinguish, put out, restrain, stifle, suppress. In the *New Jerusalem Bible* we read, "Do not stifle the Spirit."

It is possible not only to stifle but also to suppress the Spirit completely. In fact, in the history of Israel, the period following the exile was considered a time when the Spirit had been suppressed. The gift of the Spirit at that time was practically synonymous with the gift of prophecy, and prophets had disappeared. First Maccabees refers to this tragedy. "So there was great distress in Israel, such as had not been since the time that prophets ceased to appear among them" (9:27). Joachim Jeremias wrote of the experience:

> In the time of the patriarchs, all the pious and upright had the spirit of God. When Israel committed sin with the golden calf, God limited the Spirit to chosen ones, prophets, high priests and kings. With the death of the writing prophets, Haggai, Zechariah and Malachi, *the spirit was quenched* because of the sin of Israel.[30]

At the same time that there was a felt absence of the Spirit, there was a longing for its return, and the prophet Joel foretold a future time when once again, "I will pour out my spirit on all flesh..." (Joel 2:28–29).

Is such a quenching of the Spirit a real possibility? We have only to look at the history of the world, varied times and places, which are devoid of the Spirit. Or at the history of the church. There are times and places that may be devoid of the activity of the Spirit who has been suffocated.[31] Pope John XXIII convened the Second Vatican Council to inaugurate another Pentecost, to let the Spirit in. In our personal lives, in ecclesial life, or in social, political, economic, and ecological situations, we may judge that the Spirit has been rendered inoperative. This has been referred to as being in a state of mortal sin, a condition that can befall an individual as well as a society, a group, or a period of history. The Spirit ought not be taken for granted. Do not grieve the Spirit. Do not stifle the Spirit. Do not quench the Spirit. Or we may wake up one day and find that the Spirit is no longer among us.

The Synoptic Gospels speak about blaspheming the Spirit or sinning against the Spirit. We can close ourselves off or cut ourselves off from the life-giving Breath.

> "Truly, I tell you, people will be forgiven for their sins and whatever blasphemies they utter; but whoever blasphemes against the Holy Spirit can never have forgiveness, but is guilty of an eternal sin"—for they had said, "He has an unclean spirit." (Mark 3:28–30)

> And everyone who speaks a word against the Son of Humanity will be forgiven; but whoever blasphemes against the Holy Spirit will not be forgiven. (Luke 12:10)

> Therefore I tell you, people will be forgiven for every sin and blasphemy, but blasphemy against the Spirit will not be forgiven. Whoever speaks a word against the Son of Humanity will be forgiven, but whoever speaks against the Holy Spirit will not be forgiven, either in this age or in the age to come. (Matt 12:31–32)

We should not ask, "What is the sin that cannot be forgiven?" without being attentive to other aspects of the passage. There are two sources, Mark and Q, and it is difficult to determine which may be earlier, but the saying in some form goes back to Jesus himself. The Q form of the saying is more or less what we find in Luke.[32] The Matthean saying is a conflation of Mark and Q.[33] There is first the good news: sins will be forgiven, even those against Jesus himself. The statement is an overall sweeping generalization about the forgiveness of sin. The Marcan saying gives us a context for the saying that the others do not give. Blasphemy against the Holy Spirit is the refusal to see the Spirit at work in Jesus and attributing Jesus' mighty works to Satan or Beelzebul. It is to mistake the Holy Spirit for an evil spirit, to conflate God's Holy Spirit with the demonic.

Jesus could tolerate being misrepresented or misunderstood, but he could not accept a refusal or inability to recognize the Spirit. We should not take the saying about the unforgivability of sinning against the Spirit literally. It reflects Jesus' use of hyperbole to make clear the importance of the Holy Spirit. Nothing is so serious as being persistently and obstinately closed to the workings of the Spirit.[34]

In other words, sinning against the Holy Spirit may not be so much a sin as an attitude that prevents the Holy Spirit from breaking through into our lives, our institutions, our cultures and histories. It is not so much, then, a question of forgivability as of the Spirit having been so thoroughly stifled that all our actions and words become blasphemous. It is not so much that we ought to worry about an unforgivable sin as that we need to question our sensitivity to the Spirit. Are we hardened against the Spirit so that the Spirit is unable to breathe or break through?

We can refer to those texts in the Hebrew Scriptures that contrast the heart of flesh that the Spirit brings with the heart of stone that the Spirit finds impenetrable (Ezek 36:26). The Spirit is not just grieved or quenched or blasphemed, but rendered powerless. Whatever leads to this state of affairs is death: the Spirit is powerless to act. The Spirit is what true life is all about. Refusing attentiveness to the Spirit is a sin against God. The Spirit, in the end, is what the mission, ministry, death, and resurrection of Jesus were all about. Those who refuse to see the Spirit's life-giving presence in Jesus are not rejecting Jesus but rejecting the Spirit of God. It is the Spirit's mission that is at stake, not that of Jesus. Jesus is passionately concerned about the Spirit. Let no one take the Spirit lightly. The greatest sin of all is this great refusal: the refusal of the Spirit.

Gentle Breath, Blazing Fire,
Strong Wind, Holy Spirit, Atman,
Soul of my soul, Soul of the church, Soul of the universe,
cosmic Spirit, Great Spirit,
guide me to my true home in You,
where I am one with You,
one with myself and with You in myself,
where I am so totally one with You

162

that I am nothing other than You,
where I become aware that You are my true Self,
that there is no Self but you and I in You and You in me,
but One Self, the same Self that is the Self of all others,
of all creatures, of all creation,
the Self of the universe, the guide of its evolution, the
dispenser of wisdom.
My truest and deepest and inmost Self,
let there be no I, only You,
whose instruments and icons we are.
You are the pebble, we the ripples,
spreading out and out into an infinite embrace of the entire
universe.
Aware of you, we are your real presences in the world.
Help us to make your presence effective and felt. Amen.

Notes

1. Arabinda Basu, "The Hindu Doctrine of Man," *Sri Aurobindo Circle* 21 (1965): 90–91.

2. Katha Upanishad, II, 18–19. See *The Upanishads*, trans. F. Max Müller, 2 vols. (New York: Dover, 1962), 2:10–11. I have used the translation of Juan Mascaró, *The Upanishads* (Baltimore: Penguin Books, 1965), 59.

3. Heinrich Zimmer, *Philosophies of India* (Princeton, NJ: Princeton University Press, 1969), 363–78 on this metaphor as well as other metaphors.

4. Chandogya Upanishad, VI, 8–16. See Müller, *Upanishads*, 1:98–109. "Believe me, my son, an invisible and subtle essence is the Spirit of the whole universe. That is Reality. That is Atman. THOU ART THAT (Mascaró translation, *Upanishads*, 117, also 118). Also see "This in truth is That," Katha Upanishad, IV–VI. See Müller, 2:15–24.

5. Zimmer, *Philosophies of India*, 354.

6. Katha Upanishad, V. See Müller, *Upanishads*, 2:18.

7. See Juan Arintero, OP, *The Mystical Evolution in the Development and Vitality of the Church*, 2 vols. (St. Louis: Herder, 1949). He writes, "This deification, so well known to the Fathers but unfortunately forgotten today, is the primary purpose of the Christian life" (1:23). See especially 1:23–86.

8. Thomas Aquinas, *Summa Theologiae*, II/II, q. 24, a. 3, ad 2; I/II, q. 114, a. 3, ad 3.

9. Arintero, *Mystical Evolution* 1:28.

10. Cyril of Jerusalem, *Catecheses* 17 (par. 14), in *The Works of Cyril of Jerusalem*, trans. Leo P. McCauley and Anthony A. Stephenson, Fathers of the Church 64 (Washington, DC: Catholic University of America Press, 1970), 105. Two of the catechetical lectures (16–17) are devoted to the Holy Spirit.

11. Arintero, *Mystical Evolution*, 1:36.

12. Augustine, *Enarrat. in Ps 70, sermo 2*, in Arintero, *Mystical Evolution*, 1:36 n. 61. St. Augustine, *In Ps 49*: "So we have been made sons of God and even gods," Arintero, *Mystical Evolution*, 1:79 n. 48.

13. Arintero, *Mystical Evolution*, 1:114.

14. Arabinda Basu, "The Hindu Doctrine of Man," *Sri Aurobindo Circle* 21 (1965): 96; see also idem, "Introduction," to *A Greater Psychology: An Introduction to Sri Aurobindo's Psychological Thought*, ed. A. S. Dalal (New York: Jeremy P. Tarcher/Putnam, 2001), xix.

15. Raimon Panikkar, "A Christophany for our Times," *Theology Digest* 39 (Spring 1992): 3–21.

16. "Indeed what is the Spirit but the *atman* of the Upanishads, which is said to be identical with *brahman*, although this identity can only be existentially recognised and affirmed once 'realisation' has been attained?" (Raimon Panikkar, *The Trinity and the Religious Experience of Man* [Maryknoll, NY: Orbis Books, 1973], 63–64).

17. Chandogya Upanishad VIII, 1, 1 and 5. Mascaró translation, *Upanishads*, 120–21. See also Müller, *Upanishads*, 1:125–27. Also see Chandogya Upanishad VIII, 7, 1; Müller, 1:134. Also Katha Upanishad II, 12–13, 18, 20, 22, 23. Mascaró translation, 59–60. Müller, 2:10–11.

18. Teresa of Avila, *The Interior Castle*, Classics of Western Spirituality (New York: Paulist Press, 1979).

19. Claude Welch (*The Trinity in Contemporary Theology* [London: SCM Press, 1953]) emphasizes the need to distinguish the human spirit from the Holy Spirit.

20. So Theophane the Recluse, in Tomás Spidlík, *The Spirituality of the Christian East* (Kalamazoo, MI: Cistercian Publications, 1986), 32.

21. Irenaeus, *Adversus Haereses*, 5.6.1 and 5.20.2. See John Meyendorff, "Introduction," in Gregory Palamas, *The Triads*, Classics of Western Spirituality (New York: Paulist Press, 1983), 18.

22. Angelos Philippou, "The Mystery of Pentecost," in *The Orthodox Ethos* (Oxford: Holywell Press, 1964), 90.

23. See Kilian McDonnell, "A Trinitarian Theology of the Holy Spirit?" *Theological Studies* 46 (1985): 201.

24. Spidlík, *Spirituality of the Christian East*, 31.

25. Ibid., 105.

26. Ibid., 33.

27. Abhishiktananda, *Prayer*, new ed. translated from the French (Delhi: ISPCK, 1999), 53.

28. See Jerome Murphy-O'Connor, *Paul: A Critical Life* (Oxford: Clarendon Press, 1996), 172–73. These "followers of Jesus" had only received the baptism of John the Baptist, administered by Jesus while he was preaching John's baptism of repentance (John 3:22–26). They were thus disciples of Jesus, having been converted by him, but they knew him only while he was associated with John and thus knew nothing of the passion, resurrection, and Pentecost.

29. See Karl Rahner, "Do Not Stifle the Spirit!" in *Theological Investigations*, vol. 8 (New York: Seabury, 1977), 72–87.

30. Joachim Jeremias, *New Testament Theology: The Proclamation of Jesus* (New York: Charles Scribner's Sons, 1971), 80–81. Translation adjusted for inclusive language.

31. One of the accusations made by Albigensians against the medieval church was that the latter had quenched the Holy Spirit. See Ronald A. Knox, *Enthusiasm: A Chapter in the History of Religion* (Oxford: Clarendon Press, 1962), 105.

32. Ivan Havener, *Q—The Sayings of Jesus* (Wilmington, DE: Michael Glazier, 1987), 136–37. "Q" refers to a hypothetical source or lost collection of sayings common to both Matthew and Luke but not found in Mark; from the German word *Quelle* (or "source").

33. John S. Kloppenborg, *Q Parallels: Synopsis, Critical Notes and Concordance* (Sonoma, CA: Polebridge Press, 1988), 124–25.

34. Joseph A. Fitzmyer (*The Gospel according to Luke: Introduction, Translation, and Notes*, Anchor Bible 28, 28A [Garden City, NY: Doubleday, 1985], 2:964), describes the unforgivable sin as "the persistence in consummate and obdurate opposition to the influence of the Spirit."

Chapter Ten

THE ACQUISITION
OF THE HOLY SPIRIT

St. Seraphim (1759–1833), a canonized saint of the Russian Orthodox Church and *staretz*, or spiritual elder, of the monastery of Sarov, taught that no spiritual exercise is comparable to that of silence *(hēsychia)*.[1] Following the Orthodox and hesychast tradition in spirituality, his practice included the unceasing prayer of the heart, the Jesus Prayer ("Lord Jesus Christ, Son of God, have mercy on me, a sinner"). He instructed one of his disciples, Nicholas Motovilov, to whom Seraphim gave the name "Friend of God," concerning the goal of the Christian life: "I am going to try to explain to you what this goal is. Prayer, fasting, works of mercy—all this is very good, but it represents only the means, not the end of the Christian life. The true end is the acquisition of the Holy Spirit."[2] Having been given this teaching, Motovilov inquired how he might know whether he had been given this grace of the Holy Spirit. Seraphim responded that it is by an ineffable light that the grace of the Holy Spirit manifests itself, which Motovilov then experienced as radiating from the face of Seraphim himself.

Paul Endokimov described a staretz as an instrument of the Holy Spirit and St. Seraphim as an icon of Orthodox spirituality.[3] Thomas Hopko described St. Seraphim as an "icon of the Spirit."[4] Using the language of St. Basil the Great in his work *On the Holy Spirit*,[5] one could call Seraphim *pneumatikos* (one-who-belongs-to-the-Spirit). Orthodox teaching, particularly St. Athanasius (ca. 296–373) and St. Gregory of Nyssa (ca. 330–ca. 395), emphasizes that the Son reveals the Father and the Spirit reveals the Son, that the Son is the image of the Father and the Spirit the image of the Son.[6] Who, then, reveals the Spirit or is the Spirit's image? The Spirit is manifest in the *startzi*, in holy men and women.

In 1952, Ivan Michailovitch Kontzevitch (1893–1965) published a compendium of Orthodox spiritual theology and entitled it *The Acquisition of the Holy Spirit in Ancient Russia*.[7] The ascetic process of "pulling down" the Holy Spirit, which is always grace and receptivity, comprises struggling with one's thoughts[8] and passions (of which the ancients listed eight: gluttony, lust, avarice, dejection, anger, despondency, vainglory, and pride),[9] as well as the practice of unceasing prayer[10] accompanied by an attentiveness of the mind, or mindfulness.[11] The role of the elder or spiritual guide is also of major importance.[12] In the West we often speak of life in the Spirit as the mystical life. Archimandrite Cyprian suggested that the word *mysticism* is not at home in the language of the East and is better rendered by "acquisition of the Holy Spirit."[13]

Hesychasm (from the Greek word *hēsychia* meaning "stillness" or "quietude") is a prominent experiential spiritual tradition in Orthodox Christianity.[14] Originally hesychasm referred to the anchoritic life; hesychasts were hermits. They practiced absolute silence and unceasing prayer of the heart. St. Symeon the New Theologian (949–1022) is sometimes considered the father of hesychasm, but it goes back to St. Maximus the Confessor (ca. 580–662), St. John Climacus (ca. 579–649), Evagrius Ponticus (346–399), St. Gregory of Nyssa (ca. 330–395), and St. Macarius the Great (ca. 300–390). It is perhaps most associated with St. Gregory Palamas (1296–1359).

Gregory Palamas

Palamas was born in Constantinople and pursued a monastic life in the Athonite tradition.[15] During a period of Turkish incursions into the peninsula, he left Mount Athos for Thessalonica. Later he was elected archbishop there, but only after another period of monastic life on Mount Athos. He followed a hesychast way of life and practiced the uninterrupted Jesus Prayer. He is perhaps best known for his defense of hesychasm against attacks by Barlaam, a Calabrian monk. Several councils in the East (1341, 1351) endorsed his theology.

For Palamas, the goal of Christian life is the deification *(theōsis)* of the human person,[16] a goal not reserved for a few but intended for all, a reality that surpasses intellectual knowledge and leads to an experience of God as light (which is an uncreated light and often called thaboric light owing to its identification with the light experienced at the Transfiguration on Mount Thabor). Deification is a communion with God who is utterly transcendent, the God who is always "more-than-God."[17] Palamas's emphasis on the transcendence of God places him in the apophatic tradition of the *via negativa*—we only know what God is not, not what God is.[18] The unknowability of God, however, is not the same as the inattainability of God, but we attain to God only after our own transfiguration by the Spirit.[19] This transfiguration of the human person refers not only to the mind but also to the body.

Palamas defended the use of the body in prayer, specifically in the practice of the Jesus Prayer. Not following the Neoplatonic and Evagrian direction, which aimed at freeing the mind from matter in prayer, Palamas accepted the Macarian goal of the unity of body and spirit. Hence we find in the hesychasm of Palamas a defense of methods of praying that involve attentiveness to one's breathing and recognizing the heart as one's vital center.[20] Nicephorus the Hesychast (d. ca. 1340), a teacher and guide of Palamas, wrote:

> You know that we breathe our breath in and out, only because of our heart...so, as I have said, sit down, recollect your mind, draw it—I am speaking of your mind—in your nostrils; that is the path the breath takes to reach the heart. Drive it, force it to go down to your heart with the air you are breathing in. When it is there, you will see the joy that follows; you will have nothing to regret. As a man who has been away from home for a long time cannot restrain his joy at seeing his wife and children

again, so the spirit overflows with joy and unspeakable delights when it is united again to the soul....Next you must know that as long as your spirit abides there, you must not remain silent nor idle. Have no other occupation or meditation than the cry of: "Lord Jesus Christ, Son of God, have mercy on me!"[21]

Barlaam was opposed to practices such as these, and he referred to monks with this kind of spiritual practice as *omphalopsychoi*, "people-whose-soul-is in-their-navel," or later what some called navel gazers. We can note, however, similarities between the hesychast tradition and the practice of meditation in the Eastern religions. In hesychasm, the heart is the primary instrument of the Spirit.[22]

The deification of the human person is a work of the Holy Spirit, but more precisely in Palamite terms it is a work of the energies of God. Characteristic of Palamite theology is the distinction between God's essence and divine uncreated energies (the *energeiai*). The underlying dilemma is how to talk about God at all. How do we talk about God in such a way as to maintain both God's absolute transcendence and yet the reality of our human experience of God as immanent? Palamas does this by maintaining a real distinction in God between God's totally transcendent "essence," which is always more, other, beyond, and the divine "energies," which are uncreated and thus truly God. The divine energies effect our deification not with the essence of God, which always remains something more than our experience of God, but nevertheless with the one true God. In one sense, Palamas is trying to articulate God's self-revelation as being that of both "One Who Is" (Exod 3:14) and "One Who Is With Us" (Exod 33:14, 19; Isa 7:14).[23]

God remains transcendent while at the same time being self-communicating, self-revealing, and self-giving. God is both "Other" and yet given to us. There is always more to God (God's essence) than what is shared, namely, God's *energeiai*. It is through the energies that God relates to creation and enables us to partake of the divine nature. "Any confusion of the essence with the energies of

God would destroy either the ineffability of God (because God would be 'brought down' to the level of creation) or the possibility of a real participation in the life of God (because God would be regarded as totally beyond us)."[24]

The energies as Palamas understood them did not belong properly to any one of the Divine Persons, but deification, a work of the uncreated energies, was primarily a work of the Holy Spirit. The Word became enfleshed as a human being (incarnation) so that humanity might become deified (through the deifying grace of the Holy Spirit). Deification is a work of the Holy Spirit, who is in the energies. There is more to God than the God of whom we speak, and more to God than the energies of God, and more to the energies than we as human beings are able to contain or receive, although the energies really deify us and unite us to the one true God. Because of human limitations we cannot contain the divine life in its plenitude.[25] The divine energy undergirding deification is the energy of the Spirit available to all. Saints are those, to use our earlier way of speaking, who have "acquired the Holy Spirit," or to speak in a Palamite way, those who "are the instruments of the Holy Spirit, having received the same energy as He has."[26]

The doctrine of the divine energies has been explored by twentieth-century Orthodox theologians such as Georges Florovsky (1893–1979), Vladimir Lossky (1903–58), and John Meyendorff (1926–92).[27] Florovsky distinguished between essence and will in God. That which pertains to God's essence (the generation of the Son and the procession of the Spirit in the Trinity) is necessary; that which pertains to the divine will (the creation of the world) is contingent. God is trinitarian by nature, not by will. The energies pertain to the domain of God's freedom.

Vladimir Lossky indicated that real participation in God must be located within the energies as well. Deification takes place not in the divine essence (or it would be of the very essence of God), nor in a particular Divine Person (or we would all be the same as Christ), but rather through the uncreated divine energies. The energies belong to the whole Trinity, but there is a special relationship between the energies and the Spirit. "The work of our deification is accomplished by the Holy Spirit, Giver of grace."[28]

> We see that the Fathers regarded the Holy Spirit as the Person who introduces the divine energies into our souls. He comes and initiates in us the power and the knowledge and the love of God....This is not meant to imply that the divine energy is the exclusive property of the Holy Spirit but rather that it is the Spirit who initiates it in the creature, bringing about His action in the creature.[29]

The Holy Spirit not only infuses the individual human person or spirit with divine energy but also pours the uncreated divine energies into the church and through the church introduces the energies into the world. Within the church, in each sacrament, the Spirit is invoked and the sacrament receives an energy of the Spirit that comes to all who receive the sacrament.[30]

Symeon the New Theologian

St. John the Evangelist and St. Gregory of Nazianzus are the only two in the Orthodox tradition besides Symeon to have been given the title of "theologian." John the Theologian, Gregory the Theologian, and Symeon the New Theologian model what it means to be a true theologian, namely, one who has experienced God.[31] Symeon had his first vision of God as light in his early twenties before entering a monastery himself. His second such experience came when he was a novice at Stoudios. Later, at the monastery of St. Mamas, he was professed and was elected abbot, which position he held for twenty-five years. Conflict with ecclesiastical authority led him to resign. He was exiled but later vindicated.[32] For Symeon there was no substitute for the individual Christian's conscious, personal experience of God, a second baptism with the Spirit. "It is not one who does not introduce new teachings into God's Church who is orthodox, but the one whose life is in accordance with the true Word."[33]

Symeon's mysticism was apophatic: "No man has ever known anything about God, indeed neither His name nor His nature nor His image nor His form nor His substance....so, believe me, my God is hidden from us and a vast and profound darkness envelops us all."[34] Yet the Trinity shines through the darkness. The door is the Son, the key to the door the Holy Spirit, and the house is the Father.[35] The Holy Spirit is the key, and one cannot theologize without the Holy Spirit.[36]

For Symeon we are gods, gods by adoption, gods by grace, divinized, like to God, sons of God, children of God, immortals, gods united with God in the Holy Spirit, coheirs with Christ, partakers of the gift of the Holy Spirit, Christs, partakers and sharers of God's divinity and glory, friends of God.[37] The foundation of our deification is the divine indwelling effected through the Holy Spirit. This union with the Spirit through baptism is so intimate that it makes us God-conscious. Our divinity is something we can genuinely experience and of which we are conscious. The doctrines of Christ and the Spirit, the incarnation and deification, are intimately tied together.

In addition to the resurrection of Christ and the resurrection of the body at the end times, Symeon speaks of a mystical resurrection of the soul that takes place already in this life through the power of the Spirit, which resurrection is as important as the resurrection at the end.[38] "There is a death before death and a resurrection of souls before the resurrection of bodies. It is a fact, a power, an experience, a truth."[39] Symeon speaks of two baptisms as well, two gifts, by which the Spirit comes to us. In the first baptism we are sanctified but without knowing it; in the first baptism we are already born again with the Holy Spirit. Yet there is a grace of the Holy Spirit that still awaits us. The second baptism involves repentance and the gift of tears.[40]

Macarius[41] had a significant influence on Symeon the New Theologian as well as on Seraphim of Sarov. He conceived of the

Christian life as "true fellowship"[42] with the Holy Spirit, and as "mutual penetration with the Spirit."[43] When one has true fellowship with the Spirit, when one might say one's True Self has become the Spirit with whom one has become so thoroughly one, when one has acquired the Spirit, to use Seraphim's way of speaking, then one has received what Christ came to give. "For the Spirit is the life of the soul, and on this account the Lord came, in order to give his Spirit to the soul on this earth."[44] In Macarius, the Spirit and the kingdom of heaven become almost synonymous, as they do in the teaching of Symeon.

The mustard seed in the Matthean parable (Matt 13:31–32) is for Symeon the Holy Spirit, who is the kingdom of heaven within us.[45] "When a man knows that these signs and wonders are taking place within him, he is truly a god-bearer, a vessel of wonder. He has God indwelling, the all-holy Spirit himself who speaks and works in him....Flesh and blood, however, have no inheritance in the kingdom of God, for this is the Holy Spirit."[46] With Symeon we have one of those intimations that we find within Orthodoxy, the awareness that the kingdom of which Jesus speaks can be identified with the gift of the Spirit. The Spirit is the pearl, the mustard seed, the leaven.[47]

This suggestion is found already in Gregory of Nyssa (ca. 330–ca. 395)[48] as well as in Maximus Confessor (ca. 580–662).[49] Its basis is a rare variant in early manuscripts of the Gospel of Luke. Instead of "Your kingdom come" (Luke 11:2), some ancient authorities read, "Your Holy Spirit come upon us and cleanse us." This textual variant is picked up by Gregory of Nyssa in his commentary on the Lord's Prayer. Put simply, the kingdom is the Holy Spirit and in the Lord's Prayer we are in fact praying, "Thy Spirit come."[50]

The Holy Spirit in Orthodox Theology

The doctrines of the incarnation and deification are inseparable and instinctively held together in Orthodoxy. Christology and soteriology are two sides of one coin, and soteriology has as much to do with the Spirit as with Christ. Christ and the Holy Spirit are of equal importance, and emphasis ought not be given more to one than to the other. The Holy Spirit is not "third"; the Spirit proceeds from the Father, as does the Son. As Symeon argued, there is no anteriority to the Father or to the Son, even though ontologically the Father is the unoriginate source.[51] This unity of nature is manifest in the classic patristic formulation: *from* the Father, *through* the Son, *in* the Holy Spirit. This unity of *ousia* (nature) is manifest as a unity *ad extra* as well (in the activities, the *energeai*). Creation, redemption, and sanctification are a single work, not three distinctive works. It is not that creation is the work of the Father, redemption the work of the Son, and sanctification the work of the Spirit. The Word and Spirit are also Creator. The Father and the Spirit are both involved in redemption. Where one is, there is the Trinity. It is the entire Trinity that sanctifies.

St. Basil the Great (ca. 330–379), the brother of St. Gregory of Nyssa and close friend of St. Gregory of Nazianzus, wrote an early formative treatise on the Holy Spirit.[52] He wrote against those who maintained that one ought not rank the Holy Spirit with the Father and the Son, as if their equal, in other words against the pneumatomachians (##24–25). Basil argued that "in all things the Holy Spirit is inseparable and wholly incapable of being parted from the Father and the Son" (#37) The Spirit existed, preexisted, and coexisted with the Father and the Son (#49).

Much of Basil's treatise is spent defending "the Father *with* the Son *together with* the Holy Spirit" as being as appropriate a way of speaking as the classic "*through* the Son *in* the Holy Spirit" (##3, 58–68). Basil had been attacked for the former usage, and in the attack Basil detected that some understood the classic usage in an Arian or semi-Arian way, as the Son and Spirit not being equal to the Father. Both ways of speaking are orthodox for Basil. The former, *with*, conveys the full equality of the Spirit with the Son and the Father and is most appropriate when emphasizing what the three have in common. *Through* and *in* are especially apropos for expressing the activity *ad extra*, but never convey any inequality

(#16). The word *in* does not imply lower dignity than the word *with* (#58). "The preposition *'in'* states the truth rather relatively to ourselves; while *'with'* proclaims the fellowship of the Spirit with God. Wherefore we use both words, by the one expressing the dignity of the Spirit; by the other announcing the grace that is with us" (#68).

According to Dumitru Staniloae, the Holy Spirit "directs the power of God to its end by introducing this power into the creature."[53] Paul Endokimov describes *theōsis* or deification as "vivification by the Holy Spirit," "the infusion of the Spirit," and "the penetration by the divine energies of the whole human being."[54] In the Orthodox tradition one can easily associate the Holy Spirit with energy, although the Palamite doctrine of the energies is complex. Teilhard de Chardin spoke of the Holy Spirit as the radial energy of the universe. These are clearly distinct conceptions, that of Orthodoxy and that of Teilhard, but in both the concept of energy is used in order to understand God's relation to the world.

We conclude our reflection on the acquisition of the Holy Spirit as the goal of Christian life with the invocation of St. Symeon the New Theologian that begins his hymns of divine love and light.

> *Come, true light. Come, eternal life.*
> *Come, hidden mystery. Come, nameless treasure.*
> *Come, ineffable reality. Come, inconceivable person.*
> *Come, endless bliss. Come, non-setting sun.*
> *Come, infallible expectation of all those who must be saved.*
> *Come, awakening of those who are asleep.*
> *Come, resurrection of the dead.*
> *Come, O Powerful One,*
> *who always creates and recreates and transforms by Your will*
>   *alone.*
> *Come, O invisible and totally intangible and impalpable.*
> *Come, You who always remain motionless*
> *and at each moment move completely and come to us, asleep in*
>   *hell,*
> *O, You, above all the heavens.*

Come, O beloved Name and repeated everywhere,
but of whom it is absolutely forbidden for us to express the existence
*   or to know the nature.*
Come, eternal joy. Come, non-tarnishing crown.
Come, purple of the great king our God.
Come crystalline cincture, studded with precious stones.
Come, inaccessible sandal. Come, royal purple.
Come, truly sovereign right hand.
Come, You whom my miserable soul has desired and desires.
Come, You the Lonely, to the lonely, since You see I am lonely.
Come, You who have separated me from everything and made me
*   solitary in this world.*
Come, You who have become Yourself desire in me,
who have made me desire You, You, the absolutely
*   inaccessible one.*
Come, my breath and my life.
Come, consolation of my poor soul.
Come, my joy, my glory, my endless delight.[55]

Notes

1. Valentine Zander, *St. Seraphim of Sarov* (Crestwood, NY: St. Vladimir's Seminary Press, 1999).

2. Ibid., 85.

3. Paul Endokimov, "Saint Seraphim of Sarov: An Icon of Orthodox Spirituality," *Ecumenical Review* 15 (1963): 264–78.

4. Thomas Hopko, "Holy Spirit in Orthodox Theology and Life," *Commonweal* (Nov. 8, 1968): 188.

5. Basil the Great, *De Spiritu Sancto* (On the Holy Spirit), trans. Blomfield Jackson, in *St. Basil: Letters and Select Works*, Nicene and Post-Nicene Fathers, Second Series, 8 (Peabody, MA: Hendrickson, 1995), 1–50.

6. John McIntyre, "The Holy Spirit in Greek Patristic Thought," *Scottish Journal of Theology* 7 (1954): 367.

7. Ivan Michailovitch Kontzevitch, *The Acquisition of the Holy Spirit in Ancient Russia* (Platina, CA: St. Herman of Alaska Brotherhood, 1996).

8. "The essence of asceticism amounts to the struggle with thoughts" (Kontzevitch, *Acquisition*, 39). The tradition refers to different moments or stages in the development of a thought. Kontzevitch speaks of six stages, although they are easily reducible to three (pp. 39–43). Kyriacos C. Markides (*The Mountain of Silence* [New York: Doubleday, 2001], 115–46), identifies five stages in the development of logismoi. Also see Tomás Spidlík, *The Spirituality of the Christian East* (Kalamazoo: Cistercian Publications, 1986), 237–47.

9. See John Cassian, *The Institutes*, trans. Boniface Ramsey, Ancient Christian Writers 58 (New York: Newman Press, 2000), 113–279; idem, *The Conferences*, trans. Boniface Ramsey, Ancient Christian Writers 57 (New York: Paulist Press, 1997), fifth conference, pp. 177–209. Cassian speaks of eight principal vices, following the classification of Evagrius before him. Gregory the Great in the West reduced the list to seven. See Morton W. Bloomfield, "The Origin and the Concept of the Seven Cardinal Sins," *Harvard Theological Review* 34 (1941): 121–28; Spidlík, *Spirituality of the Christian East*, 248–56; Kallistos Ware, "Introduction" in John Climacus, *The Ladder of Divine Ascent*, Classics of Western Spirituality (New York: Paulist Press, 1982), 62–66.

10. This is the Jesus Prayer. See Kallistos Ware, *The Power of the Name: The Jesus Prayer in Orthodox Spirituality* (Oxford: SLG Press, 1996); and Alphonse Goettmann and Rachel Goettmann, *Prayer of Jesus, Prayer of the Heart* (Greenwood, IN: Inner Life Publications, 1996). Also see Spidlík, *Spirituality of the Christian East*, 315–20.

11. Konzevitch writes, "This ascetic endeavor is also known under various other names, giving it other shades of meaning: '*podvig* and labor of the mind' (St. Marcarius the Great, St. John Cassian), 'focusing oneself in one place' (St. Isaac the Syrian, St. Basil the Great) or else 'self-concentration,' 'concentration within' (Bishop Theophan the Recluse), 'inward activity' (Ancient Patericon, Bishop Theophan the Recluse), 'activity of the heart' (Bishop Theophan the Recluse), 'hidden activity,' 'spiritual activity' (St. Hesychius)" (*Acquisition*, 49). On this attentiveness of the mind, see especially Nicephorus the Solitary and St. Gregory of Sinai, in *Writings from*

the Philokalia on Prayer of the Heart, trans. E. Kadloubovsky and G. E. H. Palmer (London: Faber & Faber, 1973), 21–96.

12. Kontzevitch, *Acquisition*, 63–76. Also see John Cassian, *Conferences*, 90–102, on the role of the elder; as well as Ware, "Introduction," in John Climacus, *Ladder of Divine Ascent*, 36–42.

13. Archimandrite Cyprian, "Spiritual Predecessors of Gregory Palamas," in *Theological Thought* (Paris, 1942), 3, cited in Kontzevitch, *Acquisition*, 56 n. 14.

14. Ware, "Introduction," in John Climacus, *Ladder of Divine Ascent*, 48–54. Also see *Merton and Hesychasm: The Prayer of the Heart*, ed. Bernadette Dieker and Jonathan Montaldo (Louisville: Fons Vitae, 2003).

15. Gregory Palamas, *The Triads*, ed. and introduced by John Meyendorff, Classics of Western Spirituality (New York: Paulist Press, 1983), 1–22.

16. Ibid., 57–92. On deification in Orthodox spirituality, see Spidlík, *Spirituality of the Christian East*, 44–47.

17. Gregory Palamas, *Triads*, 39.

18. On apophatic theology, see Denys Turner, *The Darkness of God: Negativity in Christian Mysticism* (Cambridge: Cambridge University Press, 1995).

19. Meyendorff, "Introduction," in Gregory Palamas, *Triads*, 14.

20. Gregory Palamas, *Triads*, 41–55.

21. Translated in John Meyendorff, *St. Gregory Palamas and Orthodox Spirituality* (Crestwood, NY: St. Vladimir's Seminary Press, 1974), 59–60. Also in Nicephorus the Solitary, "A Most Profitable Discourse on Sobriety and the Guarding of the Heart," in *Writings from the Philokalia on Prayer of the Heart*, 33.

22. Spidlík, *Spirituality of the Christian East*, 103–7. What is often referred to as "heart" in Orthodox spirituality is what I often name "spirit."

23. See Donald J. Goergen, *Jesus: Son of God, Son of Mary, Immanuel* (Collegeville, MN: Liturgical Press; reprint, Eugene, OR: Wipf & Stock, 1995), 40–53.

24. Duncan Reid, *Energies of the Spirit: Trinitarian Models in Eastern Orthodox and Western Theology* (Atlanta: Scholars Press, 1997), 26. Also see George Maloney, *A Theology of Uncreated Energies* (Milwaukee, WI: Marquette University Press, 1978).

25. Meyendorff, "Introduction," in Gregory Palamas, *Triads*, 138 n. 7.

26. Gregory Palamas, *Triads*, 88.

27. Georges Florovsky, "The Concept of Creation in Saint Athanasius," *Studia Patristica* 81 (1962): 36–57; idem, "The Idea of Creation in Christian Philosophy," *Eastern Churches Quarterly* 8 (1949): 53–77. See also Reid, *Energies*, 34–46. Vladimir Lossky, *In the Image and Likeness of God* (New York: St. Vladimir's Seminary Press, 1974); idem, *The Mystical Theology of the Eastern Church* (New York: St. Vladimir's Seminary Press, 1976). John Meyendorff, *Byzantine Theology: Historical Trends and Doctrinal Themes* (New York: Fordham University Press, 1976); idem, *Christ in Eastern Christian Thought* (New York: St. Vladimir's Seminary Press, 1975); idem, *St. Gregory Palamas and Orthodox Spirituality* (New York: St. Vladimir's Seminary Press, 1974). See also George Maloney, *A History of Orthodox Theology since 1453* (Belmont, MA: Nordland, 1976).

28. Lossky, *Mystical Theology of the Eastern Church*, 66.

29. Dumitru Staniloae, "The Role of the Holy Spirit in the Theology and Life of the Orthodox Church," *Diakonia* 9 (1974): 344–45.

30. Ibid., 351, 352, 356–57.

31. On the mystic as theologian, Symeon the New Theologian, and Palamas, see Jaroslav Pelikan, *The Spirit of Eastern Christendom (600–1700)* (Chicago: University of Chicago Press, 1974), 254–70.

32. See Symeon the New Theologian, *The Discourses*, trans. C. J. de Catanzaro, Classics of Western Spirituality (New York: Paulist Press, 1980); Basil Krivocheine, *In the Light of Christ: Saint Symeon the New Theologian*, trans. Anthony P. Gythiel (New York: St. Vladimir's Seminary Press, 1986); Donald J. Goergen, *The Jesus of Christian History* (Collegeville, MN: Liturgical Press, 1992; reprint, Eugene, OR: Wipf & Stock, 1992), 167–80.

33. From a letter of St. Symeon; see Krivocheine, *In the Light of Christ*, 135.

34. Symeon the New Theologian, *Hymns of Divine Love*, trans. George A. Maloney (Denville, NJ: Dimension Books, 1976), 40.

35. Symeon the New Theologian, *Discourses*, 341–42.

36. Symeon the New Theologian, "Against Those Who Try to Theologize Without the Spirit," the Second Theological Discourse, in *The Practical and Theological Chapters and the Three Theological Discourses*, trans. Paul McGurkin (Kalamazoo: Cistercian Publications, 1982), 123–33; and idem, "On Partaking of the Holy Spirit," Discourse 33, in *Discourses*, 339–46.

37. Symeon the New Theologian, *Hymns of Divine Love*, 15, 26, 27, 29, 30, 34, 45, 53–55, 192, 204, 228, 230, 254, 260, 264, 277; *Discourses*, 146–148, 154, 162, 195, 217, 236, 263, 291, 336–38, 350–353; *Practical and Theological Chapters*, 34, 50, 56, 89, 95, 99, 136.

38. Symeon the New Theologian, *Hymns of Divine Love*, 228.

39. Symeon the New Theologian, *The Practical and Theological Chapters*, 82.

40. Symeon the New Theologian, *Discourses*, 54, 70–89, 148, 158–62, 264, 313–15. On tears, see Ware, "Introduction," in John Climacus, *The Ladder of Divine Ascent*, 23–27.

41. Or Pseudo-Macarius. His precise identity is unknown. See George A. Maloney, "Introduction," to Pseudo-Macarius, *The Fifty Spiritual Homilies and the Great Letter*, Classics of Western Spirituality (New York: Paulist Press, 1992). The homilies have been dated to the 380s.

42. Pseudo-Macarius, 56 (homily 4), 143 (homily 18), 199 (homily 32).

43. Ibid., 145 (homily 18).

44. Ibid., 192 (homily 30).

45. Krivocheine, *In the Light of Christ*, 263.

46. Symeon the New Theologian, *Practical and Theological Chapters*, 84.

47. Symeon the New Theologian, *Discourses*, 366.

48. "Perhaps the same thought is expressed more clearly for us by Luke, who, when he desires the Kingdom to come, implores the help of the Holy Spirit. For he says in his Gospel; instead of *Thy Kingdom come* it reads 'May Thy Holy Spirit come upon us and purify us.'" From Gregory

of Nyssa, *The Lord's Prayer*, Ancient Christian Writers 18 (Westminster, MD: Newman Press, 1954), 52, also 187 n. 69; from sermon 3, pp. 45–56.

49. "...'Thy Kingdom come,' that is to say, the Holy Spirit..." From Maximus Confessor, "Commentary on the Our Father," in *Selected Writings*, Classics of Western Spirituality (New York: Paulist Press, 1985), 107 #4.

50. See Endokimov, "Saint Seraphim of Sarov," 273; Hopko, "Holy Spirit in Orthodox Theology," 186; Meyendorff, *Byzantine Theology*, 169.

51. See the first and third theological discourses in Symeon the New Theologian, *Practical and Theological Chapters*, 107–22, 134–40.

52. Basil the Great, *De Spiritu Sancto*.

53. Staniloae, "Role of the Holy Spirit," 343.

54. Endokimov, "Saint Seraphim of Sarov," 271.

55. Symeon the New Theologian, *Hymns of Divine Love*, 9.

Chapter Eleven
INTERIORITY AND EXTERIORITY

The process of "acquiring" the Holy Spirit, of becoming aware of the Spirit's deep omnipresence, this process calls us to integrate our lives and the world of which we are a part, our inner being and the outer world. How do we come to that level of integration where inhaling and exhaling, interiority and exteriority, are one? Each of us is called to holiness. Each of us has a vocation in life. Frederick Buechner wrote about vocation as follows:

> Vocation comes from the Latin *vocare*, to call, and means the work a person is called to by God. There are all different kinds of voices calling you to all different kinds of work, and the problem is to find out which is the voice of God rather than of Society, say, or the Superego, or Self-Interest. By and large a good rule for finding out is this. The kind of work God usually calls you to is the kind of work (a) that you need most to do and (b) that the world most needs to have done. If you really get a kick out of your work, you've presumably met requirement (a), but if your work is writing TV deodorant commercials, the chances are you've missed requirement (b). On the other hand, if your work is being a doctor in a leper colony, you have probably met requirement (b), but if most of the time you're bored and depressed by it, the chances are you have not only bypassed (a) but probably aren't helping your patients much either. Neither the hair shirt nor the soft berth will do. The place God calls you to is the place where your deep gladness and the world's deep hunger meet.[1]

A Person's Deep Gladness

There is something within the human person that longs for something more. We call it by various names: a holy longing,[2] an ache for the infinite,[3] an openness to the transcendent,[4] or simply yearning for love (1 Thess 2:8). There is a sense of incompleteness about ourselves and an awareness that we are not whole by ourselves alone. We are structured for the other, and it is only an infinite Other that can fully satisfy what is an infinite desire.[5] This desire manifests itself as a quest for wholeness, for holiness, for Spirit. We are aware that there is something missing in life, and we often look for it in the wrong places—not that all the places are wrong; they are just the wrong places for satiating this thirst for Spirit.

Monks or nuns, vowed religious women and men, sannyasi and bodhisattvas are, in the end, no different from the rest of us. They have simply made their quest more visible so that it becomes something we can identify. The interior becomes exterior. They are transparent. This longing, seeking, yearning comes from a depth within our inner selves, and its satisfaction is the deepest joy imaginable, a gladness or delight for which we have been created. We recall Jesus' words to his disciples, "I have said these things to you so that my joy may be in you, and that your joy may be complete" (John 15:11).

This quest is rightly called mystical. Even though we do not ordinarily think of ourselves as mystics, that is what we are called to be. Mysticism is not something only for a chosen few. Evelyn Underhill (1875–1941) wrote, "Mysticism, in its pure form, is the science of ultimates, the science of union with the Absolute, and nothing else, and the mystic is the person who attains to this union, not the person who talks about it."[6] Raimon Panikkar, drawing upon his interreligious background, speaks about mysticism as the narrative of experience.[7]

The language in which we talk about mysticism does not communicate the experience itself. The experience cannot be imaged, even though the mind may attempt to translate the experience into concepts or images. Mystical experiences take place in the pneumatic core of one's being and are more often than not associated with emptiness and darkness, the Buddhist's *sunnyata* and John of the Cross's dark nights. To the mind and mental faculties the mystical experience is dark—devoid of mental comprehension.[8] There is also a purification of the soul, the psychic dimension of our being, as one comes to face one's shadow or dark side. William Johnston writes:

> In the shadow lie all the parts of our personality that we have repressed or refused to face. Here lie the fears and anxieties, the frustrations and the traumas, the hurts and the resentments that we accumulated when we were children and even when we slept in our mother's womb. Here lies the terrible fear of death we have never confronted. How great is the darkness that lies dormant in the human psyche!

And he continues:

> But if we follow St. John of the Cross we see that something very wonderful is happening. God himself is surfacing in the soul. It is as though the God who dwells in the depth of one's being is (if I may be permitted a crude anthropomorphism) pushing to the surface all the inner garbage and darkness in order that a thorough purification may take place. That is why St. John of the Cross can speak of this night as "dark contemplation" and, when it is all over, he can ecstatically sing, "O night more lovely than the dawn."[9]

Religious institutions and churches sometimes fear mysticism. Given its nature as direct experience, it undermines an understanding of authority as belonging exclusively to the institution. The *ecclesia* is the locus of Spirit, but the mystic has direct contact with the selfsame Spirit. How can you keep them down in the churches once they've been in the mind of God! The challenge for the churches is to see mysticism as an ally and not as a threat. The same Spirit is the source of each. Ecclesial and mystical life are not in opposition to each other but, rather, complementary.

Doctrine and dogma in themselves are good. Like the dharma in Asian religious traditions, they are the teaching, the way. But one can absolutize them, canonize them to the exclusion of other aspects of the spiritual life. Doctrine need not be presented with a dogmatic attitude, not even dogma in its technical sense.[10] Doctrine is different from dogmatism. The former presents mystical truth; the latter stifles the quest for truth.

Twentieth-century Western portraits of Jesus spoke about Jesus the prophet and interpreted Jesus in prophetic categories. But just as there is the prophetic Christ, so there is the mystical Christ.[11] In Jesus, prophecy and mysticism come together with the awareness that we cannot have one without the other. This aspect of Jesus, his self-identity as a Son of God who is aware that he and the Father are one, who, according to Thomas Aquinas, possesses on his earthly pilgrimage the vision of God or beatific vision, is a Jesus with whom we may be less familiar, whom we dismiss as a later theological development, without plumbing the pneumatic depths of Jesus himself as a man of the Spirit. For Christians, Jesus is "the archetypal mystic."[12]

William Ernest Hocking posited two selves, an excursive self and a reflective self, or, one might say, an extroverted self turned outward toward the world and an introverted self.[13] What the mystic has learned is that there is more to me than my self alone, that I am a part of all, that all is a part of me, that there is another Self that is my true Self, and that this *other* Self truly is *my* Self. "Inside" and "outside" disappear. A mystic's cosmic consciousness is neither inside nor outside anything. The diaphanous character of life in the Spirit reveals that the inside is outside and the outside is inside. There is no us and no them. There is only the One for whom there is no interior or exterior. That is the One I seek. That is the One I am. That is the Spirit who is the source of both mysticism and prophecy. The prophet is a God-experienced, God-conscious, God-intoxicated person, and the mystic is one who loves the world, all God's creatures, all humankind without distinction.

In the Hebrew Scriptures, the mystical journey is grounded in the *Shema:* "Hear, O Israel: The LORD is our God, the LORD alone. You shall love the LORD your God with all your heart, and with all your soul, and with all your might" (Deut 6:4–5). Likewise for Christians, following after Jesus or imitating Christ or "doing what Jesus would do" begins where Jesus began: with his heavenly Father. Jesus' love of God manifested an incomparable intimacy with the divine. The great commandment for Jesus remained the *Shema.* In Islam and the Qur'an, al-Llah, the all-merciful, the all-compassionate, is the one before whom we must all be muslims. There is but one God for the Jewish, Christian, and Muslim peoples, and that God is the God of Israel, the God of Jesus Christ, and the God of Muhammad his messenger, although the understanding of that one God may vary.

In Asian religious traditions, the One is approached not so much or so often in personal terms, although personal deities there are, but rather simply as that which is beyond any name. As the Tao Te Ching states:

> The Tao that can be told is not the eternal Tao.
> The name that can be named is not the eternal name.[14]

In Christian terms, the One beyond all names remains *agapē*, the divine lover. The twelfth-century Indian Vaishnavite poet Tukaram captures that same Spirit in personal terms.

> O save me, save me, Mightiest,
>   Save me and set me free.
> O let the love that fills my breast
>   Cling to thee lovingly.
> Grant me to taste how sweet thou art;
>   Grant me but this, I pray,

And never shall my love depart
   Or turn from thee away.
Then I thy name shall magnify
   And tell thy praise abroad,
For very love and gladness I
   Shall dance before my God.[15]

One of the great challenges facing religion and spirituality in the twenty-first century is an integration of interiority and exteriority. A dualistic consciousness has defined them over against each other. The more interior my journey or call, the less committed to the future of the earth I am, the less socially engaged, the less mindful of social injustice. Or the more committed I am to a new heaven and a new earth, to a more just social order, to the future of this world, the less called I am to undertake the journey within. Prophecy, yes; mysticism, no, or vice versa. We have dichotomized what needs to be made whole. We have all been made less whole because of it.

In theistic terms our consciousness of the One is often articulated in terms of transcendence and immanence. God is at one and the same time both transcendent and immanent. It is easy to misplace emphasis to one side or the other. In the end, however, there is no difference between the two. There are not two modes of God's being. The Immanent One is the Transcendent One and vice versa. The One could not be completely, deeply immanent without being transcendent, or transcendent without being immanent. Only a nondualistic consciousness can perceive the unity that the One is. In mental categories we often tend to see them in opposition—immanence versus transcendence. They are not opposed because they are not two. This is the mystery of the eternal godhead that is both everywhere and nowhere—everywhere, otherwise it would not be supreme, but nowhere, because there is no "where" there, no space or time when we talk about eternity and infinity.

Likewise, in a fashion paradoxical to the discursive intellect, the true Self is not many, not one. The true Self is One, the only One, the only true Self there is. But the Self is also manifest as many selves, although each of those selves is in truth the one Self.

The ground of my soul, the ground of my being, is the Ground of All Being, and that ground is both many and one. To a nondual awareness it could not be other. In a dualistic consciousness we contrast and oppose the many and the one. But the One could not be one without being the many, and the many could not be many without being the One. There is no contradiction, simply a different state of awareness required than that in which our ordinary egoistic minds live and move. This is mystical awareness, cosmic consciousness, experiential knowledge that the Father and I are one, that Brahman is Atman, that it is now not I but an Other who lives within me, that my holy spirit is the temple of God's Spirit.

This mystic consciousness, this acquisition of the Holy Spirit requires personal transformation, a deification of the person whose source of life and activity becomes God's Spirit. God's Spirit and my Spirit are the selfsame Spirit, although in an untransformed state of consciousness I am unaware of who I truly am. This transformation of consciousness is not a mental or affective or psychic transformation, although it must be all of these. At its core it is pneumatic transformation—a spiritual consciousness, pure awareness.[16] When I live permanently in that state of awareness, my joy will be complete (John 15:11).

I do not know anymore who first said, "Joy is the infallible sign of the presence of God." The interior journey through darkness and emptiness, however, culminates in a deep gladness, an incredible joy, an indescribable delight. St. Paul placed joy high on the list of the fruits that come from living in the Spirit: love, joy, peace, patience, kindness, generosity, faithfulness, gentleness, and self-control (Gal 5:22). Isaiah too envisioned a day that could only be characterized by rejoicing on the part of the meek and the lowly (Isa 29:18–19).

The association of joy with the Holy Spirit has been emphasized by the Rumanian Orthodox theologian Dumitru Staniloae, for whom the Holy Spirit is "the joy of God."[17] The joy of the First Person in the Trinity delighting in the Second and of the Second taking delight in the First is manifested in the joy that is the Holy

Spirit. As the Spirit in the theologies of Augustine and Aquinas is the mutual love of the Father and the Son, so we might say that the Spirit is their mutual joy.

God also takes delight in creation. "Delight" is also a translation of the Sanskrit word *ananda*, which we find in the Hindu name for God: *sat-chit-ananda*, or being-consciousness-delight. This third quality in the Hindu trinity, namely, *ananda* or bliss or delight, captures the Christian sense of the Holy Spirit as the delight that God is: the joy of Being Itself. Being-awareness-joy is the threefold state in which we find ourselves in our spiritual journeys through life. We are, and that is sufficient. We need not be more or other. God takes delight just in our being. I do not have to be something or someone. I just have to be. But to be requires being aware that I am, a contemplative awareness. To be and to be aware are one. Being and awareness are interchangeable. In Christian terms, God not only *is*, but God is also Logos, self-aware, pure awareness. This awareness is bliss. In terms of Indian philosophies, unhappiness results from ignorance. Ignorance creates illusions. But a process of dis-illusioning, as painful, dark, and empty as it may sometimes feel or seem, can only end up in deeper awareness, greater contact with the real, the joy of just being. Nothing has to be other than what it is, for our delight is in what is and not what is not. To learn this we pass through valleys of darkness until we see the great Light.

The World's Deep Hunger

For Jesus, as for his Jewish heritage, there is nothing in human life more important than love of God. Yet Jesus instructs us that there is something of equal importance.

So when you are offering your gift at the altar, if you remember that your brother or sister has something against you, leave your gift there before the altar and go;

first be reconciled to your brother or sister, and then come and offer your gift. (Matt 5:23–24)

As important as worship is, equally important is love of neighbor, the works of mercy (Matt 25:31–46).

This is an enduring teaching in the Judeo-Christian tradition and in its mystical traditions as well. Christian mystics never lost sight of the centrality of love of neighbor in Jesus' teaching. Their emphasis on this could hardly be more emphatic. Central in the spiritual teaching of St. Catherine of Siena is God's compassionate, ineffable, merciful, incomprehensible, unutterable love.[18] Nevertheless, for Catherine there is no virtue more important than charity, which comprises both love of God and love of neighbor.[19] For Catherine, love of God cannot exist without love of one's neighbor, and love of one's neighbor cannot exist without love of God.[20]

In the Orthodox tradition, Symeon the New Theologian made this same point.

When we are commanded to consider our neighbor as ourself, this does not mean for just one day, but all through life. When a man is told to give to all who ask, he is told to do this for all of his days. If a man wants people to do good to him, he himself will be required to do good to others. When a man really considers a neighbor as himself, he will never tolerate having more than his neighbor. If he does have more, but refuses to share things generously until he himself becomes as poor as his neighbor, then he will find that he has not fulfilled the commandment of the master. He no longer wants to give to all who ask, and instead turns away from someone who asks of him while he still has a penny or a crust of bread. He has not treated his neighbor as he would like to be treated by him. In fact, even if a man had given food and drink and clothes to all the poor, even the least, and had done everything else for them, he has only to despise or neglect a single one and it will be reckoned as

191

if he had passed by Christ and God when He was hungry and thirsty.[21]

The text may sound too demanding, or one may say that Symeon is speaking here to those called to monastic life, but the fact remains that the mystic never sees mysticism as a love of God that is in opposition to love of neighbor but, rather, sees the prophetic biblical emphases as essential to what mysticism is all about. Louis Massignon, an expert on Sufi mysticism, has written in a similar fashion. "The mystic call is as a rule the result of an inner rebellion of the conscience against social injustices, not only those of others but primarily and particularly against one's own faults: with a desire intensified by inner purification to find God at any price."[22]

This call to action, this demand to include the other within one's circle of love, this radical solidarity with all creation, all as an expression of one's love for God and the mystical quest, is well expressed in a meditation dated May 16, 1914, by the Mother of the Sri Aurobindo Ashram.

> I was interrupted yesterday just when I was trying to for-mulate the experience I had. And now everything seems changed. That precise knowledge, that clear-sightedness has given place to a great love for Thee, O Lord, which has seized my whole being from the outer organism to the deepest consciousness, and all lies prostrate at Thy feet in an ardent aspiration for a definitive identification with Thee, an absorption in Thee. I implored Thee with all the energy I could summon. And once again, just when it seemed to me that my consciousness was going to disappear in Thine, just when all my being was noth-ing but a pure crystal reflecting Thy Presence, someone came and interrupted my concentration. Such is, indeed, the symbol of the existence Thou givest me as my share, in which outer usefulness, the work for all, holds a much greater place even than the supreme realisation. All the circumstances of my life seem always to tell me on Thy

behalf: "It is not through supreme concentration that thou wilt realise oneness, it is by spreading out in all." May Thy will be done, O Lord.[23]

Enlightenment becomes compassion and compassion is enlightenment.

This same concern is manifest in socially engaged Buddhism.[24] Compassion and a respect for all sentient creatures are at the heart of the Buddha's teaching. Enlightenment is not complete without compassionate action. Engaged Buddhists recognize universal interdependence, the web of life, and the universe as an organic whole. For the Buddhist this has always implied the path of *ahimsa*, or nonviolence. Since we are one, all violence is self-inflicted violence.

The Way of the Buddha is not one of indifference to the world and one's neighbors but rather one of nonattachment: to see clearly without clinging. This perspective is manifest in the spiritual doctrine of the *Bhagavad Gita*, a spiritual classic for both Hindus and Buddhists. Krishna instructs Arjuna thus:

> Set thy heart upon thy work, but never on its reward. Work not for a reward; but never cease to do thy work.
>
> Do thy work in the peace of Yoga and, free from selfish desires, be not moved in success or in failure. Yoga is evenness of mind—a peace that is ever the same.
>
> Work done for a reward is much lower than work done in the Yoga of wisdom. Seek salvation in the wisdom of reason. How poor those who work for a reward!
>
> In this wisdom one goes beyond what is well done and what is not well done. Go thou therefore to wisdom: Yoga is wisdom in work.[25]

I often return to Sri Aurobindo's dictum: All life is yoga.[26] There can be no separation between inner work and outer work. Interiority and exteriority are mutually dependent. Depth and breadth are interconnected. The wider one's reach, the deeper one

must go, and the deeper one goes, the more expansive one's out-
look. We cannot separate God and the world. They are not two;
neither are they one. This "integral yoga" is manifest in its own
way in two contrasting Catholic thinkers: Edward Schillebeeckx
and Pope John Paul II.

For Schillebeeckx, love and holiness are "political."[27] For
those whose spiritual path is one of following after Jesus, this following is an orthopraxis, the praxis of Jesus, the praxis of the reign
of God. God's concern, as manifest in Jesus and the prophetic tradition of which Jesus was a part, is creation and humankind. The
prophet speaks out of an experience of contrast between God's
goodness and the history of excessive suffering in our world. The
prophet experiences God's no to this suffering. The praxis of the
reign of God is our own no to suffering and injustice. Jesus' understanding of holiness opposes injustice because injustice distorts our
understanding of God.

In the spiritual life, there is therefore both "a political dimension" and "a mystical dimension." The relationship between mysticism and politics is rooted in an experience of contrast between
who God is and the story of a suffering humanity. The "spiritual"
life cannot be reduced to "personal holiness." Nor can social and
political life be reduced to social and political components alone.
For Schillebeeckx, "mysticism" is an intense form of the experience
of God. "Politics" is an intense form of social engagement. Politics
without mysticism becomes barbaric; mysticism without political
love becomes sentimental interiority. Moses, a political leader who
brought his people liberation, was a mystic "who spoke to God face
to face" (Exod 33:11).

What Schillebeeckx refers to as "political love," John Paul II
called "the virtue of solidarity."[28] On John Paul's second papal visit
to Poland, in June 1983, he spoke the politically volatile word in
Czestochowa as he affirmed the "fundamental solidarity between
human beings"[29] as a basic principle of social renewal. On his third
pilgrimage to Poland in June of 1987, he returned to this theme as
he visited cities on the Baltic coast.

The seas speak to peoples about the need to find themselves together....*It speaks of the need for solidarity,* both
between human beings and among nations. It is an
important reality that *the term "solidarity"* was *expressed
right here before the Polish sea.* It is a profound reality that
was pronounced here in a new way, with a new meaning
that concerns its eternal significance. Here, along the
shore of the Baltic Sea, I too pronounce this word, this
term "solidarity," because it is an essential part of the *consistent message of the Church's social teaching....*[30]

And later, in Gdansk, a city that he had insisted be on this itinerary,
forbidden to him on the previous journey, he said, "Solidarity
means: *one another,* and if there is a burden, then *this burden is carried together,* in community. Thus: *never one against another.* Never
one group against another, and never a 'burden' carried by one
alone, without the help of others."[31]

This theme of solidarity was given a wider audience in Pope
John Paul's second social encyclical, *Sollicitudo Rei Socialis* (On Social
Concern),[32] issued February 19, 1988, dated December 30, 1987,
since it was intended to mark the twentieth anniversary of Pope Paul
VI's social encyclical *Populorum Progressio* (The Development of
Peoples). Section 5 of the encyclical moves to a moral and theologi-
cal analysis of economic, political, and ecological concerns, in which
he developed his understanding of this virtue of solidarity.

[Solidarity] then is not a feeling of vague compassion or
shallow distress at the misfortunes of so many people,
both near and far. On the contrary, it is a firm and per-
severing determination to commit oneself to the common good; that is to say to the good of all and of each
individual, because we are all really responsible for all.
This determination is based on the solid conviction that
what is hindering full development is that desire for
profit and that thirst for power already mentioned.[33]

Both Schillebeeckx and John Paul II see an inseparable inter-connectedness between love of God and love of neighbor, as did mystics and prophets of old. There is in the universe a rhythm between inhaling and exhaling, between interiority and exteriority, between interior liberation or enlightenment and social, political, economic, and ecological movements.

Jesus manifested in his own earthly life and mission this non-dual solidarity—solidarity with God and solidarity with people.[34] Jesus was one with the poor and one with the God of the poor. The poor, the outcast, the sinful were his other self: Whatever you do to the least of my brothers or sisters you do unto me (Matt 25:40). If there is any teaching from Jesus that rings true for all the religions of the world, it is that of the beatitudes in Matthew's Sermon on the Mount (Matt 5:3–10).

Each of us is a child of God and a child of the earth. Each is called to be a servant of God and a servant of humanity. We are all daughters and sons of God and daughters and sons of humanity. There is our deepest Self and our universal, cosmic body—one Self, one body. Liberation is both an interior liberation from our personal patterns of sinfulness and the exterior liberation of our world from its structures of sin. True liberation addresses both the personal and the social, not one at the expense of the other. Nor does one emphasis need to be more "Eastern" and the other more "Western."

> The two approaches, interiority and liberation, can be interpreted to offer a mutually inclusive dynamic. The interiority process is widened by the dynamism of active social involvement, while the social concerns are deepened by the inner realization of the unity of all reality. In other words, the mystic experience and the prophetic witness meet and fuse. This approach of mutual interaction between the interiority-process and the liberative-praxis offers us a new way of experiencing the reality without opposing or dichotomizing eastern and western ways.[35]

Denys Turner, in his exploration of the apophatic traditions in Christian spirituality, focuses on the images or metaphors of inwardness and ascent in the journey of the soul to God.[36] Just as the "without" and the "within" must be held in balance with each other, for one does not grow without the other, nor even exist apart from the other, so likewise with the "below" and the "above." They are to be held in harmony or at least in creative tension. In a similar fashion, for Turner, are the metaphors of inwardness and ascent. One leads to the other. He writes, in reflecting on Augustine's *De Trinitate:*

> My true selfhood is my interiority. And, as we saw, that place where the self and interiority intersect opens out to the God, the eternal light of Truth, who is *above.* The *itinerarium intus* is also an *ascensio superius.* The two metaphors of inwardness and ascent themselves intersect at the point where God and the self intersect, so that that which is most interior to me is also that which is above and beyond me; so that the God who is within me is also the God I am in.[37]

In other words, "'Within' is 'above.'"[38]

Integral Prayer: The Prayer of Martha

As a guide to the integration of one's interior journey with the demands from our external world for justice and peace, I choose Eckhart and Eckhart's interpretation of Martha in a sermon on the text from Luke (10:38).[39] Traditionally Martha had been seen as the exemplar of an active life and Mary of a contemplative life. For Eckhart, there was in Mary, to be sure, an unspeakable longing for God. Martha, nevertheless, manifested a more matured spirituality. When Martha says of Mary, "Lord, tell her to help me," it was said out of concern for Mary. Was Mary too attached to spiritual consolations? Christ was not rebuking Martha but reassuring her that Mary would come eventually to the spiritual maturity out of which

Martha now lived. A mature spirituality engages the world and does not withdraw from it. A truly Spirit-filled person, grounded in the ground of her soul but active in the world, is living a deep communion with God. Martha is not simply "in the world," she is present in the world in a different, grounded way.

Martha was maturely grounded, which grounding is put to the test in our presence to the world. This is at the core of Eckhart's appreciation of Martha. Martha was afraid that Mary would not come to the place where contemplation overflows into action, where the world's deep hunger and our own deep gladness intersect. Martha was so well grounded that her activities were not a hindrance to her; Mary was not yet so well grounded that she could take the risk of leaving her sitting. Mary had in one sense been a "Martha" of the popularly understood sort before becoming Mary, but now was being grounded more deeply in order that she might truly be a Martha, an integrated spiritual person living in the world and for the world, but in a world with both horizontal and vertical dimensions, with both a within and a without, with both personal and socially responsible dimensions. For Eckhart, to be free of the concerns of the world is neither possible nor desirable. What is possible and necessary is that our presence to the world be grounded in deeply contemplative living. As Bernard McGinn indicates, "Eckhart broke through the traditional distinction between the active life and contemplative life…creating a new model of sanctity…."[40]

We start out as Marthas in the commonly understood sense in our spiritual lives, sometimes rather smugly thinking that we can save the world, and when called to integrate Mary we flee and fail to progress toward being the mature Martha of Eckhart's understanding. One cannot become a spiritually mature Martha by bypassing interiority and jumping too quickly into exteriority. The contemplative dimension of life is not a life of leisure and spiritual consolation but, rather, a radical confrontation with one's false self, one's narcissism, one's emptiness and nothingness. C. G. Jung emphasized that "meditation" requires coming to terms with the unconscious, which means with one's shadow, which is usually a fundamental contrast to our conscious personality; and that the firstfruit of confronting this shadow is melancholy. This, for Jung, is the beginning of the *magnum opus*. If one stops here one will never get beyond this "dangerous impasse."[41] It is simply a reminder that a descent into hell must precede the ascension into heaven.

The Martha of Eckhart's understanding stands as a model for us of the possibility of integrating our interior and external worlds, of our world here below with that world beyond sense and sight, of a cosmotheandric, holistic, integral spirituality. Martha gives us hope. It is possible to be whole. Both the within and the without, both the heights and the depths, both the deep gladness and the deep hunger constitute the rhythm of life. And at the core of all is God's Holy Spirit, at the center of my life, as the soul of the church, as an energy at the heart of the cosmos, and at work from within the depths of our world, God's Gift of Love.

> *Holy Spirit, life-giving Breath,*
> *Breath of God, eternal Fire,*
> *Passion supreme, sacred Movement,*
> *delicate Dancer, enveloping Water,*
> *Water within, our indwelling Spirit, our truest Self,*
> *Water without, our divine milieu,*
> *Soul of the universe, heavenly Delight, gift of Joy, omnipresent*
> *   Presence,*
> *Power, Strength, Energy, Love, Lover, Friend,*
> *Creator of diversity, Source of unity,*
> *Oil of gladness, balm for sadness,*
> *Comforter, wise Guide, Spirit of Truth, Life Divine,*
> *we bow in awe and wonder within your Splendor,*
> *You who live in us and we in You forever and ever. Amen.*

Notes

1. Frederick Buechner, *The Alphabet of Grace* (New York: Harper & Row, 1985), 95. The word *man* was changed to *person* for the sake of inclusive language.

2. See Ronald Rolheiser, *The Holy Longing: The Search for a Christian Spirituality* (New York: Doubleday, 1999).

3. Amal Kiran, disciple of Sri Aurobindo. See K. D. Sethna, "Sri Aurobindo and Human Evolution," in *The Vision and Work of Sri Aurobindo* (Pondicherry: Sri Aurobindo Ashram, 1992), 5.

4. Karl Rahner, *Foundations of Christian Faith*, trans. William V. Dych (New York: Seabury Press, 1978), 44–89.

5. Catherine of Siena speaks about "infinite desire." See *The Dialogue*, trans. Suzanne Noffke, Classics of Western Spirituality (New York: Paulist Press, 1980), 28; see also pp. 161–83 on the gift of tears.

6. Evelyn Underhill, *Mysticism: A Study in the Nature and Development of Man's Spiritual Consciousness* (New York: E. P. Dutton, 1961), 72.

7. Raimon Panikkar, "The Mysticism of Jesus the Christ," in *Mysticism in Shaivism and Christianity*, ed. Bettina Baumer (New Delhi: D.K. Print World, 1997), 79.

8. An excellent study of apophaticism and experientialism in mysticism is that of Denys Turner, *The Darkness of God: Negativity in Christian Mysticism* (Cambridge: Cambridge University Press, 1998).

9. William Johnston, *"Arise, My Love…": Mysticism for a New Era* (Maryknoll, NY: Orbis Books, 2000), 103–4.

10. In the Roman Catholic tradition, "doctrine" is used more widely to refer to the ordinary teachings of the Catholic Church, whereas "dogma" is used more strictly to refer to solemnly defined doctrines that must be held, for example, the dogmas of the Trinity, Incarnation, Immaculate Conception of Mary, and so on.

11. See Panikkar, "The Mysticism of Jesus the Christ," 73–178; and Johnston, *Arise*, 179–201.

12. Johnston, *Arise*, 200.

13. William Ernest Hocking, *The Meaning of Immortality in Human Experience* (New York: Harper, 1957), 44–59. See Louis Dupré, "The Mystical Experience of the Self and Its Philosophical Significance," *International Philosophical Quarterly* 14 (1974): 495–511.

14. Lao Tsu, *Tao Te Ching*, trans. Gia-Fu Feng and Jane English (New York: Vintage Books, 1989), 3.

15. In A. C. Bouquet, ed., *Sacred Books of the World* (London: Penguin Books, 1954), 246.

16. Augustine writes in *De Trinitate*, "In the previous book, the twelfth of this work, we had our hands full distinguishing between the function of the rational mind in temporal matters, in which our activity as well as our awareness is engaged, and the superior function of the same mind which is engaged in contemplating eternal things and terminates in awareness alone" (*The Trinity*, trans. Edmund Hill [Brooklyn, NY: New City Press, 1991], 342 [13.1.1]).

17. Dumitrou Staniloae, "The Role of the Holy Spirit in the Theology and Life of the Orthodox Church," *Diakonia* 9 (1974): 343–47 in particular.

18. See *The Prayers of Catherine of Siena*, 2nd ed., trans. and ed. Suzanne Noffke (New York: Authors Choice Press, 2001), 1–38.

19. Catherine of Siena, *The Dialogue*, chap. 160, p. 346.

20. Ibid., chaps. 7, 55, 64, 74 78, pp. 36, 110, 121, 137, 144.

21. Symeon the New Theologian, *The Practical and Theological Chapters, and the Three Theological Discourses*, trans. Paul McGurkin (Kalamazoo: Cistercian Publications, 1982), 102.

22. Louis Massignon, "Tasawwuf," in *First Encyclopaedia of Islam (1913–1936)* (Leiden: E. J. Brill, 1987), 8:682.

23. The Mother, *Prayers and Meditations* (Pondicherry: Sri Aurobindo Ashram, 1979), 142.

24. *The Path of Compassion: Writings on Socially Engaged Buddhism*, ed. Fred Eppsteiner (Berkeley, CA: Parallax Press, 1985). On the Buddha, see also Richard H. Drummond, *Gautama The Buddha: An Essay in Religious Understanding* (Grand Rapids: Eerdmans, 1974).

25. *The Bhagavad Gita* 2:47–50, trans. Juan Mascaró (Baltimore: Penguin Books, 1962), 52.

26. Sri Aurobindo, *The Integral Yoga: Sri Aurobindo's Teaching and Method of Practice* (Pondicherry: Sri Aurobindo Ashram, 1993), 1.

27. The most complete collection of Schillebeeckx's homilies, essays, and lectures in the area of spirituality is found in *God Among Us: The Gospel Proclaimed* (New York: Crossroad, 1983). Schillebeeckx's discussion of God's opposition to human suffering can be found in *Christ* (New York: Seabury Press, 1980), 670–743. His understanding of "political holiness" and the relationship between mysticism and politics as well as liturgy and social justice can be traced in *Christ*, 762–821; *On Christian Faith* (New York: Crossroad, 1987), 47–84; and in *Church: The Human Story of God* (New York: Crossroad, 1990), 66–99, 179–86. For an introduction to the thought of Schillebeeckx, see *The Praxis of the Reign of God*, ed. Mary Catherine Hilkert and Robert Schreiter, 2nd ed. (New York: Fordham University Press, 2002). Also see Erik Borgman, *Edward Schillebeeckx: A Theologian in His History* (New York: Continuum, 2003).

28. On John Paul II, see George Weigel, *Witness to Hope: The Biography of Pope John Paul II* (New York: HarperCollins, 1999).

29. Ibid., 462.

30. Ibid., 546.

31. Ibid., 547.

32. Weigel, *Witness to Hope*, 557–60. For the text of the encyclical, see the Vatican Web site, http://www.vatican.va/holy_father/john_paul_ii/encyclicals/.

33. See "Sollicitudo Rei Socialis," par 38.6–39.7, on the Vatican Web site (see n. 32 above).

34. See Donald Goergen, *The Mission and Ministry of Jesus* (Wilmington, DE: Michael Glazier, 1986; reprint, Eugene, OR: Wipf & Stock, 1986).

35. Xavier Irudayaraj, "Interiority and Liberation," in *Leave the Temple: Indian Paths to Human Liberation*, ed. Felix Wilfred (Maryknoll, NY: Orbis Books, 1992), 123.

36. Denys Turner, *The Darkness of God: Negativity in Christian Mysticism* (Cambridge: Cambridge University Press, 1995).

37. Ibid., 99.

38. Ibid., 100.

39. Meister Eckhart, *Sermons and Treatises*, trans. M. O'C. Walshe, 3 vols. (London: Watkins, 1979), 1:79–90. Also translated in *Meister Eckhart, Teacher and Preacher*, ed. Bernard McGinn, Classics of Western Spirituality (New York: Paulist Press, 1986), 338–45.

40. Bernard McGinn, *The Mystical Thought of Meister Eckhart: The Man from Whom God Hid Nothing* (New York: Crossroad, 2001), 156.

41. C. G. Jung, "Mysterium Coniunctionis," in *The Collected Works of C. G. Jung*, vol. 14, 2nd ed. (Princeton University Press, 1970), 497–533.

Chapter Twelve
GIFT OF LOVE

We have viewed the pervasive presence of the Spirit in God's evolving creation, from within the depths of the human spirit to social and ecological movements in the world. It is a source of both unity and diversity, within the human family, among the religions and spiritualities of the world, in the cosmos itself, as breath and wind, among the prophets and the wise, in Word and sacrament, as the soul of the church, our deepest and truest Self, the goal of our quest, Grace itself, through whom we are divinized and drawn into the divine triune life.

The Holy Spirit as Gift of Love

St. Augustine (354–430) called the Holy Spirit "Gift."[1] St. Luke implied the same (Acts 2:38; 8:20; 10:45; 11:17). Can the Holy Spirit be considered a gift before actually being given? Is the Spirit already gift within the life of the triune God even before the creation of the world? Yves Congar has written, "It is true that the Spirit is only 'given' when there are creatures who are capable of 'possessing' and enjoying him, but at the same time he also proceeds eternally as 'givable' and in this sense, as Gift, so that this can be regarded as one of his attributes and one of his proper names."[2] St. Augustine had suggested the same.[3] The Holy Spirit is God, but the distinctive character of the Holy Spirit is its "givability." There is a relationship between "spirit" and "givability." The more Spirit-filled we are, the more givable we ourselves become.

"Spirit of God" thus connotes God as reaching out, as connecting, as self-giving and givable, as generous and compassionate.

God is God, but God is also Spirit and Word. As Spirit and Word we find in God an openness and freedom toward what is other than God, toward creating that which is other than God. "Spirit" and "Word" orient our understanding of God *ad extra* even if there is nothing that is ultimately "outside" God.

As significant as the name Gift is for the Holy Spirit, equally prominent in the Christian tradition is the name Love. The Holy Spirit has been understood as the bond of love between the Father and the Son, their mutual love, the love of the Father for the Son and the love of the Son for the Father. Already within the inner life of God, even before there is a history of salvation, the Holy Spirit *is* Love.

If there is any insight central to the New Testament, it is that God is love. The First Letter of John says explicitly, "Whoever does not love does not know God; for God is love"; and "So we have known and believe the love that God has for us. God is love, and those who abide in love abide in God, and God abides in them" (1 John 4:8, 16). As the doctrine of the Trinity developed in the early church, love as an attribute of God became particularly associated with the Spirit. Although it is true to say that the Father is love and the Son is love, it is particularly appropriate to speak of the Spirit as love; for the Spirit *is* the mutual love of the Father and the Son.[4] It is also true to say that God is Spirit, the Father is Spirit, and the Son is Spirit; and God is holy, the Father is holy, and the Son is holy. Yet it is the Third Person of the Trinity who is named the Holy Spirit. As with "holy" and "spirit," so with "love." Each of the Persons of the Trinity is holy and spirit and love, but it is the Third Person who is known as "Holy Spirit" and as "Love."

Augustine speaks not only of the mutual love of the Father and the Son but of their friendship, although he prefers the word *love* or *charity* as more apt. "So the Holy Spirit is something common to Father and Son, whatever it is, or is their very commonness or communion, consubstantial and coeternal. Call this friendship, if it helps, but a better word for it is charity [or love]."[5] The Holy Spirit, understood as the bond of love between the Father and the Son, was a theme variously emphasized that remained constant throughout the Western tradition. It was prominent in William of Saint-Thierry (ca. 1085–1148), Richard of Saint-Victor (d. 1173), Bonaventure (ca. 1217–74), and Thomas Aquinas (1225–74), among others.

The association of the Spirit with love can be found in Paul. "God's love has been poured into our hearts through the Holy Spirit that has been given to us" (Rom 5:5). Here the Holy Spirit is not only the bond of love between the Father and the Son within the Trinity but between ourselves and the Trinity as well. The Holy Spirit lives within us as a gift, making of us temples of the Holy Spirit (1 Cor 3:16; 2 Cor 6:16). The Holy Spirit is filling us with divine life, divine love, God's very Self. One of the effects of this being filled with the divine life is that it makes us daughters and sons of God (Rom 8:5–17).

Thomas Aquinas, following the theology of Augustine, saw both Gift and Love as proper names of the Holy Spirit. Thomas presents his mature reflection on the Holy Trinity in the first part of his *Summa Theologiae* (questions 27–43). Questions 36 to 38 deal specifically with the Holy Spirit.

Thomas writes that love can be taken either essentially or personally, insofar as it refers to the divine essence or insofar as it refers to a Divine Person. "If taken personally it is the proper name of the Holy Spirit, as Word is the proper name of the Son" (*Summa Theologiae*, I, 37, 1). There are, for Thomas, two processions in God, one proceeding by way of the divine intellect, namely, the Word, and the other by way of the divine will, which is called Love. Love expresses the relation of the lover (the Father) to the object loved (the Son, Image, or Word) and the impression of the object loved produced in the lover by the fact that he or she loves (I, 37, 1). The reciprocal love of the Father and the Son *is* the Holy Spirit. If love is taken not essentially, as referring to the divine nature, but personally as referring to a Divine Person, Love then is a proper name for the Holy Spirit.

Gift, like Love, is both a personal and proper name for the Holy Spirit. Thomas states that a gift is so called not from being actually given but from its aptitude for being given. Thus the Holy Spirit is called gift from eternity although given only in time. We have observed the same "givability" in Augustine. Something is gift because its very nature is "to be given." Thomas writes, "The word *gift* imports an aptitude for being given. And what is given has an aptitude or relation both to the giver and to that to which it is given. For it would not be given by anyone, unless it was theirs to give, and it is given to someone to be theirs" (I, 38, 1). The Spirit is thus God *as givable* and God *as given.*

For Aquinas, the heart and soul of the gospel is this gift of the Holy Spirit. He repeatedly states that the law of the gospel, "the new law" if you will, is primarily the gift or grace of the Holy Spirit (I-II, q. 106, a. 1, a. 2, a. 3; q. 108, a. 1). This gift of the Spirit, who comes to us from God through Christ, is the Gift of Love.

Christian life ultimately comes back to the Holy Spirit as its foundation. For the Holy Spirit is the Father's love for us and likewise our love for God. We could not love God apart from the gift of the Spirit. Paul says that we cannot pray apart from the Holy Spirit, who prays within us (Rom 8:14–17, 26–27; Gal 4:6). Not only is the Holy Spirit our love for God but also our love for one another. When we sin against one another, we sin against the Holy Spirit. The Holy Spirit is the bond of love between the Father and the Son, between God and ourselves, and among ourselves. Our loving God and one another is the Holy Spirit at work within and among us. As Augustine says, the Holy Spirit is "the gift of God who is love."[6] Thomas Aquinas writes in the same vein in his *Summa contra gentiles:* "The Holy Spirit constitutes us God's friends, and makes God dwell in us, and us dwell in God."[7]

We might propose another name for the Holy Spirit besides Gift of Love, and that is Friend. In the *Contra gentiles* Thomas leans on Aristotle's understanding of friendship as he explores the relationship of the Holy Spirit to the Father and the Son.[8] Augustine offered this image even though he thought friendship less to the point than the word *love* itself.[9] Yet friendship remains also an apt word for that relationship. The Holy Spirit is the friendship between the Father and the Son, their mutual love. "Friendship" describes the subsistent reality that the Holy Spirit is within the immanent Trinity as well as in the economy of creation and salvation. In relationship with us the Holy Spirit is also friendship, our friendship with the Father and the Son.

Bernard of Clairvaux, in his sermons on the Song of Songs, spoke of the Holy Spirit not simply as friendship but as the kiss that the Father and the Son mutually give one another.

> If, as is properly understood, the Father is he who kisses, the Son is he who is kissed, then it cannot be wrong to see in the kiss the Holy Spirit, for he is the imperturbable peace of the Father and the Son, their unshakeable bond, their undivided love, their indivisible unity.[10]

The Holy Spirit is their mutual love, their mutual kiss, and we can also suggest that the Holy Spirit is God's kiss vis-à-vis ourselves, God kissing us.[11]

The Two Hands of God

Early in the Christian tradition St. Irenaeus (ca. 130–200) referred to the Son and the Spirit as two hands of God.[12] The Word and the Spirit are God as reaching out, communicating and sharing their divine life. Through the two hands of God we are created and woven into the very fabric of divine life. The Trinity is a way of speaking about God that enables Christians to do justice to their experiences of God as both unknowable and known, as totally other and totally present, as beyond and yet within. In the West, of course, the discourse for talking about the Trinity was largely shaped by St. Augustine.[13]

For Augustine, the incomprehensibility of the triune God is the first principle, which incomprehensibility should not deter one from pursuing understanding as far as possible. Augustine writes, "When we think about God the trinity we are aware that our thoughts are quite inadequate to their object and incapable of grasping him as he is."[14] Faith nevertheless seeks understanding.[15]

> Why then look for something when you have compre-
> hended the incomprehensibility of what you are looking
> for, if not because you should not give up the search as
> long as you are making progress in your inquiry into
> things incomprehensible, and because you become bet-
> ter and better by looking for so great a good....[16]

A second principle in Augustine's theology of the Trinity is its affirmation of both the distinctiveness and the absolute equality of the three divine hypostases: the Father, the Son, the Spirit.

> The purpose of all the Catholic commentators I have been
> able to read on the divine books of both testaments, who
> have written before me on the trinity which God is, has
> been to teach that according to the scriptures Father and
> Son and Holy Spirit in the inseparable equality of one sub-
> stance present a divine unity; and therefore there are not
> three gods but one God; although indeed the Father has
> begotten the Son, and therefore he who is the Father is not
> the Son; and the Son is begotten by the Father, and there-
> fore he who is the Son is not the Father; and the Holy
> Spirit is neither the Father nor the Son, but only the Spirit
> of the Father and of the Son, himself coequal to the Father
> and the Son, and belonging to the threefold unity.[17]

Along with their distinctiveness and equality are their inseparability and the fact that they work *ad extra* inseparably as well.[18]
Even though one of the Persons of the Trinity may be mentioned,
it is to be taken in such a way that the others are to be understood
as included.[19] If the scriptures say "the Father loves you" (John
16:27), this is not to be understood as excluding the Son or the
Spirit. However, although they act inseparably, they cannot be
manifested inseparably because of limitations in creatures.

I will say however with absolute confidence that Father and Son and Holy Spirit, God the creator, of one and the same substance, the almighty three, act inseparably. But they cannot be manifested inseparably by creatures which are so unlike them, especially material ones; just as our words which consist of material sounds can only name Father and Son and Holy Spirit with their own proper intervals of time, which the syllables of each word take up, spaced off from each other by a definite separation. In their own proper substance by which they are, the three are one, Father and Son and Holy Spirit, without any temporal movement....But in my words Father and Son and Holy Spirit are separated and cannot be said together, and if you write them down each name has its own separate space.[20]

The Spirit and the Word are inseparable and yet distinct, but when acting *ad extra*—as the two hands of God, to use the Irenaean expression—the one is never without the other. Even in the incarnation, although it is the Word who becomes incarnate, it is the Spirit who incarnates the Word. Where the Spirit is, there are the Son and the Father.

Augustine takes as a point of departure an analysis of "the missions," that is, the "sendings," which is to say the visible manifestations of the Son and the Spirit.[21] The missions or manifestations make known *to us* the *eternal* processions within the godhead, namely, the eternal generation of the Son from the Father and the eternal procession of the Spirit from the Father through the Son.[22] Only the Son is begotten; this is what distinguishes him from the Spirit. The Father is the Unbegotten One and the Son the only Begotten One, whereas the Spirit is distinctive in that she proceeds from the Father through the Son. She is the Spirit of the Father and the Son. But these eternal relationships get us into questions of language with respect to the Trinity and remind us of our first principle, that of the incomprehensibility of the triune God. At the end of the final book of the *De Trinitate*, Augustine writes: "It still remains of course extremely difficult to distinguish generation from procession in that co-eternal and equal and incorporeal and inexpressibly unchangeable trinity."[23]

As Edmund Hill has pointed out, books 5–7 of Augustine's *Trinity* are not so much talking about God the Trinity as they are talking about how to talk about God the Trinity.[24] The utter inadequacy of language to express the mystery of the Trinity is made apparent by Augustine in his own effort to articulate the content of the word *person* (Latin *persona*; Greek *hypostasis*) as applied to the three. He quite simply says that we say three persons in order to be able to say "three something" in answer to the question of "three what?" Augustine writes:

> Yet when you ask "Three what?" human speech labors under a great dearth of words. So we say three persons, not in order to say that precisely, but in order not to be reduced to silence.[25]

We should not allow words that are necessary for speech to fool us into thinking that we have completely understood. In the end we are reduced to silence.

Through the missions of the Word and the Spirit, the scriptures reveal God as Father, Son, and Spirit. These three are one. We are not talking mathematics. We are struggling to speak the truth about the Eternal One. The "two hands of God," the Word and Spirit, are, to follow Augustine, "a certain pure outflow of the glory of almighty God" (Wis 7:25).[26] As I said earlier, the Spirit is God breaking through, God's breakthrough, God-in-us.

Given the traditional teaching about the Trinity—the unity, distinctiveness, equality, and inseparability of the Three—the Word and Spirit are not in competition with each other. St. John Damascene as well as other Greek authors speak of the Spirit as one "who accompanies the Word."[27] Where one is, there is the other. One cannot have a pneumatology apart from the Word, nor a Christology apart from the Spirit. There can be no pneumatology without Christology and no Christology without pneumatology.[28]

The Word becomes flesh through the power of the Spirit; the Spirit is unleashed through the risen Christ. Each has put its seal forever on the other. There is only a pneumatic Christ and a christic Spirit: the Spirit's Christ and Christ's Spirit. The Word assumed flesh so that we might receive the Holy Spirit! That is the teaching of Athanasius. The Spirit prepares the way for Christ, who, in turn, is the precursor of the Spirit.[29]

Yves Congar, whose work in ecclesiology and ecumenism led him eventually to the need for a more developed pneumatology,[30] whose bibliography totals over 1,700 entries,[31] following up a comment by Thomas Aquinas on John 14:26 ("the Holy Spirit will teach you everything"),[32] saw the Word, Jesus Christ, as the Teacher, but the Holy Spirit as the Teacher within, the inner Teacher.[33] According to Aquinas's suggestion, the Word gives us the teaching, but the Holy Spirit makes us able to receive it. The Word is ineffective apart from the Spirit. The two work together—hand in hand, so to speak. The Spirit interiorizes what the Word unveils.

How to formulate this "companionship" between the Son and the Spirit has been one of the difficult and disputed theological issues between East and West: the question of the *filioque* (whether the Spirit proceeds from the Father *and* the Son *[filioque]* or simply from the Father). Yves Congar maintained that the Orthodox Church and the Catholic Church are sister churches that live by the same faith and that one must allow for the coexistence of two traditions in professing that faith while at the same time adhering to the creed as formulated by the First Council of Constantinople in 381.[34] One must distinguish between the theology of the *filioque* and its inclusion in the creed. Congar insists that the *filioque* of the Latin West, properly understood, is orthodox and not heretical while at the same time acknowledging that it does not belong in the creed.[35]

The original text of the creed reads: "I believe in the Holy Spirit, the Lord and giver of life, who proceeds from the Father, who is adored and glorified with the Father and the Son, who has spoken through the prophets."[36] The Catholic West ought to return to the original authoritative statement of the creed (the *filioque* is a Western interpolation into a creed of the universal church), and the Orthodox East ought to acknowledge that the *filioque* was being taught in the West when the East and West were still in communion with each other without its being considered heretical. Charlemagne had pushed for the inclusion of the *filioque* in the creed and Pope Leo III at the time refused, although he agreed with its teaching. Pope Leo engraved the text of the creed without the *filioque* in both Latin and Greek and had them hung in St. Peter's (AD 810). The creed with the *filioque* was not introduced into the Mass in Rome until 1014.

The Son and the Spirit in the East are distinguished by two different modes of origination. The Son comes from the Father by "begetting." The Father is the Unbegotten One and the Son the only-*begotten* One. The Spirit comes from the Father by "proceeding" (*ekporeusis*), as expressed in John 15:26 ("the Spirit of truth who proceeds from the Father"). The distinction between the Son and the Spirit in the East rests with these two distinctive modes of origin. The West, however, relied also on John 20:22,[37] the sending of the Spirit by Christ (hence proceeding from the Father but sent by the Son), with the understanding that the Spirit comes *from* the Father but *through* the Son. The technicalities of this discussion, however, are not necessary for us here.[38] In 1995 there was a breakthrough in ecumenical theology when the Pontifical Council for Christian Unity published a "Clarification" on "The Greek and Latin Traditions regarding the Procession of the Holy Spirit."[39] In part, it states:

> The Catholic Church acknowledges the conciliar, ecumenical, normative and irrevocable value, as expression of the one common faith of the Church and of all Christians, of the Symbol professed in Greek at Constantinople in 381 by the Second Ecumenical Council. No profession of faith peculiar to a particular liturgical tradition can contradict this expression of the faith taught and professed by the undivided Church.

Although to most this discussion of the *filioque* may seem technical and not relevant to our lives in the Spirit, Vladimir

Lossky traced many of the differences between Catholicism and Orthodoxy back to the consequences of the *filioque*. With the *filioque*, he maintained, the Spirit is subordinated to the Son, the *perichoresis*[40] endangered, and the Spirit's role in the economy of salvation reduced to serving the Word. The goal of the Christian life then becomes an imitation of Christ, rather than deification by the Holy Spirit. The people of God become the body of Christ and charism is subordinated to institution, freedom to authority, propheticism to juridicism, mysticism to scholasticism, laity to clergy, and the college of bishops to the primacy of the pope. The creative and renewing work of the Spirit gets lost.[41]

Whether all of this can be traced to the *filioque* is debatable, but it remains true that the Latin West lacks a balanced emphasis on pneumatology and proceeds as if the Spirit is servant of the church rather than the church's being at the service of the Spirit. When it comes to the Word and the Spirit, companions *ad extra* as they are *ad intra*, there can be no either/or, no competition, no superior/inferior, no before/after. They are simply both together the two hands of God. As Nikos Nissiotis has written:

> We have to understand that according to the Scriptures, the work of the Paraclete, the Spirit of Truth, is as important as that of Christ. Without this work, nothing can exist in history, neither the reality of the Incarnation and the reconciliation in Christ, nor personal commitment to him in his community of faith.[42]

Kilian McDonnell has written in a similar vein: "If the two missions are to be kept in balance and fruitful tension, it has to be recognized that they are equal, that is, the mission of the Spirit is as important as that of the Son. Otherwise the doctrine of the Trinity collapses."[43]

McDonnell argues that to do pneumatology is to do trinitarian doctrine, that the doctrine of the Spirit cannot be separated from that of the Trinity.[44] It is true. One cannot be introduced to the Spirit without being invited into the life and mystery of the Trinity. The Trinity is the life that the Spirit lives and brings. It is also true, however, that the doctrine of the Trinity cannot be separated from the doctrine of the Spirit and that to do theology in general is to do pneumatology. Just as there can be no Christology apart from pneumatology, there can be no theology apart from it either. These three are one. Just as the Spirit is the contact point between God and creation, history, religion, the church, and ourselves and the point of entry into the christological and trinitarian mystery itself,[45] so the Spirit is also the starting point for theology, Christology, ecclesiology, and liturgy as well as moral theology.[46] If the doctrine of the Spirit ought not have a separate tract in theology because the Spirit is everywhere present, the Spirit must then be present in every tract of theology.

The Holy Spirit and Depth

> But, as it is written, "What no eye has seen, nor ear heard, nor the human heart conceived, what God has prepared for those who love him"—these things God has revealed to us through the Spirit; for the Spirit searches everything, even the depths of God. For what human being knows what is truly human except the human spirit that is within? So also no one comprehends what is truly God's except the Spirit of God. (1 Cor 2:9–11)

> Nevertheless I tell you the truth: it is to your advantage that I go away, for if I do not go away, the Advocate will not come to you; but if I go, I will send him to you. And when he comes, he will prove the world wrong about sin and righteousness and judgment: about sin, because they do not believe in me; about righteousness, because I am going to the Father and you will see me no longer; about judgment, because the ruler of this world has been condemned. (John 16: 7–11)

St. Paul writes that the Holy Spirit searches the very depths of God (1 Cor 2:9–11). The Fourth Gospel tells us that the Spirit instructs us concerning sin, righteousness, and judgment (John 16:7–11). What might this all mean?

The Spirit speaks the truth about sin. Sin closes our minds and hardens our hearts to works of the Holy Spirit, even to recognizing the presence of the Spirit in Christ Jesus. Ultimately all sin is against the Holy Spirit. The Spirit also comes to instruct us concerning righteousness, in what true righteousness consists, that it is alignment with God, solidarity with God, which is to say alignment with the Spirit of God. Sin is alignment with an evil spirit, righteousness alignment with the Holy Spirit. We cannot love both sin and the Spirit. The Spirit likewise instructs us about judgment, about God's no to evil. The power of evil is exposed for what it is—opposition to all that is truly human, to all that is from God.

Sin is a rejection of the mission of the Holy Spirit.[47] At the same time, as John Paul II indicated in his encyclical on the Holy Spirit, "convincing concerning sin" is convincing us about the forgiveness of sin.[48] Part of the truth about sin is that God forgives sin. Not only is sin an offense against the Spirit but sin is also forgiven by that same Spirit, who in the Gospel of John is both the Spirit of truth and the Spirit of forgiveness (John 14:17; 15:26; 16:13; 20:22–23). Conversion is nothing other than this discovery of the truth about sin. We need to know the truth about sin in order to comprehend the truth of the forgiveness of sin. We are wrong about sin. It is *both* evil *and* forgiven. One can easily emphasize one aspect of sin to the exclusion of the other. Either "sin is not so bad, God forgives," or "sin is evil, and unforgivable." The Spirit teaches us the truth about sin, that God is pained by it and yet forgives it. The pain of God absorbs the sin of the world, embraces and heals it, not returning evil for evil.

The Spirit who instructs us about sin and holiness also searches "the depths of God" according to Paul (1 Cor 2:9–11), penetrates the inner mystery of God itself, and reveals another truth about sin, that it is truly an offense against God, against Being itself. The Spirit searches the depths of God and reveals the pain of God.[49] John Paul II wrote, "Therefore, will not 'convincing concerning sin' also have to mean *revealing suffering?*"[50] The Spirit reveals the unimaginable and inexpressible suffering of God, the pain of being divine, even to the point that the Book of Genesis depicts God as saying, "I am sorry that I have made them" (Gen 6:7). According to John Paul II, in the very depths of the Trinity, we are confronted with God's love.[51] That which pains God is also that which is the source of our salvation, namely, a fatherly, motherly, divine love, which is what the Holy Spirit finds in the depths of God and about which she comes to instruct us.

God, the Holy Mystery, in her depths, as Spirit, is revealed as being the gift of love, given to us as the source from which our very own lives emanate, poured out among us and into the whole world and all of creation, to which the church is called to bear witness as the sacrament of Christ in which the sphere of influence of the Holy Spirit is made visible. Praised be God's Most Holy Spirit now and forever.

> *Lord, who can comprehend even one of your words? We lose more of it than we grasp, like those who drink from a living spring. For God's word offers different facets according to the capacity of the listener, and the Lord has portrayed his message in many colors, so that whoever gazes upon it can see in it what suits him. Within it he has buried manifold treasures, so that each of us might grow rich in seeking them out....And so whenever anyone discovers some part of the treasure, he should not think that he has exhausted God's word....A thirsty man is happy when he is drinking, and he is not depressed because he cannot exhaust the spring. So let this spring quench your thirst and not your thirst the spring....So do not foolishly try to drain in one draught what cannot be consumed all at once, and do not cease out of faintheartedness from what you will be able to absorb as time goes on. (Saint Ephrem)[52]*

Notes

1. Augustine, *The Trinity* (the *De Trinitate*), trans. Edmund Hill, OP (Brooklyn, NY: New City Press, 1991), 174, 196, 197–200, 231, 419, 421–24, 435 (4.29; 5.10; 5.12–16; 7.12; 15.29; 15.31–36; 15.50). In order to facilitate reference to the text of Augustine or other translations, when quoting Augustine I shall insert in parentheses book and paragraph numbers, e.g., 4.29 refers to book 4, paragraph 29.

2. Yves Congar, *I Believe in the Holy Spirit*, 3 vols., trans David Smith (New York: Seabury Press, 1983), 1:79–80.

3. Augustine, *Trinity*, 200 (5.16).

4. St. Augustine already spoke this way; See *Trinity*, 251–55, 271–75, 398, 418–26 (8.10–14; 9.2–8; 15.5; 15.27–39).

5. Ibid., 209 (6.7).

6. Ibid., 421 (15.31).

7. Thomas Aquinas, *Summa contra gentiles*, Book Four, trans. Charles J. O'Neil as *On the Truth of the Catholic Faith* (Garden City, NY: Doubleday, 1957), chaps. 21–22, pp. 121–27. For a more thorough treatment of Aquinas's theology of the Holy Spirit, see Jean-Pierre Torrell, *Saint Thomas Aquinas*, vol 2, *Spiritual Master*, trans. Robert Royal (Washington, DC: The Catholic University of America Press, 2003), 153–224. For further good insights, see Fergus Kerr, *After Aquinas: Versions of Thomism* (Oxford: Blackwell Publishing, 2002), esp. 128–33; 181–206.

8. Ibid.

9. Augustine, *Trinity*, 209 (6.7).

10. Bernard of Clairvaux, *On the Song of Songs*, I, vol. 2 of *The Works of Bernard of Clairvaux* (Kalamazoo: Cistercian Publications, 1980), 46, sermon 8, #2. Also see Yves Congar, *The Word and the Spirit* (San Francisco: Harper & Row, 1986), 108–9; also Kilian McDonnell, *The Other Hand of God: The Holy Spirit as the Universal Touch and Goal* (Collegeville, MN: Liturgical Press, 2003), 184.

11. I am reminded here of a poem by the fourteenth-century Sufi master Hafiz, in a collection called *The Gift*, trans. Daniel Ladinsky (New

York: Penguin Putnam, 1999), 40, entitled "Mismatched Newlyweds," which goes: "Like a pair of mismatched newlyweds, one of whom still feels very insecure, I keep turning to God saying, 'Kiss me.'" Also see, "You're It," 30.

12. Irenaeus, *Adversus Haereses*, 4.19.2; 4.20.1–12; 5.1.3; 5.6.1. Also Irenaeus, *Proof of the Apostolic Preaching* 11. Also see *Catechism of the Catholic Church* (New York: Doubleday, 1995), #704.

13. References to Augustine's *De Trinitate* come from the translation by Edmund Hill, OP, cited in n. 1 above.

14. *The Trinity*, 189 (5.1).

15. Ibid., 396 (15.2).

16. Ibid.

17. Ibid., 69 (1.7).

18. Ibid., 70, 79 (1.7–8, 19).

19. Ibid., 81 (1.21).

20. Ibid., 175 (4.30).

21. Ibid., books 2–4. Aquinas speaks about these missions in the *Summa Theologiae*, I, q. 43.

22. Ibid., 171–77, 435, also 147–51, 265–69.

23. Ibid., 433 (15.48).

24. Ibid., 186–88.

25. Ibid., 196 (5.10); see also 7.3, 224–30.

26. Ibid., 172 (4.27).

27. See Yves Congar, *The Word and the Spirit* (San Francisco: Harper & Row, 1986), 106.

28. Ibid., 1, 53. Also Donald J. Goergen, *Jesus, Son of God, Son of Mary, Immanuel* (Collegeville, MN: Liturgical Press, Michael Glazier, 1995; reprint, Eugene, OR: Wipf & Stock, 1995), 221–49; Walter Kasper, *Jesus the Christ* (New York: Paulist, 1976), 249; Edward Schillebeeckx, *Christ: The Experience of Jesus as Lord* (New York: Seabury Press, 1980), 534–38.

29. See Congar, *Word and the Spirit*, 130.

30. Yves M.-J. Congar, *I Believe in the Holy Spirit*, 3 vols., trans. David Smith (New York: Seabury, 1983; reprint, New York: Crossroad, 1997).

31. See Jean-Pierre Jossua, *Yves Congar: Theology in the Service of God's People* (Chicago: Priory Press, 1968), 189–241; and Aidan Nichols, "An Yves Congar Bibliography 1967–1987," *Angelicum* 66 (1989): 422–66.

32. Thomas Aquinas, *Commentary on the Gospel of John*, part 2, trans. Fabian R. Larcher (Albany, NY: Magi Books, 1998), chap. 14, lecture 6.

33. Congar, *Word and the Spirit*, 12, 22.

34. Ibid., 5, 112.

35. Congar, *I Believe in the Holy Spirit*, 3:24–56.

36. On the history of the Nicene-Constantinopolitan creed, see J. N. D. Kelly, *Early Christian Creeds* (London: Longmans, Green, 1960), 205–367.

37. See Augustine, *Trinity*, 174.

38. See, among others, Jaroslav Pelikan, *The Spirit of Eastern Christendom (600–1700)*, vol. 2 of *The Christian Tradition: A History of the Development of Doctrine* (Chicago: University of Chicago Press, 1974), 183–98, 275–78.

39. *Osservatore Romano*, no. 38 (Sept. 20, 1995): 3 and 6. Also see *Vidyajoti* 60 (May 1996): 337–49.

40. In Latin, *circuminsessio*, or being together, mutual indwelling, shared existence, interpenetration, usually referring to the doctrine of the Trinity.

41. Vladimir Lossky, *The Mystical Theology of the Eastern Church* (London, 1957), 156–57, 164–67, 184–85, 192–93, 243–44.

42. Nikos A. Nissiotis, "Pneumatological Christology as a Presupposition of Ecclesiology," in *Oecumenica* 1967 (Minneapolis: Augsburg, 1967), 239.

43. Kilian McDonnell, "A Trinitarian Theology of the Holy Spirit?" *Theological Studies* 46 (1985): 226.

44. Ibid., 227.

45. Ibid., 207–12.

46. On the Holy Spirit and moral theology, see Charles E. Bouchard, "Recovering the Gifts of the Holy Spirit in Moral Theology," *Theological Studies* 63 (Sept. 2002): 539–58.

47. Pope John Paul II's encyclical on the Holy Spirit, *Dominum et Vivificantem* 27–28; sections 27–48 are a sustained reflection on John 16:7–11. On the Vatican Web site at http://www.vatican.va/holy_father/john_paul_ii/encyclicals/documents/hf_jp-ii_enc_18051986_dominum-et-vivificantem_en.html.

48. Ibid., 31.

49. Ibid., 39–41. Also see Gerald Vann, "The Sorrow of God," in *The Pain of Christ and the Sorrow of God* (Oxford: Blackfriars, 1947).

50. *Dominum et Vivificantem*, 39.

51. Ibid., 39.

52. From the Roman Catholic Breviary, sixth Sunday in Ordinary Time (*The Liturgy of the Hours* [New York: Catholic Book, 1975], 3:199–200) from a commentary on the *Diatesseron* by Saint Ephrem.

Bibliography

An extensive bibliography on the Holy Spirit was compiled by Watson E. Mills and published in 1988 (see below). I have limited myself here to listing a few suggestions.

Augustine. *The Trinity*. Translated by Edmund Hill. Brooklyn, NY: New City Press, 1991.

Austin, Gerard. *Anointing with the Spirit: The Rite of Confirmation*. New York: Pueblo, 1985.

Badcock, Gary D. *Light of Truth and Fire of Love: A Theology of the Holy Spirit*. Grand Rapids: Eerdmans, 1997.

Basil the Great. *The Treatise De Spiritu Sancto* (On the Holy Spirit). Translated by Blomfield Jackson. In *St. Basil: Letters and Select Works*, 1–50, *Nicene and Post-Nicene Fathers*, Second Series, 8. Peabody, MA: Hendrickson, 1995.

Benoit, Pierre. *Aspects of Biblical Inspiration*. Translated by J. Murphy-O'Connor and S. K. Ashe. Chicago: Priory Press, 1965.

Bouyer, Louis. *Le Consolateur: Esprit-Saint et Vie de Grace*. Paris: Les Editions du Cerf, 1980.

Burns, J. Patout, and Gerald Fagin. *The Holy Spirit*. Message of the Fathers of the Church 3. Wilmington, DE: Michael Glazier, 1984.

Coffey, David M. "A Proper Mission of the Holy Spirit." *Theological Studies* 47 (1986): 227–50.

Comblin, José. *The Holy Spirit and Liberation*. Translated by Paul Burns. Maryknoll, NY: Orbis Books, 1989.

Congar, Yves. *I Believe in the Holy Spirit*. 3 vols. Translated by David Smith. New York: Seabury Press, 1983.

———. *The Word and the Spirit.* Translated by David Smith. San Francisco: Harper & Row, 1986.

Cooke, Bernard. *Power and the Spirit of God: Toward an Experience-Based Pneumatology.* Oxford: Oxford University Press, 2004.

Cyril of Jerusalem. *Catecheses.* Fathers of the Church 64. Washington, DC: Catholic University of America Press, 1970. Two of the catechetical lectures (16–17) are devoted to the Holy Spirit.

Dunn, James D. G. *Jesus and the Spirit.* London: SCM Press, 1975.

———. *The Theology of Paul the Apostle.* Grand Rapids: Eerdmans, 1998.

Dupuis, Jacques. *Christianity and the Religions: From Confrontation to Dialogue.* Maryknoll, NY: Orbis Books, 2001.

———. *Toward a Christian Theology of Religious Pluralism.* Maryknoll, NY: Orbis Books, 1997.

Edwards, Denis. *Breath of Life: A Theology of the Creator Spirit.* Maryknoll, NY: Orbis Books, 2004.

Fatula, Mary Ann. *The Holy Spirit: Unbounded Gift of Joy.* Collegeville, MN: Liturgical Press, 1998.

Gioia, Francesco, ed. *Interreligious Dialogue: The Official Teaching of the Catholic Church (1963–1995).* Boston: Pauline Books & Media, 1997.

Goergen, Donald J. *The Mission and Ministry of Jesus.* Volume 1 of *A Theology of Jesus.* Eugene, OR: Wipf & Stock, 1986. Previously published by Michael Glazier and Liturgical Press.

Goodwin, Rufus. *Who Killed the Holy Ghost? A Journalist Reports on the Holy Spirit.* Great Barrington, MA: Lindisfarne Books, 2005.

Gregory of Nyssa. *The Lord's Prayer.* Ancient Christian Writers 18. Westminster, MD: Newman Press, 1954.

Hilkert, Mary Catherine, and Robert Schreiter, eds. *The Praxis of the Reign of God: An Introduction to the Theology of Edward Schillebeeckx.* 2nd ed. New York: Fordham University Press, 2002.

Hodgson, Peter C. *Winds of the Spirit: A Constructive Christian Theology*. Louisville: Westminster John Knox, 1994.

Hopko, Thomas, "Holy Spirit in Orthodox Theology and Life." *Commonweal* 89 (November 1968): 186–91.

John Paul II. *Dominum et Vivificantem* (1986). In *The Encyclicals of John Paul II*, edited by J. Michael Miller, 254–339. Huntington, IN: Our Sunday Visitor, 1996.

Kärkkäinen, Veli-Matti. *Pneumatology: The Holy Spirit in Ecumenical, International, and Contextual Perspective*. Grand Rapids: Baker, 2002.

Kelly, J. N. D. *Early Christian Creeds*. London: Longmans, Green, 1960.

Kontzevitch, I. M. *The Acquisition of the Holy Spirit in Ancient Russia*. Platina, CA: St. Herman of Alaska Brotherhood, 1996.

Krivocheine, Basil. *In the Light of Christ: Saint Symeon the New Theologian*. Translated by Anthony P. Gythiel. New York: St. Vladimir's Seminary Press, 1986.

Lampe, G. W. H. *God as Spirit*. Oxford: Oxford University Press, 1977.

Lossky, Vladimir. *In the Image and Likeness of God*. Edited by John H. Erickson and Thomas E. Bird. New York: St. Vladimir's Seminary Press, 1974.

———. *The Mystical Theology of the Eastern Church*. New York: St. Vladimir's Seminary Press, 1976.

Maloney, George. *A Theology of Uncreated Energies*. Milwaukee, WI: Marquette University Press, 1978.

Mazza, Enrico. *The Celebration of the Eucharist: The Origin of the Rite and the Development of Its Interpretation*. Translated by Matthew J. O'Connell. Collegeville, MN: Liturgical Press, 1999.

McDonnell, Kilian. *The Other Hand of God: The Holy Spirit as the Universal Touch and Goal*. Collegeville, MN: Liturgical Press, 2003.

———. "A Trinitarian Theology of the Holy Spirit?" *Theological Studies* 46 (1985): 191–227.

McIntyre, John. "The Holy Spirit in Greek Patristic Thought." *The Scottish Journal of Theology* 7 (1954): 353–75.

―――. *The Shape of Pneumatology: Studies in the Doctrine of the Holy Spirit*. Edinburgh: T&T Clark, 1997.

McKenna, John H. *Eucharist and Holy Spirit: The Eucharistic Epiclesis in the Twentieth Century (1900–1966)*. London: SPCK, 1975.

Meyendorff, John. *Byzantine Theology: Historical Trends and Doctrinal Themes*. New York: Fordham University Press, 1976.

―――. *Christ in Eastern Christian Thought*. New York: St. Vladimir's Seminary Press, 1975.

―――. *St. Gregory Palamas and Orthodox Spirituality*. New York: St. Vladimir's Seminary Press, 1974.

Mills, Watson E. *The Holy Spirit: A Bibliography*. Peabody, MA: Hendrickson Publishers, 1988.

Moltmann, Jürgen. *The Spirit of Life: A Universal Affirmation*. Minneapolis: Fortress Press, 1992.

Montague, George T. *The Holy Spirit: Growth of a Biblical Tradition*. New York: Paulist Press, 1976.

Nissiotis, Nikos A. "Pneumatological Christology as a Presupposition of Ecclesiology." In *Oecumenica: An Annual Symposium of Ecumenical Research*. Edited by Frederich W. Kantzenback. Minneapolis: Augsburg, 1967.

O'Carroll, Michael. *Veni Creator Spiritus: A Theological Encyclopedia of the Holy Spirit*. Collegeville, MN: Liturgical Press, 1990.

Rahner, Karl. "Do Not Stifle the Spirit!" In *Theological Investigations*, vol. 7, translated by David Bourke, 72–87. New York: Seabury Press, 1977.

―――. "The Experience of the Holy Spirit." In *Theological Investigations*, vol. 18, translated by Edward Quinn, 189–210. New York: Crossroad, 1983.

Rayan, Samuel. *Breath of Life: The Holy Spirit, Heart of the Gospel*. London: Geoffrey Chapman, 1979.

Reid, Duncan. *Energies of the Spirit: Trinitarian Models in Eastern Orthodox and Western Theology*. Atlanta: Scholars Press, 1997.

Rideau, Emile. *The Thought of Teilhard de Chardin*. Translated by René Hague. New York: Harper & Row, 1967.

Rosato, Philip J. *The Spirit as Lord: The Pneumatology of Karl Barth*. Edinburgh: T&T Clark, 1981.

Schmitz-Moormann, Karl. *Theology of Creation in an Evolutionary World*. Cleveland: Pilgrim Press, 1997.

Pelikan, Jaroslav. *The Spirit of Eastern Christendom (600–1700)*. Vol. 2 of *The Christian Tradition: A History of the Development of Doctrine*. Chicago: University of Chicago Press, 1974.

Schillebeeckx, Edward. *Church: The Human Story of God*. Translated by John Bowden. New York: Crossroad, 1990.

Spidlík, Tomás. *The Spirituality of the Christian East*. Translated by Anthony P. Gythiel. Kalamazoo: Cistercian Publications, 1986.

Staniloae, Dumitru. "The Role of the Holy Spirit in the Theology and Life of the Orthodox Church." *Diakonia* 9 (1974): 343–66.

Steiner, George. *Real Presences*. Chicago: University of Chicago Press, 1989.

Sullivan, Francis. *Salvation Outside the Church? Tracing the History of the Catholic Response*. New York: Paulist Press, 1992.

Teilhard de Chardin, Pierre. *The Heart of Matter*. Translated by René Hague. New York: Harcourt Brace Jovanovich, 1978.

Tillard, J. M.-R. *Church of Churches: The Ecclesiology of Communion*. Collegeville, MN: Liturgical Press, 1992.

Turner, Denys. *The Darkness of God: Negativity in Christian Mysticism*. Cambridge: Cambridge University Press, 1995.

Welker, Michael. *God the Spirit*. Translated by John F. Hoffmeyer. Minneapolis: Fortress Press, 1994.

Wilber, Ken. *Sex, Ecology, Spirituality: The Spirit of Evolution*. Boston: Shambhala Publications, 1995.

Wolfson, H. A. "The Holy Spirit as the PreExistent Christ," and "The Differentiation of the Logos and the Holy Spirit." Chapters 8 and 12 of *Faith, Trinity, Incarnation*, 155–67, 192–256. Vol. 1 of *The Philosophy of the Church Fathers*. Cambridge, MA: Harvard University Press, 1964.